To Jen,

I hope you enjoy
the book!

Mike B~

CONFEDERATE POLITICAL ECONOMY

CONFLICTING WORLDS:
NEW DIMENSIONS OF THE AMERICAN CIVIL WAR

T. Michael Parrish, Series Editor

CONFEDERATE
POLITICAL
ECONOMY

❖

*Creating and Managing
a Southern Corporatist Nation*

❖

Michael Brem Bonner

LOUISIANA STATE UNIVERSITY PRESS
BATON ROUGE

Published by Louisiana State University Press
Copyright © 2016 by Louisiana State University Press
All rights reserved
Manufactured in the United States of America
First printing

DESIGNER: Michelle A. Neustrom
TYPEFACE: Whitman
PRINTER AND BINDER: Maple Press (Digital)

LIBRARY OF CONGRESS CATALOGING-IN-PUBLICATION DATA

Names: Bonner, Michael Brem, 1970–

Title: Confederate political economy : creating and managing a Southern corporatist nation / Michael Brem Bonner.

Description: Baton Rouge : Louisiana State University Press, [2016] | Series: Conflicting worlds: new dimensions of the American Civil War | Includes bibliographical references and index.

Identifiers: LCCN 2015035405 | ISBN 978-0-8071-6212-5 (cloth : alk. paper) | ISBN 978-0-8071-6214-9 (pdf) | ISBN 978-0-8071-6213-2 (epub) | ISBN 978-0-8071-6215-6 (mobi)

Subjects: LCSH: Confederate States of America—Economic conditions. | Confederate States of America—Economic policy. | Confederate States of America—History.

Classification: LCC HC105.65 .B66 2016 | DDC 330.975/03—dc23 LC record available at http://lccn.loc.gov/2015035405

This book is dedicated to Roger Ransom—
one could not ask for a better mentor.

Contents

Preface

The author is indebted to many individuals and institutions for generous assistance in this project's completion. Roger Ransom deserves special mention for believing in the project and providing continual inspirational support through graduate school and into the first phases of a career in history. Many thanks go to T. Michael Parrish, who encouraged me at several key points and exhibited a courteous patience as I plodded away on the manuscript between job changes and teaching duties. Mike is a gentleman and a genuine Civil War scholar. At several points in the writing process, Mike pointed out additional resources like little-known articles and even pamphlets on specific subjects related to the topic at hand. I dare say that Mike's knowledge of Civil War scholarship is unmatched when it comes to Confederate source materials. It has been a pleasure working with him and I am proud to be added to the list of authors in his edited series at LSU Press.

My colleague at the University of South Carolina Lancaster, Dr. Richard Van Hall, deserves special thanks for reading parts of the manuscript and providing useful feedback on several themes.

An Archie K. Davis fellowship from the North Caroliniana Society allowed me to extensively research Confederate political culture at the Southern Historical Collection in 2011. A Research & Productive Scholarship Grant from the University of South Carolina Lancaster helped me to research the Shelby Iron Company at the W. S. Hoole Special Collections Library at the University of Alabama and perform additional research on the Confederate domestic passport system at the National Archives in Washington, D.C., in the summer of 2012. Donnelly Walton and the staff at the University of Alabama's W. S. Hoole Special Collections were wonderful and helped me track down documents about the Shelby Iron Company from that vast collection.

Useful comments after presentations at the All UC Economic History Conference and the Southern Historical Association helped refine some points. Mary DeCredico, Sean Patrick Adams, and especially John Majewski provided constructive comments in the early stages of the work. Several students at the University of Arizona—Sean Harvey, Joel Childers, and Guru Simran "Goose" Khalsa—provided vital research assistance.

Kristina Dunn Johnson at the South Carolina Confederate Relic Room and Military Museum went beyond the call of duty with assistance in tracking down specific documents. Judy Bolton at Louisiana State University's Special Collections promptly and courteously fulfilled long distance requests for important documents. Orville Vernon Burton helped me sort out some of the details about the origins of state-level conscription.

In using primary source materials from the Civil War era, one encounters a variety of often poorly handwritten words that are misspelled or grammatically incorrect. To promote an improved reading flow, I decided against using [sic] after misspelled words and corrected them to prevent unnecessary distraction. In my opinion, this does not detract from an authentic experience. Since the historian is frequently the liaison between the primary source materials and the readers, I believe it is the author's duty to eliminate mistakes and clutter in conveying historical information. In short, I believe the accuracy of historical content is not compromised by correcting the spelling and grammatical errors of past voices for the benefit of the reading audience. Any errors are the sole responsibility of the author.

CONFEDERATE POLITICAL ECONOMY

---·❖·---

INTRODUCTION

---·❖·---

T he Confederate experience continues to be a source of fascination
for general audiences and professional historians alike. Scholars of
Confederate history typically explore various compelling themes of
adaptation, endurance, dissent, and tragedy on both the military and home
fronts. After many volumes, however, the nature of the Confederacy remains a somewhat elusive and controversial topic, and several questions require deeper investigation. Did the Confederate States of America meet the
requirements of nationhood? Did coercive Confederate government policies bolster nationalism or exacerbate popular dissent? How did southern
civilians react to increasing centralization and onerous wartime burdens?
The main goal of this study is to describe Confederate political culture, the
political system in action, wartime industrial policy, and railroad policy in
order to establish a new model for an improved understanding of Confederate political economy.

Political economy is a field of investigation that developed alongside the
other social sciences in the early nineteenth century. Intellectuals posited
hypothetical changes in economic systems in hopes that they could scien-
tifically predict and improve society. American writers like John Taylor,
Daniel Raymond, Jacob Cardozo, and Thomas Cooper contributed to, and
built upon, the growing field previously dominated by European thinkers
like Adam Smith, Thomas Malthus, David Ricardo, and Robert Owen. For
these authors, political economy was a philosophical endeavor endowed
with scientific certainty.[1] The academic musings of political economists
were intended to produce blueprints for an improved social system, but
most theories, although intellectually stimulating, did not easily translate
into social reality. Thus for historians, political economy diverges into two

distinct fields: the first is a theoretical discourse of how society should be organized and the second interprets the actual political and economic relationships between existing institutions. This study focuses on the latter approach, and seeks to describe the nature of the Confederate system and how the government, bureaucrats, industrial leaders, and citizens interacted to construct their own distinctly Confederate political economy.

The concept of modernization has received widespread historical usage since the second half of the twentieth century. Some historians utilize the concept as an explanatory tool for discussion of national transitions to either industrialized states or at least a less traditional society. Theorist of comparative modernism C. E. Black defined the concept as "the process by which historically evolved institutions are adapted to the rapidly changing functions" of social circumstances. In political and economic terms, modernization precipitated "the desire . . . in both government and private enterprise to mobilize and rationalize the resources of society with a view to achieving greater control, efficiency, and production."[2] Modernization theory allowed for a more universalized approach to interpret developmental stages outside the Western European contexts of colonialism. Scholarly disagreement naturally arose about the utility of the new concept. Proponents believed modernization could be useful to analyze practically any society that underwent drastic change, and critics typically attacked the overt generalization of modernization theory as being virtually devoid of substantial meaning. Still today, the concept of modernism is difficult to define and not firmly established as an unambiguous interpretive model.

By the 1960s, a standard school of modernization theory developed that allowed historians to construct comparative studies based on a widely accepted definition of modernization and opened a new conceptual framework for Civil War scholars. Other scholarly works that deal with specific aspects of Civil War modernization are too numerous to list here, but it might suffice to say that historians have thoroughly explored and are still examining modernist themes.[3] This work will add to the long list of scholarship on Civil War modernization and will attempt to explain Confederate political economy in relation to other modern political and economic systems.

An ideology of southern modernization existed well before 1861. Prominent southern writers and political leaders advocated government intervention into agriculture, trade, and internal improvements.[4] Prewar modernist schemes, however, usually achieved negligible results until secession allowed for an experimental atmosphere of centralization. The enduring suspicions of many large-scale planters prevented prewar modernization, but secession forced slaveholders to reconsider modernist policies in a war for survival. After secession, planters hoped modernization could be controlled by the traditional elite through political means. Thus Confederate modernization was ironically facilitated by a largely antimodern group of slaveholders who sought to limit and define southern industrialization on their own terms through the Confederate state. In the absence of powerful bourgeois competition for political and economic control, southern slaveholding elites dictated the political parameters of their counterrevolution, but their dominance was contested by private sector industrial leaders during the war.

Wartime circumstances pushed Confederate leaders to adopt a centralized, but flexible, system to support national survival, but this new structure was not simply a "top-down" command economy as some historians suggest.[5] During the Civil War, Confederate modernization involved a complicated process of give-and-take between bureaucrats and industrial managers, with each group liable and responsible to the other for mutual success. Labor was a vital element in later corporatist arrangements but less influential in the Confederacy's expedient corporatist state because skilled industrial workers were not widespread and much of the Confederacy's industrial labor was performed by slaves. The existing southern industries could not produce sufficient war materiel, so Confederate bureaucrats developed a constellation of armaments industries that depended on a curious mixture of private and government ownership. Both sectors shared the same goals of national survival but squabbled over access to supplies, labor, and profits. By 1865, Confederate modernization had progressed in ways that prewar industrial boosters could not have anticipated. The plans of antebellum industrial advocates were accelerated and warped by the war effort to points of unforeseen direction and extent. The experience of Confederate modernization represented a brief foray into twentieth century–style corporatist organizational state methods, a system of powerful interest blocs partnered with government institutions for mutual benefit.

Explaining the Confederate system is daunting and often unwieldy, so it is important to admit the limitations of this study and to mention what it will not cover. This is not a narrative on specific Confederate military operations, yet it fully recognizes the importance of military contingency in any wartime study. If the Civil War teaches us anything, it is that few policy makers foresaw the eventual scale of the conflict, and unanticipated daily events often dictated long-term policy decisions. The ebb and flow of military operations directly affected Confederate policy development, but battlefield events will only be mentioned with regard to their specific influence on political and economic decisions. Confederate leaders and civilians understood that their fledgling nation could only exist so long as rebel armies remained in the field. This is the story of how the Confederate government organized its political, economic, industrial, and human resources to ensure that enough military materiel was available to continue that tenuous existence. The fact that the Confederacy endured for four years was somewhat of a minor miracle, considering the numerous disadvantages and obstacles that confronted the aspiring nation. One point that warrants repetition is the obvious fact that the evolution of Confederate political economy occurred in the context of a war for national survival, and all other considerations were deemed secondary by devoted southern nationalists.

This work is also not a social history of the wartime South, and thus some readers may be disappointed by the lack of detail on the popular experience. Other scholars have already provided a rich background of Confederate social history. Underrepresented groups in the historical documentation pose a serious concern for scholars of the Confederacy. The lack of written material is particularly frustrating when one attempts to assess the vital position of slaves, and historians are also hindered with regard to women's influence on political and economic developments.

White women of all classes certainly represented a pivotal category of southern support. However, as historian Stephanie McCurry points out, "all of the new developments in the political culture" of the Confederacy "proceeded from the view, universally held, that women were not parties to war, that they played no role in the politics that had brought it on and would take no part in waging it."[6] Southern women possessed significant influence over soldier morale and even organized, especially during the food riots of early 1863, to protest Confederate policies. These protests exhibited the common dynamics of moral economy as described by social historian E. P. Thompson. Southern bread riots, headed by charismatic and well-organized middling and lower-class women, "were triggered . . . by soaring prices, by malpractices among dealers, or by hunger," but were fundamentally motivated by "a popular consensus as to what were legitimate and what were illegitimate practices" with regard to accessing enough food.

Hunger initiated the riots, and the ineffective system of food distribution forced women into the streets and pushed them to challenge social and economic norms. The women's sense of moral economy sustained their purpose and justified their efforts to the larger southern population. E. P. Thompson pointed out the nebulous political nature of this type of riot and noted, "this moral economy cannot be described as 'political' in any advanced sense, nevertheless it cannot be described as unpolitical either." Josiah Gorgas, the observant Ordnance Department head, aptly described the motivation for the 1863 women's riot in Richmond and believed "their pretence was bread; but their motive was really license."[7] State reaction depended on whether political leaders believed the women's grievances to be legitimate, which most eventually tacitly acknowledged, but the riotous discourse conducted in the spring of 1863 on the streets of Richmond, Salisbury, Mobile, and other southern cities, was motivated by common sentiments of moral economy that had been consistently eroded by Confederate policies. In other words, during the 1863 food riots, "the moral economy of the crowd" defiantly confronted Confederate political economy.

This ongoing exchange between the people and the government lay at the heart of an evolving and flexible Confederate nationalism. Protesting soldiers' wives claimed entitlements from state governments, but their actions stemmed from impending starvation and were carried out in the context of legitimate demands as citizens. State welfare for orphans and widows was a common-sense solution to the wartime exigencies of the home front, not necessarily undertaken because the Confederacy recognized a new era of women's political activity. Women caused policy alteration and measured reform in paternalist policies, but their public activities were symptomatic, and not aimed at producing fundamental changes in Confederate political economy. As always, the instinct of national survival propelled Confederate policy decisions, and women were swept into the evolution of an ad hoc Confederate system.

African American slaves primarily influenced Confederate policy by being a potential fifth column that could undermine the war effort. In

Charleston, five days before the firing on Fort Sumter, the well-connected and opinionated South Carolinian Mary Chesnut "had it out on the subject of civil war" with the wife of Texas secessionist Louis Wigfall, as they both contemplated "what we had a right to expect, with Yankees in front and negroes in the rear." Longtime southern nationalist Edmund Ruffin openly admitted in February 1861 that southerners "all know, that if our slaves so choose, they could kill every white person on any farm, or even through a neighborhood, in any night," but Ruffin also complained that few communities were taking precautions against such possible insurrections.[8] Even if many Confederates would not openly admit it, white southerners understood they might face an internal slave insurrection of unknown degree at some point during the upcoming struggle.

Secession and the tide of war prompted different forms of slave action, some aggressive and others passive, against the Confederate state. Slave rebellions varied from simply running away to the more direct action of joining Union armed forces, but overall the Confederacy avoided a simultaneous "general strike" by slaves. Decades of experience assisted the slaveholding regime and allowed it to maintain some semblance of social control over the slaves if masters could keep their servants away from the vicinity of Union armies. Preemptive violence, as discussed by historian Winthrop D. Jordan, like the hanging of twenty-seven or more slaves in response to a rumored rebellion outside Natchez, Mississippi, in September 1861, typified the constant threat to slaves who understood the risks involved in open rebellion.[9] For slaves with no access to the protection of Union armed forces, the risks of overt rebellion might outweigh the immediate rewards, especially when a bit more patience could lead to the cherished goal of emancipation.

As the war progressed, slaves understood that the Confederacy was losing and emancipation was eventually inevitable, so individual slaves were forced to weigh their desire for immediate freedom against the possibility of bodily harm or death should they rise up against their masters and the Confederate state. Many slaves exhibited a more defiant attitude towards masters during the war, and some did employ extreme measures of resistance towards state authority, but a significant number of slaves realized that the safest and most sure method to obtain freedom was to wait for Union armies to destroy the Confederacy. Had a majority of the slave population engaged in a simultaneous general strike, at any point in the war but especially in the later stages from 1863 to 1865, the Confederacy likely could not have continued the struggle for more than a few months. The Confederacy was overly dependent on slave labor in several economic sectors, and a general strike would not only have crippled many forms of production, but also would have created an internal security threat to assist encroaching Union forces in the final destruction of the Confederate system.

Both the Union and the Confederacy sought to utilize the slaves as a war resource, and both sides had distinct advantages based on time. In the short term, the Confederacy possessed the advantage of a strong slave labor system, relied on the momentum of perpetual tradition, and harnessed slave labor to assist in home-front duties. Some southern nationalists believed slave labor would be an asset and would free up white male laborers for military service. In January 1845, James Henry Hammond, outspoken paternalist advocate of slavery as a "positive good," lectured British abolitionist Thomas Clarkson on the wartime benefits of race-based slavery. Hammond warned Clarkson "it is a great mistake to suppose . . . that in case of war slavery would be a source of weakness" and asserted "if, as I am satisfied would be the case, our slaves remained peaceful on our plantations . . . in time of war under the superintendence of a limited number of our citizens, it is obvious we could put forth more strength in such an emergency, at less sacrifice, than any other people of the same numbers."[10] This overly confident assumption was widespread among slave owners and southern rhetoricians by 1861. As the war progressed, the scale of mobilization shifted white male labor resources to the armies, and productive slave labor became even more vital. The balance between home-front labor needs and maintenance of adequate southern armies increasingly tilted in favor of military service, and although the Confederacy needed a consistent labor supply, by 1865, the military manpower shortage had become so acute that southern leaders even considered using slaves as soldiers.

The North also possessed an advantage in the contest to access the power of African American slaves. The Union's momentum increased as the Confederacy's advantage of perpetual tradition eroded. Abraham Lincoln summed up this crucial competitive element in the bid to utilize the massive resources of four million African American slaves in his famous July 1862 phrase, "we must free the slaves or be ourselves subdued." The Union eventually enrolled roughly 150,000 former slaves as soldiers and was assisted by the labor of other freedmen and freedwomen to support the war effort. The Union clearly possessed the superior ideological position in this contest for African Americans, but the Confederacy did attempt to maintain control of this vital human resource through controversial policies like the exemption of large slaveholders from military conscription. The South's slave population was an essential element in the formation of Confederate political economy, but it was misunderstood and mismanaged by southern power brokers. Confederate leaders simply could not conceive of the slave population as an active influence on policy formation until too late.

Women and African American slaves played important roles as factors in policy development, and their actions certainly helped to shape the limits of Confederate political economy. When applicable, their experiences enhance the narrative of a desperate Confederate government constantly trying to juggle all the nation's problems in the midst of war. Both groups represented important components of southern society, but neither was a foundational element in the construction of Confederate political economy because political leaders refused to fully acknowledge their potential contributions.

Every historian of the South must eventually contend with one major theme of the region's past: continuity. The fundamental question can be stated: What elements of antebellum society survived the Civil War and continued during the postwar era to become staples of the New South's identity into the twentieth century? There are several sub-themes within the continuity argument and various methods can be used to reinforce conclusions, but the two main elements of the historical dispute are race and economics. The historical literature on both of these sub-themes is extensive and the interpretations seem endless, yet inevitably historians of the South must address these issues. The most popular sub-theme, what might be termed the constant of racial hierarchy, or white supremacy, will not be covered in this study. The war simultaneously shattered paternalist notions of slave loyalty and also reinforced white supremacy among southern whites.

Economic histories of the South often focus on the transition from the slave labor system to the postwar era of debt peonage resulting from sharecropping and tenancy. This work will largely ignore agricultural developments and focus on Confederate industrial policies crafted to meet the constant crises of wartime supply. The topics of political control and economic development are central to comprehension of the Confederate experience, but this study will not attempt to draw long-term conclusions from wartime events. Historians who emphasize continuity tend to pick and choose the portions of the Confederate experience that prove their arguments and neglect to interpret the totality of the war years. Confederate political economy was vastly different from any system implemented before or after the war, so some students of southern political economy tend to treat the Confederate era as an aberration. Although defeat precluded many potential long-range developments, the methods and achievements of the Confederate system allowed for the nation's immediate survival and established precedents for governance that directly foreshadowed other modern forms of national organization. The Confederacy was a severe break with the antebellum past and Confederate political economy did not carry over into the postwar decades, although some scholars assert that it did. Therefore in terms of political economy, the Confederacy represents a stark example of discontinuity in southern history.

This work will argue that the Confederacy implemented one of the world's first examples of a corporatist political economy and provide a new synthesis to better understand the short-lived nature of the Confederate state in terms of "expedient corporatism." Confederate leaders did not possess a preconceived political blueprint for their nascent government and did not intentionally create a corporatist state. Instead, they were dominated by circumstance and typically used ad hoc methods to temporarily satisfy wartime demands.

Corporatism is a model used to describe governments over a wide range of historical eras and geographic locations. The flexibility of corporatist doctrine might evoke criticisms of its use as a "catchall" for disparate political forms, but there are basic common aspects of all corporatist states regardless of geography or historical era.[11] Corporatism is an arrangement of shared governance and responsibility between the public and private sectors in which government, business, and labor provide direction for mutually beneficial economic policies. Other interest groups can also be important members of corporatist organizations, but in all cases each group must be sanctioned by the state. Each interest group is given some authority in policy formulation under the auspices of the corporatist state.

A major task of this study will be to describe and analyze these categories of interest groups and their relationship with the Confederate state. Prioritization meant that some groups possessed greater political influence and powers of policy creation than others. However, the relationship between each interest group and the government was always symbiotic; each group needed the other for survival.

In addition to this functional definition of an active corporatist state, there are several other requirements for the term's application. First, corporatism is an organizational method for societies with capitalist backgrounds. Corporatist philosophy is founded in the attempt to utilize government for a more orderly market system. A corporatist nation embraces markets but only if they are overseen by the partnership of government, business, and labor. Although capitalist, corporatist states stifle laissez-faire traits in exchange for a more controlled system predicated on an integration of government needs and private sector goals. Corporatism also represents a reactionary, or counterrevolutionary, political-economic model that seeks to reverse the perceived excesses of liberal capitalism. Adherents to corporatist political systems often denounced the lack of structure in a laissez-faire economy and the incipient class conflict in an uncontrolled society. For corporatist theorists, unlimited market capitalism threatened the traditional political and social order and thus needed to be bent to the will of ruling elites.[12]

Corporatist states foster the growth of distinct interest groups that greatly influence, and often direct, state policy. Vital economic sectors are not dictated to, or commanded, by the state, but instead become quasi-partners in government operations. In corporatist regimes, private economic sectors assume roles that conflate with public sector duties.[13] Private interest groups serve as important channels for policy creation and thus become protected hybrid sectors of public and private power. Policy formulation and government implementation are therefore dependent on private sector acquiescence in exchange for continued state support.

Corporatist organization can be sparked from a central state apparatus or initiated in response to a crisis. Confederate leaders certainly operated under the behavioral influence of economic and political crises, and the development of the Confederate state evolved in an ad hoc manner based on wartime contingencies from 1861 to 1865.[14] What began as an experiment with new modes of organization evolved into a centralized state that implemented policies to deal with each emerging crisis with the available economic, industrial, political, and human resources at hand. Confederate political and economic systems were directly shaped by the rapidly changing circumstances of war.

Twentieth-century corporatism is typically associated with bourgeois governmental movements that sought to reassert control over society. For example, historian Charles Maier brilliantly explained how bourgeois leaders in France, Germany, and Italy utilized corporatist methods to briefly regain command of their respective national political economies in the early interwar period after 1919.[15] Confederate leaders might be termed conservative reactionaries, but most were part of a semi-aristocratic class of slaveholders wary of rising bourgeois power. From their perspective, northern bourgeois society had initiated the evils of rampant liberalism, unrestricted industrial capitalism, and antagonistic abolitionism. Confederate leaders did not represent the bourgeois counterrevolution typically associated with early twentieth-century corporatist movements and likely would have cringed at the association.

Critics of the term *expedient*, when used with regard to the description of political systems, point out its potential wide application and argue that every government is, at least to some degree, expedient in nature. Most, if not all, self-professing democratic republics like the Confederacy must operate within the realm of the possible, keeping both policy goals and public support in mind. Every law is the result of an expedient system of give-and-take between political leaders and their constituents. This is a legitimate interpretation of peacetime governance, but in this study, the term *expedient* is meant to reemphasize the importance of wartime circumstances that underlay each government decision. Confederate leaders relied on an ad hoc method of policy construction mainly because they were under the duress of an all-consuming war. Also, the title *expedient* allows historians to explain the improvised dichotomy of private and state-owned industrial facilities that cooperated to provide vital war materiel to southern armies.

The word *expedient* also exonerates Confederate leaders from accusations by conspiracy-minded historians who might dismiss them as inherently undemocratic. Confederate leaders were conservatives, and many even believed in a more limited white male franchise based on property qualifications, but they were not antimodern tyrants who intentionally created a proto-fascist state. Application of the word *expedient* is vital to our understanding of the southern wartime experience and the development of the Confederate corporatist system.

Two assumptions about antebellum southern society must be clear before one applies a corporatist label to the Confederate experiment. First, one must agree with the assertion that antebellum southern political economy was capitalist in nature and that the leaders of the southern secession movement might be termed planter or agricultural capitalists.[16] The notion that the southern slave system represented a semifeudal or precapitalist labor system is incompatible with wartime corporatist development, since only societies with capitalist backgrounds typically implement this political-economic model.

The reader must also accept the assertion that secession was not a revolution but a reactionary counterrevolution. Southern leaders sought to protect the antebellum paradigm in which southern interests, especially the protection and possible growth of slavery, could be provided for by the new Confederate state.[17] If one can accept that southern society and the economy were capitalist and that secession represented a preemptive counterrevolution, then one might proceed to argue that the Confederacy exhibited the requisite characteristics of a society and economy open to corporatist development.

Confederate political culture initially developed against a background of well-defined antebellum ideological positions but evolved into new dimensions as the war dragged on past the expectations of southern political leaders in 1861. Secession prompted an accelerated process of constitutional construction, but Confederate delegates possessed a ready-made foundation in the U.S. Constitution. Most southern leaders were comfortable imitating the founding fathers' contract because they believed correct interpretation would remedy the ills that pushed them to rebellion. However, if government centralization in Washington, D.C. in the Old Republic was the primary reason for secession, then the delegates responsible for the new nation's Constitution not only refused to correct the centralizing features of the U.S. Constitution but created a system that allowed for extensive authoritarian governance.

Constitutional delegates did not necessarily intend to consolidate national power, but several aspects of Confederate political culture fostered an environment of centralization. The Confederate Constitution allowed for extensive presidential powers, including six-year terms of office, a line-item veto, and executive control over government expenditures. Although some Davis administration critics attacked the president's policies due to personal animosity, accusations of despotism could be legitimately supported by the unprecedented expansion of executive powers. The constitution also called for creation of a supreme court, but Confederate leaders failed to implement this potentially powerful instrument and thereby assured judicial branch impotency. The lack of national judicial review implied that the president and Congress could exert unchallenged dominance over policy creation and legal interpretation.

Delegates to the February 1861 constitutional convention in Montgomery, Alabama, mimicked the creators of the U.S. Constitution through the use of secret sessions to fashion their document. Desires to project a united front against the incoming Lincoln administration and to attract the undecided Upper South states provided a legitimate reason for Confederate delegates to use secret sessions. However, the permanent Congress continued the practice of secret deliberations ostensibly in the interest of national security for the remainder of the war. At times the Congress had valid reasons to meet in seclusion, especially when specific discussions of troop strengths and military topics dominated debates, but secrecy raised suspicions among citizens and drew criticism from government watchdogs, especially the press.

An environment of antiparty sentiment among Confederate political leaders developed during the constitutional convention and carried over into wartime political culture, stifling political dissent. The lack of established parties fostered the notion of a legislative monolith bent to the will of the executive and arguably unresponsive to the people's needs. The acrimonious partisan experiences of the antebellum decades gave way to apparent unanimity and an obsequious Congress that merely validated executive power and government consolidation.

Confederate delegates did not intentionally develop an autocratic government. However, the aspiring nation's constitutional foundations provided for the potential creation of a more centralized state, combined with greater executive powers, lack of judicial review, the prevailing antiparty sentiment, and the use of secret sessions. As a result, the Confederate government appeared, if not functioned, as an authoritarian state.

The Confederate system was a remarkable engine of state survival but required controversial public policies to maintain sovereignty. At various stages of the war the Confederate government was forced by circumstance to implement policies such as a domestic passport system, suspension of habeas corpus, and military conscription. These policies defined the relationship between the southern citizenry and the Confederate government. If the southern populace defied government authority or withheld popular support in reaction to these measures, then the Confederacy could not sustain the war effort for any appreciable time. Thus a consensual relationship between the Richmond government and the people was crucial to eventual success, and southern nationalists largely consented to this centralization. Perhaps no Confederate policy exemplified the power of the expedient corporatist state like conscription. The necessity of maintaining a standing army forced Confederate leaders to enact and expand conscription laws in April 1862, October 1862, and February 1864. Conscription provided the Confederate government with unprecedented power to control not only the size of its military, but also to directly control private access to labor through exemptions. As the war progressed, fewer draft exemptions were allowed and some became subjects of popular dissent, like the "twenty slave clause" passed in the fall of 1862. Some historians attempt to track waning Confederate nationalism by analyzing the growth of dissent against conscription from 1862 to 1865. Despite considerable popular resistance, Confederate leaders were compelled by circumstances to continue with conscripted mobilization as an expedient necessary for continued state existence. If some civil liberties had to be temporarily set aside, then Confederate leaders proved willing to pursue the interests of the state over individual rights. This is not to say that Davis and other Confederate leaders conspired to foist an undemocratic plot on the southern people and force them to participate in the war. Leaders resorted to policies like conscription, domestic passports, and suspension of habeas corpus as temporary expedients, but these controversial policies symbolized the logical results of an authoritarian political culture. Centralized implementation of such government policies embodied the Confederacy's shared characteristics with later corporatist regimes.

Confederate political culture and policies also influenced southern wartime industrial development. This aspect of Confederate political economy perhaps best symbolized the creation of an expedient corporatist state. Historians have been forced to come to terms with a mixture of both state-owned, or nationalized, and privately owned industries when attempting to describe the South's industrial sectors. This has usually caused analysis to focus solely on either government-owned industries or the private sectors, and rarely have the two distinctly different categories been combined into one comprehensive interpretive model. Application of the term *expedient corporatist* state is an attempt to explain the dichotomy of Confederate industrial production and how the two styles coexisted during the war. Vital private industries, like the Tredegar Iron Works, received government patronage and competitive protection in exchange for war-based production priority. If the private sector was unable to meet the government's wartime needs, then state ownership became an option to fill the production gap. Confederate state ownership helped to fill vital sectors of industrial production, some of which did not exist before the war, while others were purchased and expanded by government officials. For example, to maintain a sufficient supply of crucial resources like gunpowder, the Confederacy constructed and managed a massive gunpowder plant in Augusta, Georgia. In other examples of state ownership, however, the Confederacy purchased private industries unable to profitably operate in the wartime economy and expanded production with government investment and management. By utilizing extant private facilities and creating state-owned industrial sites, the Confederacy was able to produce sufficient munitions to wage war for four years against a vastly superior industrial foe. The accomplishments of Josiah Gorgas and the Confederate Ordnance Bureau during the Civil War should be regarded as little short of miraculous.

Private economic sectors and industries played key roles in the Confederate war effort such that their contributions and experiences also symbolized the actions of a corporatist state. In addition to being capitalist, counterrevolutionary, and resistant to liberalism, corporatist states allow powerful private-interest blocs to provide leadership in policy formation in return for government support and production priorities. Important private industries, especially those vital to the war effort, possessed great leverage in dealing with Confederate authorities, and influenced policy creation for their economic sector. The term "patriotism for profit" used by historian Mary DeCredico to describe Georgia's wartime urban entrepreneurs might also be applied to larger private interest blocs, which arguably placed profits before patriotism. Far from being a simple "command economy," the relationship between the state and these private interest blocs was symbiotic: Both parties received benefits from the other and depended on the other for survival. This relationship was meant to assure Confederate leaders of sufficient munitions and other products, and in exchange, select private industries received government subsidies, patronage, protection from competition, and occasionally a direct role in Confederate policy formation.

Confederate railroad policy has typically been interpreted by historians as little short of disastrous and a significant aspect of defeat, but these same historians rarely delve into the organizational elements of this policy, preferring instead to point out its confusing nature. Southern railroad corporations were vital to the Confederate war effort and directly formulated state railroad policy. During the antebellum period, southern railroad companies enjoyed a close operational relationship with individual states, including Georgia and North Carolina, each of which also directly owned and operated some railroads. Despite the resistance of planters and Democratic leaders, the southern states had increased their railroad mileage by a higher percentage than the North in the decade before the war. Obviously, competent management and operation of the South's extant railroads would be an important factor in the Confederate war effort, especially in terms of utilizing interior lines of defense and ensuring proper supply of armies at the front. As a result, one might have expected the Confederate government to implement a centralized plan for state management of the rail system.[18] Government control of the railroads did not occur until 1865, but a valid Confederate railroad policy did exist from 1861 to 1865, although it did not strictly conform to laissez-faire principles. Confederate railroad policy consisted of an ad hoc approach designed and submitted by the managers of private rail companies and was approved by the state. Due to the primacy of private concerns in the development of public policy, Confederate railroad policy is one of the best examples of expedient corporatism in action.

Confederate leaders understood that drastic measures were necessary in their bold bid for independence and resolved to cooperate on policies crafted to promote state survival. With a centralizing political culture, they implemented an expedient corporatist state to mobilize the southern populace and develop an industrial base sufficient to wage a modern war. This style of governance was a forerunner for later governments that also sought to roll back the perceived negative consequences of liberal modernism. The Confederacy was not a nineteenth-century aberration but the first of many modern conservative counterrevolutionary movements to battle the rise of liberalism and unfettered industrial capitalism. Confederate leaders attempted to break away from the liberal democracy of the North and preserve their peculiar vision of republican government. In the process, they created a centralized modern government with expedient corporatist qualities.

1

POLITICAL CULTURE

The best known public Measures are . . . seldom adopted from
previous Wisdom, but forc'd by the Occasion.
—Benjamin Franklin, *The Autobiography of Benjamin Franklin*

Confederate political economy must be discussed in terms of southern political culture as it evolved from 1861 to 1865, years that provided a foundation and encouraged the maturation of an expedient corporatist state. One must begin with a functional, widely accepted definition of political culture to set a standard for further investigation. Political culture in nations with democratic traditions can be defined as the substance of political thought and action derived from interaction between the individual and the state.[1] In other words, political culture is the ongoing relationship between citizens and the government, both directly and through elected representatives, with both groups constantly negotiating the terms of their mutual existence. Political culture derives impetus from popular reaction to government policies and the resultant state adaptations to maintain legitimacy in the eyes of political participants. As a unifying medium of discourse between the people and the state, political culture can thus promote or hinder the development of nationalism. This chapter focuses on the milieu of Confederate politics and analyzes the modernist political bedrock of the Confederacy's expedient corporatist state.

Various methods of examining nineteenth-century political culture exist and can be divided into roughly three categories: statistical, social, and organizational studies.[2] Statistical works usually look at election returns to measure popular support of government policies and often extrapolate analyses from winning percentages and voter turnout. Social investigations of political culture focus on family and community development of political participation, partisan education, political symbols and campaign ephemera, and even the sociology of voting at the ballot box. Organizational studies tend to describe the creation and function of the political system, the nature of the constitution, legislation, bureaucracies, and policy development. This work falls under the organizational category with a special focus on the Confederate political environment. The goal is to construct an interpretive framework based on the nature and foundations of Confederate politics in order to achieve a synthesis of political economy. The foundational elements of Confederate political culture require deeper investigation before one can analyze the specific policies and popular reaction.

THE CONFEDERATE CONSTITUTION

To understand Confederate political culture, one needs to investigate the underlying philosophies of the Confederate Constitution. In many respects, the Confederate Constitution is relatively easy to analyze because scholars are not obliged to deal with issues of original meaning that often cloud the historical interpretation of the U.S. Constitution. Since the Confederate Constitution only operated for roughly four years, historians need only to glean the immediate intent of the constitutional framers and not worry about long-term political ideology. Historians disagree over minor points of original intent, but many agree with the basic interpretation that the Confederate Constitution was simply an adapted version of the U.S. Constitution. This adherence to the old Constitution was not unusual, since most southerners believed that the national document, when interpreted in terms consistent with southern state ratification in the 1780s, protected slavery. Secessionists believed the new Confederate document restored the true meaning of the U.S. Constitution without the abolitionist taint. However, the Confederate Constitution, despite scholarly arguments that it merely mimicked the U.S. document and added safeguards for slavery, was fundamentally different from the U.S. Constitution in several respects.

What was the intent of the Confederate Constitution's framers? When one assesses the sectional disagreements over constitutional interpretation from the early republic through 1860, it becomes easy for historians to link the various episodes with the sectional battle over slavery's future. Slavery was the most important point of disagreement and represented a fundamental regional dispute. By 1860 southern slaveholders understood their dim prospects for long-term economic protection within the federal framework. Through secession they could create a system that continued their political control and institutions. Secessionists were intent on continuing their economic dominance with slave labor and possible expansion in the new Confederate system.[3]

Delegates to the February 1861 Montgomery convention confronted a complex situation that required simultaneous decisiveness and prudent deliberation. Lower South secessionists needed to act quickly to construct a government, but more importantly, it was absolutely necessary that they fashion a constitution to coax the Upper South states into the Confederacy. On both counts, the delegates achieved fantastic success. In order to rapidly construct a legitimate government, delegates adopted the Georgia Plan and, as described by historian Don Fehrenbacher, "assumed the multiple role of provisional congress, electoral college, and constitutional convention."[4] From the initial gathering of representatives on February 4th to the adjournment of the provisional congress on March 16th, delegates created the Confederate States of America in a mere forty-one days! By contrast, the U.S. Constitutional Convention, May 25th to September 17th, 1787, required 116 days, although it arguably had a more difficult task. Delegates worked at a frantic pace but also sagaciously deliberated and incorporated moderate aspects into the constitution to attract the Upper South slave states into their new republic. Issues like renewal of the African slave trade and regional protective tariffs were explicitly denied in hopes of attracting the Upper South, especially Virginia, into the Confederacy.

Detailed day-to-day histories of Confederate constitutional construction highlight the debates, issues, and leaders responsible for the quick creation of both the provisional and permanent constitutions.[5] The most obvious addition to the Confederate Constitution, when compared to the U.S. document, was the explicit protection and guaranteed perpetuation of slave property, but alternate solutions to other issues like strict construction, protective tariffs, internal improvements, and increased executive powers also symbolized Confederate constitutional construction.

Confederate constitutional delegates decided to close some of the vaguely phrased loopholes that allowed for centralization in the U.S. Constitution. Fundamental differences in the Confederate Constitution included the attempted alteration of national supremacy and the omission of broad construction clauses. In the U.S. Constitution, the primary justifications for strong national powers and broad construction can be found in the "supremacy" and "general welfare" clauses. Confederate framers included a "supremacy" clause in Article VI, but simultaneously added states' rights protection almost identical to the Ninth and Tenth Amendments in the U.S. document.[6] Thus, delegates did not decisively resolve the issue of state versus centralized authority but merely carried the debate over national supremacy and original state sovereignty into their new republic. States' rights eventually evolved into a greater philosophical dilemma for the Confederacy than it was for previous American generations.

To overturn broad construction, the framers omitted the general welfare clause. According to the U.S. Constitution's preamble, one of the government's primary purposes is to "promote the general welfare," which could be widely interpreted to mean a variety of policies determined by the current political majority. Confederate framers replaced promotion of the general welfare with an assurance to "secure the blessings of liberty to ourselves and our posterity."[7] Over the next four years, circumstances ensured that the philosophical debate over supremacy and sovereignty continued among southern political thinkers, but the constitution clearly curbed many of the elastic constitutional interpretations possible under the U.S. Constitution.

Refusal to continue the broad construction clauses represented a deep ideological belief in strict construction and linked the Confederacy with similar ideologies from the early republic. Thomas Jefferson's principles of limited government founded this historically cherished constitutional principle, even though many southerners ignored, or selectively interpreted, Jefferson's views on equality. Andrew Jackson and John C. Calhoun reinvigorated strict construction principles during the 1820s and 1830s and passed them along to the next generation of southern politicians. Thus by 1861, secessionists could tap a rich history of limited government principles. Confederate constitutional framers almost universally believed in the sanctity of strict construction and sought to avoid a loose construction of their governing document. The omission of broad construction clauses marked a fundamental difference between U.S. and Confederate constitutional development.

If delegates expected the absence of broad construction clauses to seriously hamstring the national government's powers, they were ultimately disappointed. The Confederate Constitution positively affirmed the Confederate government's supremacy. The delegate's omission of broad construction elements was no impediment to government centralization but merely a homage to bygone constitutional principles of strict construction. Historians tend to overemphasize the states' rights and decentralizing principles in the Confederate Constitution, and, for that matter, in the Confederate experience as a whole. Moreover, historians rarely mention the fact that the Confederate Constitution failed to prevent centralization.[8]

Most Americans knew that slavery was the root cause of antebellum sectionalism and was the sine qua non of the secession crisis. Whether it was nullification, internal improvements, or American expansion, the heated sectionalist arguments of the antebellum decades centered on differing constitutional interpretations of slavery. Southerners believed, at the very least, that slavery symbolized a constitutionally protected property right. In particular, zealous slaveholders argued that their property rights extended beyond local areas and into the territories or wherever the federal government could enforce them. Abraham Lincoln and other northern constitutional interpreters disagreed with their claim. Regardless, by 1860 many southern politicians insisted that the U.S. Constitution implied universal protection for slavery and, if that status could not be guaranteed, secession was the only remedy. It was no surprise that Confederate constitutional delegates included explicit protections for slavery in the nation's founding document.[9]

Several issues united Confederate delegates in early 1861, but the legal protection of slavery held primacy. Secession provided a unique opportunity to perpetuate slavery, and the men present at Montgomery were perfect for the task. Nearly 85 percent of the delegates had formal legal experience, two-thirds were agricultural planters, and all but one were slaveholders. Thus the constitution established nationwide protection of slave property. Article IV, Section 2, declared that "the citizens of each state shall be entitled to all the privileges and immunities of citizens in the several states; and shall have the right of transit and sojourn . . . with their slaves and other property; and the right of property in said slaves shall not be thereby impaired." Delegates also included an indisputable fugitive slave clause stating that "no slave or other person held to service or labor in any State or Territory of the Confederate States . . . escaping or lawfully carried into another . . . [shall] be discharged from such service or labor: but shall be delivered up on claim of the party to whom such slave belongs, or to whom such service or labor may be due." No Confederate state could enact personal liberty laws to thwart the return of fugitive slaves to their rightful owners. In case the Confederacy expanded, its constitution required that "in all such territory, the institution of negro slavery . . . shall be recognized and protected . . . and the inhabitants of the several Confederate States . . . shall have the right to take to such Territory any slaves lawfully held by them."[10] From the Confederate perspective, this clause finally rectified the sectional dispute over slavery in the territories. All three clauses, a "privileges and immunities" protection for slaveholders, an enforceable fugitive slave clause, and a guarantee of slavery in potential territories, were reactions to divisive issues that precipitated the sectional crises of the 1850s.

The debate over prohibition of the African slave trade held important political ramifications for the Confederacy's future. South Carolina members Robert Barnwell Rhett and James Chesnut opposed the immediate ban and were willing to consider future prohibition, but moderate delegates who worried that importing slaves would depress slave values carried the debate and inserted a clause that expressly forbade further importation of slaves from outside the United States.[11] To maintain this important commercial link between the Upper and Lower South, Article I, Section 9, banned "the importation of negroes of the African race from any foreign country other than the slaveholding States or Territories of the United States." To further coax the slave-exporting states, the document declared, "Congress shall also have the power to prohibit the introduction of slaves from any State not a member of, or Territory belonging to, this Confederacy."[12] This clause might be interpreted as a veiled threat. Unless the slave-exporting states, from both the Upper South and Border States, joined the Confederacy, access to sell slave property in Lower South slave markets could be terminated. The slave import/export link between the

Upper South and Lower South defined their mutual interest in the peculiar institution's perpetuation, even if their political views and economic interests did not always coincide on other issues. Confederate constitutional delegates handled the debate over banning the African slave trade with a politic sense of future prosperity.

Slavery was the economic, political, and social glue that connected the southern states. Many nonslaveholding southerners did not believe that the protection of slavery represented sufficient reason to secede. However, the absence of the peculiar institution portended a southern future that neither the slave owners nor poor white yeoman farmers wanted to contemplate—a society with no racial controls. Confederate constitutional delegates understood that reinforced guarantees for slavery alone might not attract the lukewarm Upper South states. The coveted conditional unionists of the Upper South, however, were not likely to side with the alternative of Lincoln's Republican-styled Unionism. Confederate framers gambled correctly and predicted that, given the choice, the Upper South would side with the Confederacy and long-term protections for slavery. The issue was masterfully manipulated by the Montgomery constitutional delegates and eventually yielded the vital strategic results of upper southern membership in the Confederacy.

In 1861 many southern political leaders espoused an antitariff ideology that stretched back forty years. John C. Calhoun and the South Carolina nullifiers founded the antitariff philosophy in the 1820s and 1830s, but later writers like Muscoe R. H. Garnett and John Townsend further developed the concept into southern dogma. Some Confederate delegates from the Lower South supported the traditional free trade doctrine and included their antitariff philosophy in the Confederate Constitution. Article I, Section 8, provided for the natural right of Congress to "collect taxes, duties, imposts, and excises" but also declared no "duties or taxes on importation from foreign nations be laid to promote or foster any branch of industry; and all duties, imposts, and excises shall be uniform throughout the Confederate States."[13] According to the constitution, no subregion or specific industrial interest of the southern states could profit from tariff protection.

The free trade philosophy was the first of several cherished antebellum doctrines to be conveniently scrapped for the sake of southern unity. In order to attract the vital and more industrially developed Upper South states like Virginia, the Provisional Congress almost immediately retracted its antitariff stance. The first legislation passed by the Provisional Congress maintained the prewar 24 percent duty on imported manufactured items. To moderate the tariff's effects, a law passed on February 18, 1861, exempted certain commodities like food, "gunpowder and all the materials of which it is made, lead in all forms, arms of every description, and munitions of war." By March 15th, delegates decided to readjust the tariff with an "ad valorem duty of fifteen per cent" on coal, iron products, and railroad construction supplies. This lower tariff represented a compromise between free trade supporters and the goal of attracting Upper South industrial interests. Congress passed comprehensive tariff rates on May 21st that divided the duties into six separate schedules. The tariff did not take effect until August 31st, but virtually every conceivable imported commodity was listed at various rates. The tariff on iron products, so vital to luring support from Virginia industries like the Tredegar Iron Works, remained at 15 percent.[14]

Wisely, free trade doctrine was sacrificed on the altar of national unity. Virginia's importance to the war effort demanded that the Confederacy institute a protective tariff to attract industrial interests into what appeared to outsiders in early 1861 as a confederation of Lower South agricultural capitalists intent on perpetuating their assets in land and slaves. The onset of war and the Union blockade disrupted normal trade relationships, which makes Confederate tariff policy difficult to analyze. Eventually the Confederate Congress, not content to indirectly aid specific economic sectors with a protective tariff, directly subsidized vital war industries. All governments, especially new ones facing impending war, need to raise revenue, but to so quickly contradict decades of established ideology proves that national survival easily trumped the power of antebellum free trade philosophy.

The Confederate Constitution also specifically forbade nationally funded internal improvements. Southern opposition to national support for internal improvements was closely linked to the antitariff philosophy and the long cherished sectional complaint against northern business interests. According to the argument, the northern economy unfairly benefited at the expense of southern tax dollars. The lion's share of antebellum improvements furthered northern economic development and simultaneously increased the South's dependence on northern manufactures and transportation. To prevent regional economic discrimination in the Confederacy, the document declared that no "clause in the constitution, shall ever be construed to delegate the power to Congress to appropriate money for any internal improvement intended to facilitate commerce."[15] Much like the repudiation of antitariff policy, the Confederate government largely ignored the anti-improvement ideology and eventually initiated clearly unconstitutional policies that directly subsidized railroad companies. One could make the legal argument that these subsidies were directed at the war effort and not commerce, but the constitutional prohibition against nationally funded internal improvements did not withstand the rigors of war.

One of the most modern aspects of the Confederate Constitution was the allowance for wide-ranging executive powers. Southern delegates did not want to repeat the partisan political gridlock of the antebellum years and thus cloaked their president with powers, including six-year terms of office, a line-item veto, and control over government expenditures. Article II, Section 1, established six-year terms for both the president and vice president, but these lengthy tenures were counterbalanced by the rule that they could only serve one term. Six years, however, afforded the Confederate executive ample time to implement policy before being turned out of office. Jefferson Davis, thanks to his appointment by the Provisional Congress in February 1861, which was confirmed by his election in November 1861 and official inauguration in February 1862, would have served seven full years as chief executive had the Confederacy survived that long.

Most historians interpret the single six-year presidency as a check on executive power.[16] There is little doubt that Confederate constitutional delegates intended to use the single term to check executive power, but whether they succeeded or not is an entirely different question that cannot be answered with any degree of certainty. Six years afforded the Confederate executive a dominant role in policy development. Compared to the U.S. president, the Confederate executive also possessed greater opportunity to successfully achieve policy objectives because he did not have to worry about reelection three years into his administration. In addition, the Confederate Constitution was easier to amend, requiring only "the demand of any three states" to call a convention and then a two-thirds vote of the total states, so Davis might have been able to muster enough support in his first term to amend constitutional term limits.[17]

The Confederate Constitution also allowed for a line-item veto. This was a powerful executive privilege and symbolized the constitutional subordination of the legislative branch to the president. Article I, Section 7, allowed the Confederate president to "approve any appropriation and disapprove any other appropriation in the same bill" sent to him by the Congress. Support for the line-item veto originated in antebellum southern complaints about federal spending. To prevent unnecessary expenditures in the Confederacy, the constitutional delegates willingly gave up their prerogative to attach "pork" to priority legislation. The line-item veto provided the Confederate president with immense power over the legislative process since the Congress was forced to pass bills that were completely amenable to the chief executive. The temptation to attach superfluous additions to legislation was also discouraged by Article 1, Section 9, Clause 20, which stated, "every law . . . shall relate to but one subject and that shall be expressed in the title," so the executive did not have to scan lengthy bills for objectionable material.[18]

Perhaps the greatest power of the Confederate president, often overlooked by historians, was the ability to control appropriations. This power has usually been the main role of legislative bodies in the American system. The president's power of appropriation derived from Article I, Section 9, clause 9 of the Confederate Constitution. It stated, "Congress shall appropriate no money from the treasury except by a vote of two-thirds of both Houses . . . unless it be asked and estimated for by some one of the heads of departments, and submitted to Congress by the President." If Congress could not achieve a two-thirds majority in both Houses, which was a difficult task, then financial appropriations would have to be requested by the president and the array of bureaucratic department heads. This gave the executive branch extensive control over the "purse strings" of the Confederate government.[19]

The notion that the Confederate Constitution was simply the U.S. Constitution with added protections for slavery is misguided. Secessionists utilized the American document as a foundation and attempted to correct some of its alleged shortcomings. The war forced Confederate political leaders to abandon many previously sacrosanct constitutional principles. The clauses regarding antebellum issues like opposition to internal improvements and protective tariffs contained an implicit qualifier that such policies would only be pursued in peacetime. The one new constitutional aspect, however, that flourished under wartime pressure was the increased strength of the executive branch. The Confederate Constitution provided a foundation for centralization despite the rhetorical advocacy of state's rights. The constitution's explicit protection of slavery and development of increased executive powers defined Confederate political culture and overshadowed other constitutional principles. Confederate constitutional historians tend to focus on aspects of the document that sought to remedy prewar conflicts but sometimes failed to recognize that those very principles were quickly scrapped after secession.

Alexander Stephens, constitutional delegate and acting vice president, possessed one of the South's keenest constitutional minds. After the Montgomery convention's conclusion, Stephens returned to his native Georgia to inform the anxious citizenry about the new Confederate government and to provide some insight into aspects of the constitution. Stephens's visceral, and oft-quoted, constitutional analysis, however, deserves close scrutiny because it was developed immediately after the convention in an emotionally charged atmosphere.

At the Athenaeum in Savannah, on March 21, 1861, Stephens described the improvements of the new constitution and also summed up the importance of slavery to the aspiring nation in his famous "cornerstone speech." Stephens began with a melodramatic reference to recent events and remarked that "the last 90 days will mark one of the most memorable eras in the history of modern civilization." He reassured the audience that "all the essentials of the old Constitution which have endeared it to the hearts of the American people have been preserved and perpetuated," and the new aspects "form great improvements." Like most southern constitutional delegates, Stephens found admirable qualities in the U.S. Constitution, but now the perceived flaws had been corrected, resulting in a near-perfect governing document for the Confederacy. Referencing the distributive politics of the antebellum era, Stephens remarked, "The question of building up clans, interests, or fostering one branch of industry to the prejudice of another . . . which gave us so much trouble under the Old Constitution, is put at rest forever under the new." Industry, theoretically, could not use the government to promote self-interested policies under the new system. Ironically, Confederate industrial policy eventually fostered a system that indeed favored certain economic sectors over others, not through the tariffs that Stephens inferred, but instead through direct government incentives and subsidies. He also apparently did not view slave-based plantation agriculture as an "interest" that qualified for special government protection, although that was exactly what the Confederate Constitution established.

Stephens also praised the increased executive powers. On the topic of executive representation in the Senate and House, he actually "preferred that this provision should have gone farther." Stephens cited the six-year presidential term as proof of a "decidedly conservative change . . . [that] will remove from the incumbent all temptation to use his office [to] exert the powers confided to him for any objects of personal ambition." For now, Stephens did not believe that increased executive powers threatened southern liberties, but he quickly evolved into one of the most outspoken critics of the Davis administration's alleged despotism.

The most cited aspect of Stephens's speech dealt with the new constitution's position on slavery. Stephens proudly stated that "the new Constitution has put at rest, forever, all the agitating questions relating to our peculiar institution—African slavery" and defined "the proper status of the negro." After a brief discussion about the misguided and erroneous rhetoric of equality by the founding fathers, Stephens frankly declared: "Our new government is founded upon exactly the opposite idea; Its foundations are laid, its cornerstone rests, upon the great truth, that the negro is not equal to the white man. That slavery—subordination to the superior race, is his natural and moral condition. This, our new government, is the first in the history of the world, based upon this great physical, philosophical, and moral truth."

Stephens's frequently quoted "cornerstone" declaration represented a pivotal and fundamental pillar of Confederate political culture. It was the common belief in inequality that provided an initial degree of unifying stability to the young republic among white southerners in the Upper and Lower South.[20]

The most remarkable aspect of this speech was Stephens's bold style. Fresh from the constitutional convention in Montgomery, he exhibited genuine enthusiasm for the new government but an amazing lack of restraint considering the circumstances. Confederates still needed to lure the upper southern states into their government, and these areas possessed a relatively weaker commitment to slavery than the lower southern states. Stephens's speech showed an incredible departure from his typically politic style but allows a glimpse into his original analysis of the Confederate Constitution. If Stephens and the vocal approval of the crowd were representative, then the vast majority of southerners also approved of the new measures adopted. To be sure, not everyone read it or fully understood the differences from the U.S. document, but there was no significant protest in 1861 to any of the ideologies and structures outlined in the Confederate Constitution. If slavery's centrality to the new republic or the consolidation of power in the executive branch—both lauded by Stephens as improvements—worried southern citizens, then they refused to consider reform or repeal in 1861. Confederate citizens actively consented to the constitutional concepts laid out by the Montgomery delegates. Ironically, both during and after the war, Stephens spent a great deal of time lambasting President Davis for exercising too much power, and he also categorically denied that slavery was the cause of the conflict, yet both were clearly supported and even exalted in the "cornerstone speech" of 1861.

The Confederate Constitution was not a wholly original document but more of a composition of southern ideas etched around American constitutional principles. As in all new constitutions, the authors corrected the perceived flaws of past governance: they prohibited nationally funded internal improvements, denied protective tariffs, and created overt protections for slavery. These backward-looking modifications righted the constitutional defects of the Old Republic but were almost immediately overshadowed by the forward-looking aspects of the document, particularly a much stronger executive branch. The Confederate Constitution was far more than a replica of the U.S. Constitution with added safeguards for slavery, as some historians suggest. It symbolized the ideals and aspirations of the secessionist counterrevolutionaries, who erected it and fostered what they hoped would be nothing less than the dawn of a new era for the South.

The foundations for an expedient corporatist state were also established, albeit unintentionally, by the Confederate Constitution. Executive dominance proved to be perhaps the most useful wartime expedient for national survival. Although the Confederate Constitution dropped government support for internal improvements, it allowed for corporatist-style private sector leadership, for example in management of the railroad system, and eventually granted government subsidies for vital industries like iron and munitions, a distinctly corporatist development. Many scholars interpret the Confederate Constitution in terms of *what the Confederacy wanted to become,* instead of analyzing *what the Confederacy actually became,* a centralized modern state driven by an exceedingly powerful executive branch. The Confederate Constitution was far more modern than many historians admit, and it outlined the future development of an expedient corporatist state in the Confederacy.

A preeminent constitutional historian of the Civil War era, Mark Neely Jr., points out several important aspects about the Confederate Constitution that bear further discussion and analysis. For Neely, the "republican ideal" was just as important, if not more so, to Confederate constitutional framers as the institution of slavery to the aspiring nation's founding philosophy. Neely refers to the particular brand of southern slave society republicanism formulated over several decades in the nineteenth century, which represented a pillar of southern political thought by 1860. On the influence of slavery upon Confederate political construction, Neely correctly asserts that "slavery did not necessarily make the Confederacy authoritarian and undemocratic in politics."[21] There is little doubt as to the importance of slavery to the Confederate nation, as pointed out in Alexander Stephens's "cornerstone speech," but this importance manifested itself more in economic and social terms than in political ones. It was not the presence of slavery, but instead the creation of an expedient corporatist government that gave the Confederacy its authoritarian tendencies. Although Confederate leaders, including Jefferson Davis, continued to use the language of republicanism, it was this "republican ideal" that was sacrificed for national survival and gave way to more modern forms of governance over the course of the Confederacy's brief life span.

SECRET SESSIONS

The Confederacy's founders set an important precedent for government proceedings with the use of secret sessions. They readily mimicked the 1787 Constitutional Convention's use of secret sessions and allowed the practice to continue throughout the deliberations of the provisional and regular congress. In Article 1, Section 5, the U.S. constitution allows for "each house" to debate and publish deliberations "excepting such parts as may in their judgment require secrecy." A common nineteenth-century use of Senate secret sessions typically occurred during controversial treaty ratification debates. The option to seclude proceedings, however, remained little used by the U.S. legislative branch because leaks to the press easily undermined the original purpose.

In contrast, Confederate political leaders learned to frequently use secret sessions to shield controversial topics from not only enemy observers but also the southern people. During the 1861 Montgomery constitutional convention, delegates had legitimate reasons for secluded debates and proceedings. The new government played a high stakes game for upper southern support and could not afford to provide the incoming Lincoln administration with information about issues that might disrupt southern unity before Confederate consolidation could be completed. Secret sessions cloaked controversial debates like renewal of the African slave trade and denied Union leaders access to the details of southern preparations.

South Carolina delegate Robert Barnwell Rhett, editor of the *Charleston Mercury*, criticized the newly established government for not being as open to public scrutiny as that of their northern enemies. Rhett initially joked about the private nature of Confederate decision making and satirized proper Victorian etiquette when he playfully declared: "Don't they know, every man of them who has a wife in town, that he can't sleep until he tells her, every night, all . . . that takes place in the Congress? What the deuce, then, can be the meaning of all this affected secrecy, unless it is to bring together discordant couples, who . . . have two beds in their room."

This humorous poke at congressional privacy eventually transitioned into a serious concern for openness in the young republic. Looking back and without the humor, Rhett later complained that "almost all important business was transacted away from the knowledge and thus beyond the criticism of the people."[22]

Popular disapproval of secret sessions remained a concern for some members and observers as congressional culture transitioned from a provisional status into a permanent institution. In July 1861 Texas congressman William Ochiltree worried about the public perception of secrecy and queried whether "there is a resolution now in force requiring all snob bills to be acted on in secret session."[23] Ochiltree foresaw that the southern public might view secret sessions as haughty, elitist affairs that excluded popular input. In August 1861 a recurrent critic from the *Charleston Mercury*, most likely Rhett, complained, "Congress continues its mysterious work clothed in secrecy . . . which gives room for speculation and exaggeration, producing a worse effect than a knowledge of the whole truth would." From this perspective, the mere existence of secret deliberations, even if innocently undertaken, might foster wild speculation and harmful rumors that could undermine the public's trust in Congress. Foreshadowing how southern citizens might construe the continuation of such secretive behavior, the author reminded readers that "members of Congress are the servants, and not the masters of the people." This congressional critic believed "secret legislation" set "a bad precedent . . . in the initiatory stages of the existence of our Government." As a final warning to remove secret deliberations in Congress, the author declared, "the intelligent people of the Southern Confederacy will recognize no juntas as their masters."[24] Secrecy could potentially sour southern popular opinion towards the Congress.

Secret sessions were wise policy in 1861, and even in certain circumstances during the war, especially when the legislative discussion specifically concerned military preparedness. A practice that began as a legitimate way to protect the young republic, however, evolved into a habitual method to temporarily minimize popular influence on congressional deliberations. In both the provisional and regular congresses, Confederate politicians continued to conduct numerous debates behind closed doors and thereby engendered an environment of legislative secrecy.

An obvious problem for true secrecy was the dubious ability of the 133 members to remain silent on the volatile issues discussed. With only twenty-six members, the Senate could more easily protect its confidentiality, but the House found it necessary to pass a resolution "that the proceedings . . . in secret session, shall be held . . . until the injunction of secrecy has been duly removed by the consent of the Congress." In addition to the actual members, ancillary congressional workers like stenographers and printers were also required to maintain secrecy. No potential leaky loophole was left unplugged and even the "Assistant Doorkeeper . . . was sworn not to divulge or disclose any matter . . . [of] the secret sessions of the Senate."[25] Considering the number of knowledgeable witnesses to the secret material, the Confederate Congress did a commendable job of hiding specific policy debates, at least temporarily, from northern observers and the southern public.

Secret sessions evolved into a congressional bad habit. It was relatively easy for representatives to close off legislative debate from public scrutiny. The provisional congress set the precedent that was followed by the regular congress. At the request of two members, either chamber of the Confederate congress might be removed into secret deliberations. The ease of reclusion into secret session meant that southern politicians could not be forced to fully debate controversial policies in the presence of a public gallery or newspaper reporters.[26]

In early 1862, however, it remained to be seen whether the regular congress would continue the provisional practice of secret sessions. Critics hoped the incoming Permanent Congress would do away with frequent sequestration and allow public observers and the press to access the daily debates. One detractor declared that without open sessions, "representation is a farce." Some congressmen also condemned the renewal of secret sessions as detrimental to public freedoms. The Permanent Congress convened on February 18, 1862, and the next day witnessed the first protest against secret sessions. When outspoken Tennessee congressman Henry S. Foote requested to investigate the recent military setbacks in his home state, John Crockett, representative from Kentucky, recommended these matters "be considered in secret session." Foote responded that "he was for freedom of discussion and freedom of the press." According to Foote, constant use of secret sessions undermined the democratic process and he personally did "not come here to be submitted to any gag law."[27]

Several legislators wanted to reform the rules to mitigate the frequency of closed sessions. On March 4th, Louisiana representative Lucius Dupre attempted to change House rules so that "a majority . . . shall be required to go into secret session," but the resolution to consider alteration was voted down 53 to 29. Foote suggested that secrecy should require at least one-fifth of the representatives. Louisiana congressman Duncan Kenner remarked that secret sessions were logical for the Provisional Congress, "but these reasons no longer existed." Speaker of the House Thomas Bocock, chairman of the Rules Committee, countered that secret sessions prevented Yankee spies from gleaning vital information and "the rule adopted was the same as that in the old Federal House of Representatives." Members voted down Foote's one-fifth resolution by a 55 to 33 margin.[28] In the first session of the Permanent Congress, from February to April 1862, the original rules for secret sessions remained unchanged despite protests from a minority of Confederate congressmen.

The second session convened on August 18th and opponents immediately attacked continued use of secret sessions. In the House of Representatives, the ever-loquacious Foote again requested that a majority be required to induce legislative secrecy on the grounds that "the people . . . had a right to know, whether their servants . . . were doing their duty." By the second session, significant support existed for a rule change on secrecy. Texas representative Franklin B. Sexton noted that "Foote spoke as usual an hour or so . . . [and] made an onslaught on secret sessions, to which I am also opposed." On August 19th, the House secret session debate continued between Foote and James Lyons of Virginia, who supported continuation of the current rule to initiate secrecy. Alabama congressman William Chilton requested a majority vote for secrecy, and to prevent ceaseless wrangling asked that secrecy only be considered once for each motion. On August 19th the resolution easily passed the House of Representatives by a vote of 56 to 15 and instantly made it more difficult for the body to meet in secret.[29] At some point between April and August 1862, a minority of congressmen turned into a majority in favor of tougher requirements to induce secret sessions. The impetus was likely a heightened political sensitivity among Confederate representatives about potential criticism of policies, like conscription, implemented since the first session. With regard to secret sessions, the House of Representatives exhibited a remarkable sense of self-awareness that possibly prevented further development of negative popular opinion about legislative practices.

The Confederate Senate simultaneously addressed the issue of secret sessions. William Lowndes Yancey attempted to change the rules so that a two-thirds vote would be necessary to initiate secret sessions. After discussion, the Senate agreed that "after the doors shall be closed, the Senate shall take a vote, a majority to decide whether the subject shall or not be considered in secret session." Senators did not even want to make a public decision about whether to devolve into secrecy and redundantly desired an additional secret vote to decide if an issue should be deliberated in secret session! A frustrated Yancey asserted that an open vote should be required but was voted down and so he withdrew his motion.[30] Due to other pressing matters, the Senate did not reconsider secret sessions and maintained the original rules. Since the Senate consisted of only twenty-six members at any given time, the ability of two members to initiate secret sessions was not as egregious as the original House rules that allowed two members to devolve all 107 members into a secret conclave.

The controversial policy of secret sessions continued to spark debate even after the rule changes in the House. In September 1863 North Carolina congressional candidate James T. Leach told a Johnston County audience that he was "opposed to secret sessions and closed doors" because they were "anti-republican . . . and should not be tolerated by a free people." Leach won the election as an antiadministration candidate who would consider a negotiated end to the war. Even if secret sessions were not the primary issue of concern to war-weary voters, Leach's attack on secrecy in Congress showed that criticism of closed-door political tendencies proved a successful rhetorical attack against incumbents. True to his campaign promise, Leach "introduced a joint resolution 'condemning secret sessions'" in November 1864, but the resolution was sent to committee for further discussion. In late 1864 the Confederacy certainly faced more pressing concerns than House rules on secrecy, but Leach's resolution shows that he believed constituents deserved a more open legislative culture.

Despite successfully altering the rules in 1862 and making it more difficult to call secret sessions in the House of Representatives, Henry Foote renewed his assault against the secrecy policy in May 1864. He hoped to increase the existing majority requirement and moved that secrecy require a seven-eighths vote. Two days later, sensing that the percentage of consent was too high, Foote issued a revised resolution that lowered the requirement to two-thirds. It was referred to the Rules Committee. On May 17th the committee recommended that Foote's resolution "not pass," after which a vote showed only twenty-five members in support of the rule change and fifty-one against.[31] The House kept the 1862 rules intact and retained the simple majority assent to initiate secret sessions.

What types of legislation were discussed in secret session? Significant disagreement arose over which issues required private debate. On February 24, 1862, the Senate adopted rules "that all propositions on foreign affairs or questions relating to the public defence should be considered in secret session." This was a legitimate use of wartime legislative secrecy but could be abused since almost any topic might be construed to fall under the category of public defense. The next day, Duncan Kenner requested that the rules of secrecy be suspended and the matter was sent to the Rules Committee. On April 8th the House created a special committee to "decide what matters shall be considered in secret session."[32] Majorities in both chambers continued to support a flexible interpretation of the topics eligible for secret discussion. The Confederate Congress could interpret most topics as being in the interest of national security and as a result, it held an unchecked power to debate policies without simultaneous public scrutiny.

Legislators used secret sessions for discretionary reasons like minimizing frank discussion of military events. Some congressmen were apparently reluctant to speak openly about battlefield defeats and assign blame. On March 1, 1862, Mississippi representative Reuben Davis requested that the House sequester itself to discuss recent military disasters in Tennessee because he believed discussion would deflate public morale. [33] When contrasted with the U.S. Congress's Joint Committee on the Conduct of War, the Confederate Congress, at least in this case, appeared to be timid about assigning blame and a bit more considerate of military careers.

Topics of military intelligence were legitimate candidates for secret session. In March 1862 Tennessee senator Landon Haynes requested a report on the number of troops and their readiness for service. A month later, the House sequestered itself to discuss a letter from Navy secretary Stephen Mallory that dealt with construction of Confederate ships abroad. Mallory requested additional funds in March 1863, and Texas congressman Franklin Sexton noted that the House, "in secret session, appropriated $5,200,000 to pay for ironclad ships in Europe" and again on April 27th, "in secret session too, a bill was passed appropriating . . . $20,000,000 . . . to buy steamers abroad."[34] The Congress also discussed funding for the various clandestine operations that sought to bring the war directly to the northern people in 1864. This type of privacy was well warranted and meant to prevent Yankee spies from obtaining any useful military intelligence from legislative discussions.

In some instances, congressmen could use their knowledge of closed door sessions for personal benefit. In late 1863 Treasury secretary Christopher Memminger hatched a plan to combat rampant inflation by reducing the amount of currency in circulation. His plan to replace "outstanding currency for a new issue of 6 percent, 20 year bonds," was to be completed by April 1, 1864, and with the exception of notes $2 or under, "any note not funded or registered would be repudiated."[35] Archibald Arrington, outgoing representative from the Fifth District of North Carolina, sought to protect his economic interests from pending Confederate monetary policy. On January 4, 1864, he requested that his wife Kate "save all the Five dollar Confederate bills and all under Five dollars you have [and] don't pay any of them out for change." He insisted that she "must not let any body know that I have written you on the subject, because if they were to find out that you were trying to save the Five dollar bills they might have something to say about it, as Congress is acting upon that question in secret session." It is unclear who the proverbial "they" were, most likely his constituents or possibly even some of his peers in the House of Representatives, but it is very clear that Arrington used his privileged position and knowledge of secret debates to protect his family's liquid assets. He later explained his otherwise strange rationale to his wife: "in a short time I am afraid no one will take Confederate notes above Five dollars." Arrington's example proved that discreet congressmen could use inside information to anticipate and benefit from secret policy deliberations.[36]

When it was deemed necessary, Congress used secret sessions to deliberate on sensitive issues like suspension of habeas corpus. Congress authorized temporary suspensions in February and October 1862 in response to corresponding military reverses, but in both instances debates were conducted in open sessions. In the fourth and final session of the First Congress from December 1863 to February 1864, legislators utilized secret sessions to veil deliberations on habeas corpus suspension.

Secrecy was warranted for several reasons, not the least of which was the fact that the 1863 congressional elections signaled a partial shift towards antiadministration candidates, so there would likely be no smooth transition into the Second Congress scheduled to convene in May 1864. In addition, desperation to reverse the tide of war meant legislators were forced to consider measures like suspension of habeas corpus to protect loyal Confederates from disloyal elements, bolster the war effort, and solidify Confederate nationalism. Despite the necessities of national survival, on the eve of the habeas corpus debates Henry Foote continued to worry about popular perceptions of Congress's lack of openness since "sessions were so often secret, and the reporters so often excluded, that editors could say nothing of the proceedings." According to Foote, "the people came to the conclusion that the members were a luxurious set of men, indulging in the fashionable dissipations of the day, and doing nothing for the country at large."[37] Congressional leaders did not have time to dabble in abstractions like altering secret session rules, but they did go forward with plans to restrict civil liberties for this pivotal fourth year of the war.

On February 3, 1864, President Davis requested habeas corpus suspension because "the zeal with which the people sprang to arms at the beginning of the contest has . . . been impaired by the long continuance and magnitude of the struggle," and he also wanted to lessen desertion rates and crush pockets of disloyalty. Davis justified the suspension as "a sharp remedy, but a necessary one," and for the next nine days, Congress discussed Davis's request in secret session. On February 15th, Davis signed the bill into law with the entire request, deliberation, and vote conducted in secret sessions. Two days later, some representatives wanted "the injunction of secrecy [to] be removed," and the Judiciary Committee recommended the cloak of secrecy be removed. Davis's request for suspension of habeas corpus rights and Congress's authorization remained hidden from the public purview a total of fourteen days, enough time to deliberate and pass the law without considerable popular backlash. In 1862 congressional leaders felt comfortable enough debating suspension of habeas corpus in open session, but by 1864 their preemptive move to significantly curb civil liberties for an indefinite period was cautiously deliberated behind closed doors. Throughout 1864 and 1865, congressional discussion of the controversial policy of habeas corpus suspension continued to be held in secret session. Sequestration allowed legislators to limit pre-passage scrutiny by newspapers and at least temporarily prevent public protest.[38]

Due to congressional covertness, politicians away from Richmond might not know the full breadth of legislative debates unless a colleague elaborated upon the limited information in newspapers. William Yancey departed from Richmond in April 1863 before Congress's adjournment, and after surviving a horrible train wreck outside Augusta, Georgia, he arrived home in Alabama but wanted to know more about ongoing congressional debates. Yancey queried his senate colleague from Alabama, Clement Clay, about political events in Richmond and "all matters of interest which have transpired in secret session."[39] Yancey was a critic of secret sessions, so the irony of his inability to penetrate the legislative veil was somewhat lessened, but the point remains that even well-connected politicians like Yancey could be denied access, at least temporarily, to congressional deliberations if they were absent.

Most politicians understood that legislative secrecy was intended to provide some breathing room for policy formulation and a head start for implementation so that congressional decisions would not be hampered by popular criticism. Closed debates partially shielded politicians from the press and constituent backlash but also countered democratic political rhetoric. In a cogent analysis of secret sessions, Robert Barnwell Rhett claimed that "the people of the Confederate States have been kept in profound ignorance of all debates by their representatives . . ." in order to hide "the inefficiency of the Administration." Even if secret sessions served legitimate uses of unity in the early stages of political development, they later assumed a less noble purpose that "covered up the weakness . . . of [the Confederate] Government." According to Rhett, secret sessions were no minor flaw of political culture but indicative of the Confederate government's general lack of transparency. Closed legislative debates also implied that President Davis might privately request unpopular policies of the Congress, and, as Rhett pointed out, if "the public voice is stifled" under such a system, "a small body of men . . . are subjected to Executive drill, and act in obedience to Executive dictation, without criticism . . . or responsibility to their masters, the people."[40] This allegation of undemocratic governance and the continued use of secret sessions allowed critics like Rhett to make claims of tyranny, whether fully warranted or not. Secret sessions also symbolized an embarrassing weakness to claims of voluntary Confederate nationalism but by the fall of 1862 secret sessions were an established aspect of Confederate political culture.

Most historians of Confederate political culture do not devote much attention to the secrecy of legislative deliberation. Historian Mark Neely Jr. points out that secret sessions during the secession conventions of 1861 "might well be grist for the mill of those historians who see . . . a conservative coup, working behind closed doors to accomplish changes in government the people would not like."[41] If the secrecy had ended with the secession crisis, then Confederate leaders might be forgiven for their lack of transparency, the same way that the delegates to the Philadelphia Convention of 1787 have largely been forgiven, but the Confederate Congress continued to meet in secret when controversial issues came up for discussion. Even if rebel political leaders did not conspire behind closed doors to pursue policies detrimental to the Confederate citizenry, it certainly appeared suspicious to critics. Congressional secret sessions allowed for speculation of collusion and inserted an implied atmosphere of potential authoritarianism into Confederate political culture. However, for a government that, out of necessity, became increasingly centralized, secret sessions allowed for serious policy disputes to be resolved without public scrutiny and fostered a sense of unified purpose between the legislative and executive branches.

ABSENCE OF A SUPREME COURT

Montgomery delegates' formulations of executive and legislative constitutional powers were only slight changes from American constitutional precedent when compared to the Confederate judicial branch, especially the lack of a Supreme Court. Technically the judicial branch might be considered outside the purview of political culture, but the absence of a Supreme Court was a direct result of Confederate political construction. Some secessionists proudly pointed to the antebellum U.S. Supreme Court as a bulwark of slaveholders' property rights. The primary antebellum legal obstacles to slaveholders' property rights were personal liberty laws in northern states that subverted application of the U.S. Constitution's fugitive slave clause, enforcement of the 1793 Fugitive Slave Law, and the 1850 strengthening law.

Two major cases prior to the Dred Scott decision had indicated that the court might eventually support slaveholders' property rights. In *Prigg v. Pennsylvania* (1841), the majority opinion allowed northern states to opt out of returning fugitives but also simultaneously reinforced the legal duty of the federal government to enforce the fugitive slave law. The second important precedential case was *Strader v. Graham* (1851). Proslavery chief justice Roger Taney and the other justices denied jurisdictional authority and thus upheld the Kentucky Supreme Court in favor of slaveholders' property rights.[42]

The highly controversial case *Dred Scott v. Sanford* (1857) finally confirmed slaveholders' noninterventionist arguments. Taney's majority opinion delivered a powerful guarantee of slaveholders' property rights. The majority opinion held that Dred Scott was a slave and thus unable to sue, and further opined that all African Americans, not just slaves, were not and could not be citizens. In addition, Taney declared that slavery in the territories was protected by the due process clause of the Fifth Amendment and that the Thomas Proviso portion of the 1820 Missouri Compromise, which banned slavery north of the 36°30′ line, was unconstitutional. In February 1861 a North Carolina secessionist summed up the faith southerners placed in the Supreme Court. He told an audience that the Republican "majority claims to be governed by a higher law and to be bound by the constitution of the United States, which they have sworn to support, and tramples under foot the decisions of the Supreme Court . . . because the decisions of that court recognized rights as guaranteed to us under the constitution."[43] For like-minded southerners, the U.S. Supreme Court vindicated the right to slave property and had evolved into an important bulwark of defense in the Old Republic. Secessionists had good reason to support creation of a Confederate Supreme Court to continue the legacy of judicial support for slavery.

Southern critics of the U.S. Supreme Court grounded their arguments in the well-developed theories of state supremacy. For these individuals, the U.S. Supreme Court, and specifically the arch deacon of national power John Marshall, epitomized the movement to strengthen national powers at the expense of state sovereignty. A long tradition of states' rights thinkers, beginning with Jefferson, continued by fellow Virginians John Randolph and Spencer Roane after Marshall's *McCulloch v. Maryland* (1819) decision, and carried to fruition in John C. Calhoun's nullification theories, informed a generation of dogmatic states' rights acolytes who held powerful political positions in the Confederacy. In their opinion, the preponderance of antebellum U.S. Supreme Court decisions consolidated national powers at the expense of individual rights, and despite decisions like *Dred Scott v. Sanford*, the high court represented a repressive institution in the Old Republic.

Enough secessionists, however, were pleased with the antebellum high court to ensure a smooth transition of the institution into the Confederate judicial system. The U.S. judiciary was almost exactly copied by Confederate constitutional delegates in 1861. Just like the U.S. version, Article III of the Confederate Constitution mandated that "the judicial power of the Confederate States shall be vested in one Supreme Court, and in such inferior courts as the Congress may . . . establish." In Section 2, delegates dropped the superfluous phrase "in law and equity" but in cases "between a State and citizens of another state" they added the phrase "where the state is plaintiff." Confederate founders removed the power to oversee cases "between citizens of different states," ostensibly to satisfy notions of state sovereignty. The phrase on the legal domain "between citizens claiming land under grants of different states" was reworded to prevent northern creditors from overwhelming the new nation's courts, and delegates added that "no State shall be sued by a citizen or subject of any foreign state." The Confederate high court was almost identical to the U.S. Supreme Court and was granted similar powers to resolve disputes between states and had final "appellate jurisdiction."[44] The high court assumed appellate powers over the district courts but did not possess the power of judicial review. It should be remembered that neither the U.S. Constitution nor the Judiciary Act of 1789 granted the U.S. Supreme Court the ability to deem laws unconstitutional. Judicial review was later asserted by John Marshall in the landmark case of *Marbury v. Madison* (1803). Many southern political leaders apparently did not wish to continue Marshall's precedent of a strong high court that might overturn legislation by using powers of judicial review.

On March 16, 1861, the Provisional Congress passed the Judiciary Act, which allowed for creation of a Confederate Supreme Court. The high court was required to convene each year on the first Monday of January and stay in session until all business was complete. The act established a system of district courts in which "each of the Confederate States shall constitute one district." Traditional judicial powers were included so that "both the district and supreme courts . . . shall have the power to issue writs of injunction . . . and *habeas corpus*."[45] This was legal precedent for judges to release prisoners arrested by Confederate military authorities for avoiding conscription. The judicial power to issue writs of habeas corpus, and more specifically the prerogative of Congress to suspend the writ at executive request, eventually proved to be a point of contention between local jurisdictions and the central government in Richmond. A national Supreme Court would have possessed the power to decisively resolve the legal debate over habeas corpus, but in the absence of a high court the controversy festered and caused considerable disagreement between the Davis administration and state authorities.

In addition, the Judiciary Act created Supreme Court appellate jurisdiction for writs of error, civil decisions, and maritime prize claims over $5,000, civil cases "where a state is a party," and "proceedings against ambassadors or other public ministers."[46] Cases pending before U.S. courts were transferred to the Confederate judicial system along with standing judgments and prison sentences. Plaintiffs seeking transition of their cases onto the Confederate Supreme Court docket would ultimately be disappointed because their cases would never be heard by a high court. The Judiciary Act intentionally created a Confederate legal system that was very similar to the U.S. version.

The first meeting of the Confederate Supreme Court was scheduled to convene in January 1862 but it did not meet as anticipated. On July 31, 1861, the Provisional Congress repealed the scheduled January meeting and decided that the Supreme Court should not meet until the Permanent Congress convened. The reasoning for postponing assembly of the high court was plausible but unusual. On March 16th, the same day the Judiciary Act passed the Provisional Congress, delegates began signing the permanent Constitution, thus beginning the transition to perpetual legitimacy. According to this argument, a Supreme Court organized by the Provisional Congress and scheduled to convene before the first meeting of a Permanent Congress would be somehow unofficial or illegitimate. But this was an excuse. The Provisional Congress established and empowered other Confederate institutions vital to government function prior to inauguration of the permanent government in February 1862. Apparently by July 1861 a sizable portion of the Provisional Congress did not believe creation of a Supreme Court to be important and delayed empowerment. Another excuse for delay was "that Western judges would have difficulty making the long trek to Richmond for its sessions," which seems absurd given the ample time to plan for the trip between July 1861 and January 1862. Regardless, between March and July 1861 some Confederate leaders apparently reconsidered their commitment to empower the highest court of the judicial branch and indefinitely postponed the Supreme Court's existence.[47]

In early 1862 significant support still existed for empowerment of the

Confederate Supreme Court. In a message to the first Permanent Congress on February 26th, Jefferson Davis urged legislators to create a Supreme Court. Both chambers of Congress revisited the matter as requested by the president. Louisiana senator Thomas J. Semmes offered a bill on March 11th to construct a high court with a chief justice and three associate justices, which would meet twice annually in January and August. After generous salary suggestions of $7,000 and $6,000 for the chief and associate justices respectively, Bill S. 19 was added for future consideration. After a brief attempt to reintroduce the bill on March 26th and April 10th, the Senate decided again to postpone debate indefinitely.[48] In early 1862 it appeared that the judicial plans for a high court might succeed, but both the Senate and House bills failed to come to a vote.

The debate about enabling a Supreme Court was rejoined in the second session. On September 17th Congressman James Lyons requested that the Judiciary Committee craft a Supreme Court bill. House supporters of enabling the high court, however, were in no hurry and merely recommended the committee report in the next session, which would not be until January 1863. The Senate undertook a more forthright effort to empower the Supreme Court, this time led by Benjamin H. Hill of Georgia. Hill was a savvy, some might say crassly opportunistic, political figure. Known as a staunch supporter of the Davis administration, Hill believed a Supreme Court would validate controversial congressional policies he deemed necessary for national survival. On September 26th, Hill's request to reconsider empowering the high court passed by a vote of 10 to 8 but was set aside for further deliberation until the next day. Much to Hill's dismay the bill was again postponed, this time indefinitely, on the motion of Edward Sparrow, which was approved by a vote of 11 to 8. Hill's faction could not maintain the two crucial swing votes that originally brought the bill to the floor. If the Congress would indeed authorize the Supreme Court, it would have to wait, at least, until the third session in January 1863.[49]

During the congressional break, the executive branch again suggested that Congress act to create a Supreme Court. Attorney General Thomas Watts reminded returning congressional leaders that the permanent Constitution had "been in operation nearly one year . . . [and] the many conflicting decisions . . . show but too plainly the necessity for prompt action on the part of Congress." Multiple state supreme court decisions on the constitutionality of national laws caused confusion and lack of "uniformity in the construction of statutes." Furthermore, Watts argued, the lack of a Supreme Court meant that there was no appellate system for District Court decisions.[50] If the current situation remained unresolved then the state supreme courts would be the "courts of last resort" and the national government could only hope that state judges would uphold the constitutionality of Confederate laws. Attorney General Watts presumably spoke for Davis in this request, and their main Senate advocate in the upcoming session was Benjamin Hill.

As chairman of the Judiciary Committee in 1863, Hill argued that a high court was a national necessity. Not only was the Supreme Court a constitutional mandate, but to continually block its existence, Hill insisted, might hinder the Confederacy's ability to implement important policies successfully. On January 19th Hill offered another bill to create a Supreme Court, which came to the floor for debate on January 26th, and again opponents attempted to postpone deliberation indefinitely. Thomas Semmes lamented further postponement and recalled that "he had the honor to report this bill from the committee nearly a year ago . . . [but] did not press its passage . . . because the state of the country did not seem to demand it." Harkening to the position of national necessity, Semmes argued, "the state of the country was now very different, and there were many questions likely to arise which could only be decided by a Supreme Court." A functional Supreme Court might reflect well upon the aspiring nation to outside observers, and Semmes believed "the moral effect of the passage of this bill would be great, as showing . . . the stability of our institutions." Despite contrary arguments by Henry Burnett and Robert Barnwell, Hill and Semmes's argument prevailed and postponement was soundly voted down 18 to 3.[51]

The first issue in the attempt to establish a Supreme Court centered on the number of judges to be appointed. The bill called for one chief justice and three associate justices to meet twice a year, in January and August. Hill hoped to increase the number of associate justices from three to four. William L. Yancey opposed expansion and attempted to amend Hill's proposal by reducing the number of associate justices to two. Yancey and his supporters argued that a smaller court would likely increase agreement. Yancey, frequently the antagonist of President Davis, also argued that "executive patronage . . . would be reduced by forty per cent" if the court was constricted. Hill's goal of three associate justices won and the bill was held over to the next day.[52]

The second issue, justices' salaries, also caused heated debate. The original bill called for annual salaries of $7,000 for the chief justice and $6,000 for each associate justice. Alabama senator Clement Clay believed this amount too generous and attempted to reduce the chief justice's salary to $5,500 and each associate justice's to $5,000. Hill opposed the reduction because the Supreme Court needed to attract brilliant legal minds, and it forced justices to move to Richmond. Texan Louis T. Wigfall protested higher salaries because he "did not think it desirable to have the first talent in this court." Yancey worried about undermining the "main pillar of this Confederacy," the sovereignty of state courts, and wanted to reduce the chief justice's salary by $500 so that all justices would receive equal pay. The reductionists carried the vote 11 to 10.[53]

By far the most contentious aspect of the Supreme Court debates involved appellate jurisdiction over state courts. Clement Clay's amendment to repeal sections 45 and 46 of the 1861 Judiciary Act set off a firestorm of debate that ultimately aborted the Confederate Supreme Court. Semmes had recommended this same repeal on March 8, 1862, but the idea withered in the Judiciary Committee, and thus the jurisdiction battle lay dormant until 1863. Hill did not want the jurisdictional debate to undermine Supreme Court organization, and he understood the inherent dangers of appellate jurisdiction deliberation at this point in the enabling process. He reminded his fellow senators that "the bill under consideration was one to establish the Supreme Court and not to fix its jurisdiction." Hill pleaded, "Let us first organize the court," and he protested that Clay's amendment "would open a new field of argument and embarrass the passage of the bill." Presumably Hill would have the Senate create the high court but not fully define its powers. The Clay amendment did more than just "embarrass" passage; it completely unraveled Hill's long-standing efforts to create a Confederate high court.[54]

Sections 45 and 46 of the Judiciary Act dealt specifically with the Supreme Court's powers to overturn state court rulings. From January 28th to March 18th, the Senate postponed a vote on the Clay amendment no less than sixteen times due to the heightened level of disagreement between factions and the fact that the Senate had other contentious policies to debate, like exemptions and impressment. This was no mere gentlemanly discussion of constitutional abstractions but a hotly contested struggle for power at the highest levels of Confederate governance.[55]

Opponents of the repeal typically utilized some form of national necessity argument. Mississippi's James Phelan argued that "the opinions of the State Courts were mere opinions, and not entitled to more respect than the opinion of the Supreme Court." Phelan worried that "if each State was entitled to its own construction of what laws were constitutional, the Confederate government was at an end." Gustavus Henry simply reminded his colleagues that the Constitution provided for a Supreme Court, presumably with appellate powers, "and Senators had no right to change the words" to fit their states' rights arguments. Supporters of the Clay amendment, Henry argued, wanted "to rob the Supreme Court of all power and efficacy to do good," and those "who claimed to be strict constructionists . . . would by their construction destroy the rights of the citizen, while pretending to maintain the rights of the States." Henry concluded that to prevent creation of a Supreme Court or to deny it appellate jurisdiction would be "the fatal stab . . . to our new Government." Opponents of the Clay amendment argued that an empowered Supreme Court would contribute stability and legitimacy to the Confederate government. Without an authoritative high court, these leaders feared interpretive anarchy might ensue and allow for local disputation of national laws.[56]

Supporters of the Clay amendment based their arguments on some variation of states' rights or fear of increased government centralization. Thomas Semmes argued that allowing the Confederate Supreme Court to overturn state decisions represented the first step down the slippery slope toward judicial review of congressional policies. Yancey derided the very idea of a Supreme Court as "an evil incident to the hasty formation of this Government," and believed that the strong-court faction "sheltered themselves under the great names of another generation." Far from resuming the traditions of the U.S. Supreme Court, Yancey argued, southern leaders "had reflected more deeply . . . upon this question" of a strong Supreme Court. Georgia senator Herschel V. Johnson adopted a strict constructionist position and argued "the constitution" allowed for a "Supreme Court . . . [with] appellate jurisdiction over such inferior courts as Congress shall . . .

establish," but since the Congress did not create state courts then it had no authority to empower a high court with conclusive powers. Clay amendment supporters viewed national supremacy over state court decisions as anathema and counterproductive to the essence of state sovereignty. They claimed that an empowered Confederate Supreme Court threatened popular liberty and increased national centralization at the expense of local and congressional powers.[57]

On February 4th, the Supreme Court debate sparked the only incident of physical violence witnessed in the Confederate Congress. Benjamin Hill and William Yancey had a history of mutual distaste for each other as a result of an antebellum exchange of insults that evolved into a contentious relationship in the Senate. Hill allegedly "attacked Yancey's character and morals" in a speech that solicited a caustic response from the hot-tempered Alabama senator. After Yancey's demeaning response, Hill snapped. He picked up a "heavy glass inkstand [and] hurled it with all his might and power at the head of Mr. Yancey," striking the unsuspecting statesman in the right temple. The wound caused significant bleeding but did not prevent Yancey from further taunting his attacker. In a frenzy, Hill picked up a chair with the intention of smashing the still defiant Yancey but was restrained by colleagues. The attack symbolized the intense debate over enabling the Supreme Court and might have been an extremely embarrassing episode had the Senate not sworn both men to secrecy about the incident. Contrary to the humorous retrospectives offered by some historians, the Hill-Yancey incident was no laughing matter in terms of its impact on political culture. This violent episode symbolized the tense imbroglio and power conflicts involved in creation of a Supreme Court and highlighted Congress's inability to resolve simple disagreements effectively.[58]

On March 18th, after nearly two months of intermittent and heated debate, the Clay amendment finally came to a vote. Supporters of the resolution denying appellate jurisdiction to the Supreme Court won by a decisive 16 to 6 margin. This meant any high court would be impotent. As a result of the better than 2 to 1 majority in favor of the amendment, Hill had to decide whether to go forward with the bill to create an emasculated Supreme Court, and he voted with his former antagonists in a 14 to 8 approval to create a weak Supreme Court. Although it never convened, the court was supposed to have a chief and four associate justices who would meet twice each year and receive $5,500 salaries. The strong-court faction had failed miserably in the face of determined opposition headed by Barnwell, Wigfall, and Yancey. Any high court organized after this Senate defeat would be a powerless shell of national authority, disrespected by the other branches and unheeded by state judges.[59]

Some members of the House of Representatives continued to press for Supreme Court organization. Congressman Burgess Gaither from western North Carolina was disturbed by Senate votes in early 1863 and held Clay amendment supporters responsible for derailing the Supreme Court. Gaither complained to North Carolina governor Zebulon B. Vance that the obstructionists "have attempted to organize and establish . . . legal nullification of any and all the powers of the Confederate Government, by the State Courts, by organizing the Supreme Court without the power of appellate jurisdiction." Gaither fretted that there was "no hope of establishing the Supreme Court, without yielding to this miserable doctrine, while the senate is composed of its present members."[60]

In December 1863 House members reconsidered Supreme Court creation. Arkansas congressman Augustus Garland reminded colleagues that "courts were the safeguards of . . . liberties and rights." For Garland and like-minded supporters a Supreme Court served as a protector of, not a threat to, civil liberties. Henry Foote disagreed on grounds of low priority, states' rights, and personal animosity. Foote argued that the decision to empower the high court could wait "whilst the pending war was in progress." The Confederacy, he insisted, "had no use for a supreme appellate tribunal" and asserted "the establishment of the court, with appellate power over the supreme courts of the States, would be utterly subversive of . . . State sovereignty." The final reason to delay creation of a high court came in the form of an acerbic personal attack on the secretary of state. Foote declared he would "never consent to the establishment of a supreme court . . . so long as Judah P. Benjamin shall continue to pollute the ears" of the president "with his insidious counsels." Much like the now-deceased Yancey had argued the previous spring, Foote viewed the high court as an extension of executive power and patronage, not a coequal branch. Foote worried about an overzealous executive branch using the high court to coerce states into compliance with unconscionable policies.[61]

Two more attempts were made in the House of Representatives to create a high court in 1864. On May 5th a bill to create a Supreme Court was introduced and instantly referred to committee. Twenty-one days later, Virginia representative Charles Russell delivered the committee's decision that the bill had not passed. Supreme Court organization was reintroduced on November 18th by William Chilton but the bill was sent to the Judiciary Committee. On November 29th, the House voted 45 to 34 to devolve into secret session, presumably to further discuss the Supreme Court issue. A final last-ditch effort on behalf of high court creation occurred on March 14, 1865, but, like so many times before, was tabled for a future deliberation that never came to pass. The House did not even proceed far enough to debate the contentious jurisdictional issues that had gripped the Senate in early 1863. In fact, with knowledge that the Senate had already rejected an empowered Supreme Court, House members' support for creation was likely as much political posturing as a serious attempt to get the court under way.[62]

A powerful collection of congressional leaders in both chambers, headed by states' rights activists in the Senate, did not wish to contend with judicial review of legislation; thus a viable and reasonably powerful Supreme Court was never allowed to exist. The Davis administration openly supported the Supreme Court early in 1862 and again through department heads like Attorney General Watts and Treasury Secretary Christopher Memminger in early 1863, but the executive branch eventually acquiesced in the congressional decision not to enable a high court.

With no Supreme Court, most judicial review and Confederate constitutional interpretation devolved to the state courts. As pointed out by historian John G. de Roulhac Hamilton, the Confederate district courts held "no final jurisdiction under the Constitution . . . and at best had only concurrent jurisdiction with the state courts over which they had no authority, appellate or otherwise."[63] Most state supreme courts upheld the controversial Confederate policies like conscription even if the decisions quibbled with particular elements of implementation. The Alabama, Georgia, Virginia, and Texas supreme courts all upheld conscription's constitutionality, but serious resistance came from North Carolina. Without the clear-cut national supremacy of a Supreme Court, the possibility of interpretive friction existed with state judges and could undermine Confederate laws, much to the chagrin of Davis and the Congress.

North Carolina jurist Richmond Pearson, and his mouthpiece Governor Zebulon Vance, symbolized the potential for legal dissent at the state level. Both men maintained the prerogative of the North Carolina Supreme Court to interpret the constitutionality of Confederate policies. In May 1863, when Secretary of War James Seddon complained to Governor Vance about the state court's subversion of conscription policy, Vance replied that "it is certainly no fault of this Government that there exists no proper tribunal to decide these issues . . . and it is certainly not unreasonable for the State of North Carolina to object when a decision of its Chief Justice is ordered to be disregarded by a Department of the Confederate Government invested with no judicial power whatever." A frustrated Seddon responded that Pearson's dissenting "opinion contradicts the practice of the department, the assent of Congress . . . and also . . . decisions by other judges." Vance reminded Seddon that he was "bound by the judicial decisions of the State Courts . . . and in the absence of a Court having a Superior and appellate jurisdiction, deciding to the contrary, that they are . . . the supreme law of the land." Over time, the Confederate government gained the upper hand in dealing with Pearson, Vance, and annoying judicial decisions that leaned more toward individual liberty than Confederate policy.[64]

State-level resistance crumbled in the face of constant executive pressure to implement centralized policies, and in 1864 the state courts deferred to Confederate policies. Congress's failure to create a functional Supreme Court opened an interpretive loophole for recalcitrant state judges and governors to legitimately subvert Confederate policies by deeming them unconstitutional. However, the power of state supreme courts eventually faded and allowed for even more centralization in the face of wartime pressures.

Another source of constitutional interpretation emanated from the Confederate attorneys general. President Davis relied on five attorneys general, both appointed and de facto, during the war. Judah P. Benjamin served as the first attorney general but took over as secretary of war in September 1861. Wade Keyes provided interim service until Thomas Braggs's appointment in November 1861. Bragg abruptly retired in March 1862 and Thomas Watts, a jocund, well-respected Alabamian, took charge of the Justice Department. Watts's tenure witnessed a rise in appeals for legal clarification of Confederate policies that traditionally would have been interpreted by a

Supreme Court. Watts performed admirably in this capacity but returned to Alabama in the fall of 1863 to serve as governor. Wade Keyes again stepped in for interim duty until former North Carolina senator George Davis assumed the post in January 1864 and served until the end of the war.

The attorneys general provided a source of legal clarification and temporary interpretation until the Supreme Court could disseminate judicial interpretations to government officials and the wider public. These opinions constituted a valuable source for other cabinet members to argue for the legitimacy of controversial policies. The breakdown of opinions of attorneys general as requested by department, "35 per cent . . . to the secretary of war; 27 per cent to secretary of the treasury; 17 per cent to the President; 12 per cent to the secretary of the navy; 4 per cent to the postmaster general; 2 per cent to the secretary of state; and 2 per cent to the bureau chiefs of the Department of Justice," generally reflected the need to legitimize controversial areas of Confederate governance like conscription, impressment, tax policies, and executive authority.[65]

The opinions of the attorneys general did not overtly side with the executive branch, but it was obvious that decisions were not completely independent. For example, in a decision concerning the wages of War Department clerks, Watts stated that "it is the duty and appropriate sphere of the Legislative Department, to make, alter, or repeal laws [but] it has no authority to interpret or define the meaning of laws." As a final justification of his interpretive function, Watts asserted "the Judicial Department is assigned the . . . power of declaring what the law is . . . and cannot be controlled in the exercise of its power interpreting laws, by the declarations of the Legislative Department." In his mini-civics lesson Watts correctly pointed out that the legislative branch possessed no interpretive powers, but he failed to mention that the executive branch, which is typically responsible for enforcement, should not be expected to interpret laws. Watts was no opponent of Supreme Court organization per se, and he was not going to allow national interpretive duties to lay dormant.[66]

George Davis expressed a similar interpretation of national powers in February 1864. In a decision on district judge salaries, Attorney General Davis declared, "the Congress are to ordain laws, the Judiciary to interpret them, and the President to execute them [and] neither department can trench upon the functions of the other." By using the word *neither* and the singular *other* instead of *others*, Davis implied that only two branches, legislative and executive, vied for legal interpretive powers in the absence of a Supreme Court. Just like Watts, Davis apparently did not see judicial review by an executive appointee as a conflict of interest among the Confederate branches of government.[67]

In September 1864 Assistant Attorney General Wade Keyes frankly summarized the Justice Department's powers of judicial review "in the execution of laws" to Treasury Secretary George Trenholm. Keyes asserted that "the Executive Department has the right . . . to execute [the laws] according to its own interpretation, until that interpretation has been fixed by the Judicial Department." According to Keyes, until a Supreme Court was created and vested with interpretive powers, executive department heads could unilaterally construe the laws to their benefit. Without a Supreme Court, the attorneys general represented the highest national authority for legal interpretation, and they combined the important powers of law enforcement and judicial review into one executive post. None overtly abused their considerable powers, and this promoted legitimacy for their legal opinions, but President Davis and the department heads could certainly depend on the attorneys general for reliable decisions to uphold controversial Confederate policies.[68]

Why did Confederate leaders decide not to empower the high court? One valid reason was low priority. Congressional leaders pointed to other more pressing war-related issues that needed resolution before completion of the judicial branch. This reason implied that a high court was a legal luxury, not a necessary component of Confederate governance. If the executive branch had viewed the high court as a vital governmental entity, then surely Davis would have pushed harder for implementation of the Judiciary Act. The longer the war dragged on, the more difficult it became to establish a high court, and wartime exigencies supported arguments that a Supreme Court was indeed superfluous. Once independence had been gained then judicial branch powers could be reexamined by the Congress, but during the war all policies needed to be predicated on immediate needs. For most congressional leaders, Supreme Court empowerment did not qualify as a matter of national survival.

Some opponents denied empowerment and worried that a strong Supreme Court might be easily influenced by the executive branch. Yancey in particular viewed the high court as an extension of executive patronage and not a coequal branch buttressing the checks and balances of Confederate power. Surely Yancey understood that without a Supreme Court, the Davis administration could indirectly interpret national laws through the attorney general. From this perspective, arguments against a Supreme Court for reasons of increased executive patronage seem unusual. There is little doubt, however, that some members of Congress opposed creating a Supreme Court due to animosity towards President Davis.

Confederate justices would be required to undergo the same selection process as did their U.S. counterparts as outlined in Article 2 of the Confederate Constitution, and after presidential nomination justices had to be confirmed by two-thirds of the Senate. It would be difficult to imagine the Confederate Senate holding lengthy modern-style confirmation hearings given the heavy workload required for other more pressing issues, but senators had the option to block undesirable judicial candidates. Speculation arose that Davis would appoint former U.S. Supreme Court member John A. Campbell as chief justice. This upset hard-core nationalists because Campbell was a reluctant secessionist and had been too friendly with prominent "Black Republicans" like William Seward during the secession crisis. Some congressional leaders chose not to enable a Supreme Court for fear it would become another manifestation of executive power.

Another reason to prevent a Supreme Court was to protect legislation from judicial review. Senators like Wigfall and Yancey, and representatives like Foote, often played the role of petulant obstructionists towards the Davis administration and attempts to create a Supreme Court while simultaneously protecting their congressional power fiefdoms. These men wanted to either "rule or ruin" and in this case they much preferred the "ruin" of the Confederate judicial branch to any potential diminishment of their powers. If any of the individual state supreme courts ruled a law unconstitutional, then the executive branch could be depended on to eventually force compliance.

The states' rights doctrine was also a major reason the Confederacy never enabled a Supreme Court. This interpretation is easily supported by congressional arguments against enablement of a Supreme Court with final jurisdiction over state courts. Failure to create a Supreme Court, according to this oft-cited argument, derived from recognition of state sovereignty and the need to protect the supremacy of the states.[69] Congressional leaders did proclaim adherence to states' rights but did not craft policies in anticipation of state supreme court decisions. Policy deliberations, when possible, took into account popular support, but political leaders were confronted with far more vexing problems than the approval of state courts. The states' rights interpretation has been accorded far too much consideration with respect to the absence of a Confederate high court.

Objections to the Supreme Court based upon states' rights doctrinal objections were more complicated than the simplistic rhetorical appeals to state sovereignty delivered by contemporaries. Opponents used the states' rights argument to refuse even the most basic powers to the high court. Opposition leaders like Yancey, Wigfall, and Foote were true believers with impeccable states' rights credentials, but their opinions also derived from their jealous natures and enjoyment of playing power politics. These congressional leaders did not fear a dependent judicial branch as much as a truly independent one that might undercut their considerable power to craft policy. Former U.S. Supreme Court chief justice John Marshall, no stranger to combat with the theory of state supremacy, could have been describing Confederate Supreme Court obstructionists when he stated that opposition was "more about agitating the publick mind, and reviving those unfounded jealousies by whose blind ambition climbs the ladder of power."[70] In some respects, states' rights has always been used by secondary power brokers to frustrate the policies of those in control. The states' rights opposition to Supreme Court empowerment was partially a visceral reaction against the potential restructuring of Confederate power relationships, and not solely a principled objection on behalf of state sovereignty. Unfortunately the catchall states' rights argument, although certainly prominent and not merely a pretext, disguised other more nuanced reasons for denying the existence of a Supreme Court.[71]

There are two fundamentally different ways to analyze the absence of a Confederate Supreme Court. The first interpretation views the lack of a high court as an attempt to make the government more democratic because local state courts might better protect the rights of citizens against authoritarian policies from Richmond. Unlike national Supreme Court justices who served for life, judges on the state level were elected and thus inclined to be more responsive to voters. Determined states' rights advocates believed individual liberties were best protected at the state level and that state sovereignty was the only foil for centralization. Therefore the absence of a high national tribunal promoted preservation of local liberties.[72]

The second interpretation, the centralization interpretation, views the failure to organize a Supreme Court as an attempt by the executive branch to deny judicial review. The executive branch, an early supporter of Supreme Court enablement, seemed contented knowing that national policies could not be undermined by unpredictable justices. President Davis showed no signs of being more than annoyed when he realized Congress would not empower a Supreme Court, probably because he could depend on his loyal attorneys general to fill the jurisdictional vacuum by issuing decisions on the constitutionality of Confederate policies. Without a co-equal institution in the judicial branch, the executive branch wielded more centralized power over Confederate policy.

The failure of Confederate leaders to establish a functional Supreme Court allowed for increased centralization in the political culture. The jurisdictional void created by the absence of a high court fostered a negative projection of national legitimacy and sparked bitter legal battles over states' rights that epitomized the conflict of centralized power versus local dissent. The absence of a Supreme Court also meant that the executive and legislative branches could enact and implement policies unimpeded by any institution with national standing. This two-branch system represented a form of bilateral authoritarianism. Confederate political leaders made a short-sighted decision and grievous error by not empowering a Supreme Court that could ratify necessary nationalist policies. Although many governors and local officials would have contested Confederate policies using states' rights arguments under any circumstances, President Davis and the Congress exacerbated the antagonistic relationship between state and national sovereignty by not empowering a Supreme Court that could rule on Confederate policies.

ANTIPARTY SENTIMENT

The Confederate government operated in an atmosphere of antiparty sentiment that provided the image, if not the actuality, of unity between the executive and legislative branches. Many Confederate politicians were veterans of the hyper-partisan divisions of the 1850s, and their devotion to a national party waned in proportion to their increasing loyalty to the South. As a result, strong national partisan affiliations left over from the second party system struggled to maintain political primacy in the decade before the Civil War. Sectionalism irreparably eroded the local competitiveness of national parties by 1860, with southern Democrats and northern Republicans unilaterally dominating their respective regions.

Southern antiparty ideology did not openly manifest itself until after secession, but the distaste for competing party organizations did grow from events in the 1850s as southern Whigs and Democrats combined in a less partisan and more sectional effort to protect slavery from outside interference. Antiparty sentiment continued throughout the secession crisis, carried over into wartime southern politics, and evolved into a fundamental tenet of Confederate political culture.[73]

Notions of slavery-based republicanism also promoted antiparty sentiment. Republicanism can be defined as a broad social and political ideology intended to create criteria for responsible citizenship in a democratic republic. Tenets of republicanism carried over into the secession crisis and arguably prompted antiparty sentiment.[74] For secessionists, the best example of partisan evil was the rapid antebellum rise of the "Black Republican" party in the North. Many Confederate political leaders recalled the breakdown of bisectional partisan affiliations over slavery in the 1850s and perhaps worried that similar factionalism might destroy the southern bid for independence.

In the North, slavery and republicanism were antonyms, but in the South, slavery and republicanism were not antithetical concepts but compatible with the goals of Confederate nationalism.[75] For southern republicans, slavery represented the one institution that held society together and informed southern identity. Thus secessionists viewed themselves as carrying on the American tradition of slave society republicanism in their bid for national sovereignty, and the ideal way to preserve this ideology was to stifle partisan differences.

Political leaders in both houses of Congress repeatedly warned that parties should be avoided at all costs. In reference to the potential effects of secret sessions on partisanship, Duncan Kenner remarked that "if this mysterious policy was persevered in, parties would arise." William Yancey reminded his colleagues that "party had been the bane of the old Government, and . . . would be the bane of the new" if partisan allegiances trumped political consensus. In an excellent historical analogy, Yancey observed, "Pompey had his party, and Caesar his Party, but Rome had no party."[76]

In January 1864 Congress passed a joint resolution designed to encourage the people to "surrender all personal and party feuds . . . [and] every exhibition of factious temper." The statement declared that "we ignore all party names, lines and issues, and recognize but two parties in this war—patriots and traitors." In another example, Georgia senator Herschel V. Johnson vacillated on the February 1864 vote to suspend the writ of habeas corpus and explained to his friend Vice President Alexander Stephens that he acquiesced in the suspension because "there was no room for but one party—the party of the country— . . . in time of peace, we might engage in party squabbles—but in time of war I would stand by the government right or wrong." In this instance, Johnson's nationalism trumped his political principles and he noted it would "be delightful to the enemy to see us torn by partisan associations or factions."[77]

Congress's only delineation of partisanship was based upon whether politicians supported or opposed the Davis administration, but this could hardly be defined as a party system with the requisite local organizations, election committees, and disbursement of patronage. Antiparty sentiment consisted of more than just the rhetoric of political unity. It symbolized the lengths to which congressional leaders were willing to go, by fighting their old habits of partisan bickering for the sake of Confederate nationalism.

National parties did not form during the Confederacy's short existence, but well-organized local and state party systems continued during the war in isolated pockets. North Carolina represents the sustained existence of a two-party system. According to Congressman Burgess Gaither, the political lines in North Carolina were redrawn in early 1861 when "two parties sprang up . . . and its fruits [have] been evil." Gaither traced the origins of the wartime two-party system to the February 1861 secession convention in which "eighty gentlemen elected were opposed to secession and forty in its favor." This division became the foundation for wartime political disagreement between "the secession [Confederate] and conservative parties."[78]

The 1861 November elections for the Confederate Congress further crystallized North Carolina's emergent two-party political system. The pro-Confederate party, pejoratively referred to as the "Destructives," harnessed the momentum of pro-secession Democrats while the Conservative party constructed an opposition platform that criticized the political leaders of secession. The 1863 Congressional elections reflected popular views of the war. North Carolinians suffered grievous casualties in the 1863 military campaigns at Chancellorsville, Gettysburg, and Bristoe Station, all of which took an unusually heavy toll on North Carolina troops and their families back home. These casualties likely played an important role in the overwhelming victory in the fall congressional elections in which Conservative candidates won nine out of ten districts.[79] North Carolina's two-party system mirrored the progress of the war, and if rebel armies had won more military victories in 1862 and 1863, antiparty sentiment might have stifled partisanship in North Carolina.

Confederate antiparty attitudes evolved from the basic necessity of unity in the face of an overwhelming national crisis. Often against their divisive and contentious natures, Confederate congressional leaders wisely maintained some semblance of monolithic agreement on vital policies. Even if they disagreed about aspects of legislation, they tended to conform to the requirements of national survival. This does not mean there were not serious policy differences between the president and legislators, but each necessary measure became a test of Confederate nationalism. The only semblance of opposition to the executive branch emerged from legislators who accused the Davis administration of despotism.[80] Unity in the face of an external threat continually trumped abstract policy disagreements, and antiparty sentiment provided an important element to Confederate political culture, which created a strong impetus for government centralization.

CONCLUSION

In some respects, the political culture of secession from December 1860 through May 1861 differed from the fully developed Confederate political culture that followed, the newly drafted constitution being the common denominator to both. In 1861 the Confederate experiment was not yet confronted with the full realities of wartime policies. Political culture at this early stage manifested the enthusiasm of hopeful southern nationalists. On his journey from Montgomery to the new Confederate capital in Richmond in May 1861, President Jefferson Davis was feted by "throngs of men, women, and children . . . and was received with the wildest enthusiasm," according to one reporter. At one stop, Davis's dining area was allegedly attended by "beautiful girls . . . bedecking him with garlands of flowers, while others fanned him." The reporter's hyperbole symbolized the genuine popular enthusiasm for the new government and its leaders. The reporter concluded that "the whole soul of the South is in this war."[81] The "soul" of the majority of the southern population had indeed been delivered up to the assumed good judgment of Confederate leaders.

By June 1861 the halcyon days of national creation, during which abstract principles like internal improvements, free trade, and states' rights could be remedied with the stroke of a pen, soon gave way to the practical realities of wartime policy implementation. The foundations of Confederate political culture ensured that leaders could pursue the primary goal of national survival without major internal interference from institutional obstacles. What remained to be seen was how the southern populace, the reactive but powerful element of Confederate political culture, would respond to the leadership of Davis and other Confederate leaders once the hysteria and exhilaration of secession transitioned into the problems of daily governance.

The basic structure of Confederate political culture comprised several components that allowed for the creation of a centralized state. A strong executive branch established by the Confederate Constitution was made more powerful by lack of judicial review and antiparty sentiment in the legislative branch. The Congress, through the continued use of secret sessions, mainly complied with executive prerogative and even hid crucial policy debates from Confederate citizens. Critics of the national government argued that the methods of governance were authoritarian in style, despite the fact that southern constituents had elected these same leaders to office. The essential elements of Confederate political culture provided the foundation for a powerful modern-style government designed to sustain state survival. A centralized political culture is the framework of corporatist development, and the modern elements of Confederate political culture were key cornerstones in the implementation of an expedient corporatist state. The constant problem faced by Confederate political culture was how to successfully mobilize the southern populace and to develop an industrial base sufficient to wage a modern war.

2

———— ✦ ————

CORPORATIST INDUSTRIAL POLICY
IN THE CONFEDERACY,
PART ONE

Private Munitions Industries

———— ✦ ————

We must now place the Manufacturer by the side of the Agriculturalist.
—Thomas Jefferson to Benjamin Austin (1816)

If Thomas Jefferson was dismayed by the erosion of his eighteenth-century vision for an independent and virtuous citizenry based on an agrarian lifestyle at the dawn of the Market Revolution, he would have been seriously disturbed by the rapid industrial expansion of the Confederacy. In addition, the Sage of Monticello would have been particularly upset by government subsidies to encourage the necessary industries to supply the massive armies mobilized for southern defense. Confederate leaders defined themselves by the norms of a long-standing agrarian society based primarily on slave labor and often boasted about their agricultural roots, but the conflict necessitated a drastic increase in the South's industrial sectors, especially those related to war materiel production.

The historical debate about the paucity or sufficiency of southern prewar industrialization provides a basis for understanding the extent of wartime development. Historians of the underdevelopment school argue that full-scale southern industrialization was prevented by factors like the absence of a reliable domestic market and dependence on slave labor, but this so-called "deplorable scarcity," as described by economic historians Fred Bateman and Thomas Weiss, was caused primarily by slaveholding planter elites who opposed industrialization and refused to allocate surplus cash resources to manufacturing ventures.[1] Investment in land and slaves represented the proven method for continued profits in the South, so widespread financing of industrial concerns remained a secondary avenue for excess capital.

Historians who argue that there was comparative industrial sufficiency assert that southern manufacturers comprised a respectable portion of the region's economic leadership and created a viable manufacturing base despite the anti-industrial bias of the planter class. This "antebellum renaissance in Southern manufacturing," as asserted by historian Harold Wilson, provided the Confederacy with a stable industrial foundation even if the slave states lagged behind northern capacity in several sectors. Statements about antebellum southern industrial stagnation, according to this argument, have been overstated, and when compared to other regions around the world in the mid-nineteenth century, the southern states initiated their bid for independence with a relatively strong industrial core.[2]

The debate will continue until historians agree upon a uniform definition and degree of industrialization, and then it will likely go on anyway, but this matter is only important for this study as a point of departure. The salient fact underlying the prewar industrialization debate is that the South, no matter how developed compared to other world regions, especially the industrialized North, was severely deficient in industries needed to fight a protracted war against another industrial power. To be sure, southern textile manufacturing flourished during the antebellum period, but cotton and woolen factories would not directly help to destroy invading Yankee armies.[3] If the Confederacy expected any reasonable chance of success, it needed to rapidly construct a productive military industrial system across the agrarian-oriented South while it simultaneously fought Union armies with the available means at hand. This was a herculean task that, at the outset, stood little chance of success. The fact that the Confederacy adapted its resources to wartime military production so quickly is a testament to the resolve and ingenuity of southern leaders and the expedient corporatist system they created.

During the 1850s, manufacturing boosters in southern newspapers and other periodicals like *DeBow's Review* warned of the long-term consequences associated with continued reliance on imported products, but few heeded these warnings so long as cotton prices, land, and slaves remained highly profitable. Prophets of economic diversification took no perverse pleasure in being correct once the war began, and some even viewed secession as an opportunity to fulfill a long-awaited program of southern industrial development.

Few held any illusions about the difficult task ahead, but there was hope for success. "Everywhere and all around us are seen the proofs of our widening industry," one Richmond observer remarked; the "privations that turn our industry into these new courses" was a beneficial aspect of "the existence of war." From this viewpoint, secession liberated the southern economy from the doldrums of antebellum stagnation by forcing southern capital into industrial development, since the region could no longer depend on northern manufactures. However, this same optimistic commentator realistically cautioned that "though we are doing much, we are yet doing too little . . . [and] there is no room for an idler in the whole South."[4] The war required Confederate political and industrial leaders to rapidly construct an industrial manufacturing base in a cooperative manner fostered by the state. The primary goal of Confederate industrial policy was not profit, long-term sustainability, or creation of a state-owned network of facilities, but instead the basic task of immediate national survival.

This study does not pretend to cover the entire scope of Confederate industrial experience, but the simple goal is to better understand the creation and operation of southern heavy industries responsible for production of vital war materiel like iron and gunpowder. The term *munitions*, in this study, refers to the ingredients of war materiel production and not necessarily to the finished products themselves, like artillery and ammunition. Focusing on several firms involved with munitions production does not mean, by implication, that other industries were considered unimportant to the Confederate war effort, but in reality they were less vital to the immediate survival of southern armies.

For example, the primary manufacturing sectors in the antebellum South continued to churn out products for the Confederacy. These manufacturing interests, as described by economic historians Bateman and Weiss, consisted largely of "cotton ginning, sugar refining, rice milling, and tobacco processing," all of which were pivotal for agricultural exports and local consumption.[5] These industries could reap peacetime profits, but as manufacturing sectors they were less valuable when it came to repelling Union armies.

In addition to these agricultural processing industries, the southern states did possess a growing textile manufacturing sector. Southern cloth manufactures rivaled northern firms with factories "such as E. M. Holt's in North Carolina, which produced the so-called 'Alamance plaids'; and . . . Edward McGehee's Woodville (Mississippi) Manufacturing Company . . . William Gregg's Graniteville Manufacturing Company . . . [which had] 9,000 spindles and 300 looms." In Alabama, Daniel Pratt had built up "the Prattville Manufacturing Company, [into] a cotton cloth factory with nearly 3,000 spindles."[6] When war broke out, the Confederacy did not suffer from the inability to spin cotton into cloth. Home textile production with cotton cards, however, was still encouraged because southern textile operators knew that eventually there would be a shortage of machine parts and perhaps labor, both of which came to pass.

During the war, southern textile magnates, so powerful and vocal in the antebellum era, were generally not accorded the same priority status created for owners of vital munitions industries. Instead of individual sweetheart deals and government advances, southern textile industries attempted to band together under the auspices of the "Manufacturers Association of the Confederate States" to protect their interests and pool resources to minimize government intervention. In many ways, the "Manufacturers Association" was an attempt to create a corporatist bloc, but it simply did not possess the same clout with the Confederate government as southern munitions firms.

These "less vital" manufacturing firms of agricultural products provided some support to southern armies in the form of military attire, consumer tobacco products (particularly good for trading with Yankees desperate for a nicotine fix), and rebel foodstuffs, but when compared to the continual need for munitions, these products were viewed by Confederate leaders as of secondary importance. The manufactured products of cotton gins, textile factories, and tobacco processors were not inconsequential, but they were considered less vital for rebel battlefield victories. As a result, managers and owners in these manufacturing sectors typically experienced stricter forced compliance with government policies, were allowed less leeway when it came to conscription and resource allocation, and more fully felt the brunt of government regulations.

Scholars consistently interpret the relationship between the Confederate government and industrial leaders as "statist" or a "command economy." This phrase describes a mostly one-way dictatorial link in which the Confederate government forced southern firms to bend to its will by controlling access to vital resources like commodities and labor.[7] Statism is one example of a modernist approach to the problems of industrial development, but the methods of that development require further explanation.

The terms *command economy* and *statism* are valid when describing the Confederate government's relationship with less-essential manufacturing firms, but these terms are not as useful when applied to other critically important industrial sectors like munitions production and railroads. There is no question that the Confederate government possessed the necessary tools to coerce southern industries, but what the "command economy" thesis overlooks were the numerous means for essential firms to leverage their indispensable products against state pressure. The "statist/command economy" model, although useful for describing some aspects of Confederate industrial economy, has been too broadly applied to the overall nature of southern industry. Statist principles certainly contributed to the expedient corporatist system, especially with regard to policies like conscription and impressment, but they were not successfully or uniformly applied across the entire southern industrial landscape as some historians suggest.

Wartime industrial policy, especially with regard to munitions, symbolized the creation of an expedient corporatist state in microcosm and was a defining aspect of Confederate political economy. Historians have been forced to come to terms with a mixture of both state-owned, or nationalized, and privately owned industries when attempting to describe the South's industrial sector. This has usually caused analysis to focus solely on either the state-owned or the private sectors, and rarely have the two distinctly different categories been combined into one comprehensive interpretive model. Application of the term *expedient corporatist* state is an attempt to explain the dichotomy of Confederate industrial production and how the two styles coexisted and reinforced one another during the war.

PRIVATE MUNITIONS INDUSTRIES

At the outset of the war it was unclear how the Confederacy would develop sustainable munitions industries to support rebel armies. In March 1861 an anonymous contributor to the *Charleston Daily Courier* mused on the nature of future southern armaments industries and knew that either private or state action would be necessary to jump-start the munitions sector. "Experience has shown," the author asserted, "that it is cheaper and better for a Government to buy (under proper inspection) whatever they want from private establishments." This position represented more than adherence to laissez-faire doctrine, and it outlines a fundamental doubt about competent government management. The author accurately predicted a system of unified production in munitions facilities, but he later warned that desperately needed munitions "should be supplied by State or Confederate action," and he warned "there are strong objections derived from experience and observation, against any undertaking by government of duties that can be fulfilled by private enterprise."[8]

Why the great opposition to government control of the emerging munitions sector? The first possibility was a legitimate distrust of state-run institutions. Some southerners clung to the Jeffersonian small government doctrine and believed that eventually government control could only end up in destruction of liberty or corruption of republican principles. Another possible reason for opposition was profit. The anonymous *Charleston Daily Courier* author who so adamantly opposed state ownership also aggrandized one "Thomas E. McNeill, Esq., who has come home to the South . . . for this special purpose." The author claimed McNeill was "thoroughly trained and tried as a constructive engineer and inventor . . . for the manufacture of arms . . . and all military materials."[9] The relationship between McNeill and the author is unclear, but the articles about the superiority of private ownership suddenly sounded more like a public request for investors than a principled ideological stand against state management. The McNeill story shows historians that sometimes arguments against state ownership perhaps had as much to do with private profits as they did with any laissez-faire attitude in the South.

Confederate leaders understood from the outset of their experiment in 1861 that southern munitions industries required government assistance. On February 20, 1861, the founding delegates at the Montgomery convention created a foundational relationship of government support for firms that could "provide Munitions of War." President Davis and Secretary of War Leroy Pope Walker were "empowered to make contracts for the purchase and manufacture of heavy ordnance and small arms."[10] Since the Confederacy did not possess the apparatus of the yet-to-be-established Ordnance Bureau, this type of direct executive power was necessary if the Confederate government expected to immediately begin collecting armaments. After Josiah Gorgas's appointment to head the Ordnance Bureau in early April, Secretary of War Leroy Pope Walker could now rely on responsible oversight of munitions contracts and focus on the myriad other duties of the burdensome office.

Extant production facilities were obviously insufficient to meet demand. This situation was remedied by a government promise to "employ the necessary agents and artisans for these purposes." Congress also apparently recognized the looming southern gunpowder shortage and allowed the War Department "to make contracts for the establishment of powder mills and the manufacture of powder."[11] As it turned out, private firms were never able to produce enough gunpowder to sustain Confederate needs, and eventually the government resorted to the highly successful state-owned operation in Augusta, Georgia.

The final aspect of the munitions support law allowed for executive initiative. That meant President Davis could "make contracts . . . in such a manner and on such terms as in his judgment the public exigencies may require."[12] President Davis's involvement in the details of making contracts with munitions factories may have appealed to his micromanagement style, but these types of negotiations were conducted by War Department officials as proxies for the executive branch. During the formative stages of the Confederacy, political leaders recognized government's role in aiding creation or expansion of the South's military manufacturing capabilities. Confederate politicians were not deluded by rhetoric but instantly empowered the executive branch with powers to promote munitions industries.

The 1861 victories at Wilson's Creek, Manassas, and Ball's Bluff reinforced southern stereotypes of rebel battlefield prowess, but the problems of supplying massive armies had not abated in the opening year of the war. When Ulysses S. Grant's Union armies captured Forts Henry and Donelson and then the crucial industrial center of Nashville, Tennessee in February 1862, southern leaders realized an accelerated program of industrial development was required. Confederate leaders renewed and expanded the policy of government advances and subsidies that could help jump-start or broaden private production.

In April 1862 the Confederate Congress initiated another round of government support and subsidies for industrial expansion of the South's munitions capacity. Any manufacturer of "saltpeter and of Small Arms," and in addendum legislation two days later, "all establishments or mines for the production of coal and for the production and manufacture of iron," were given a 50 percent government advance, interest-free upon repayment, "for the erection and preparation of the works and machinery necessary." Applicants were required to get President Davis's approval and to pay at least 25 percent of the costs upfront; then "the amount so advanced shall be paid in installments as the works shall progress." Repayment of the government advance could be in "merchantable article manufactured, to be delivered at such times and in such quantities as may be agreed upon" or could be repaid in full at any time with cash assets. Phrasing of the laws indicated that Confederate leaders desired a long-term symbiotic relationship with these munitions firms. President Davis, through his agents in the War Department and Ordnance Bureau, was given the power to contract for coal and iron, and government agents were also allowed "to make advances . . . not exceeding one-third of the amount of such contract."[13] This series of legislation passed into law on April 17 and April 19, 1862, established a major cornerstone of the Confederacy's expedient corporatist policies by creating a codependent economic relationship, or public-private partnership, between munitions companies and the government.

Confederate lawmakers offered relatively shortsighted subsidies to important military production sectors, including coal producers, iron manufacturers, and foundries. Contracts between the Confederate government and essential industries were typically based upon minimum production quotas and did not include production incentives. For example, the government contract with the Shelby Iron Company forwarded $75,000 to the owners and set agreeable prices, but merely required the "manufacture [of] the largest quantity of iron practicable" up to "twelve thousand tons per" year.[14]

That type of contract did not "incentivize" maximum production. A wiser contract might have tied increased productivity to a graduated price scale in which the company would receive higher profits for increased production. The prototypical munitions contract required only a minimal promise of future production and cooperation with government needs, a tendency of corporatist relationships. The Confederate war effort would have been better served if politicians and bureaucrats had crafted a more incentivized subsidy system of production contracts with the private sector. The Confederate government's corporatist contract style of offering industrial subsidies to essential industries was formulated under desperate circumstances and, in the absence of more incentivized contracts, possibly hampered maximum production. Also in a corporatist fashion, shortsighted subsidies provided private management with the loophole of meeting minimum production quotas for government contracts and then selling any surplus products on the open market for higher profits.

As the Confederate Congress initiated additional subsidies for vital munitions industries in April 1862, it was evident that large-scale government capital outlays would be required to create nationally owned plants in the South or expand extant iron facilities. The political competition to land these valuable economic assets in home states began before the subsidy legislation was even passed. On April 1st Senator Benjamin Hill of Georgia brought a resolution concerning "the Iron Interest [and] a National Foundry" to the floor and recommended generous government support, which eventually took the form of the April 17th and 19th subsidy legislation. Hill's resolution also called for the Committee on Military Affairs to "enquire into the proper localities for the erection of such furnaces, rolling mills, and other machinery." Instead of going to work on subsidy details, Confederate senators instead debated which state should receive this substantial Confederate investment. Hill lobbied for expansion of existing iron works in Georgia, and Senators Gustavus Henry and Landon Carter Haynes of Tennessee supported government investment in Chattanooga and Knoxville. After harsh debate the resolution was referred to the Military Committee for further discussion.[15] Fortunately for the benefit of the Confederate war effort, the allocation of resources was left up to the War Department and Ordnance Bureau, not carping politicians.

Although some private iron firms were eventually nationalized, the War Department did not construct large-scale national foundries but instead opted for subsidies to extant, privately owned iron companies. Thus the Confederate munitions manufacturing network was a curious entity in which private corporations operated alongside state-owned facilities. Historians might interpret the coexistence of state-owned and privately owned firms in one economic sector as an antagonistic system of socialism versus capitalism, but in this case, the Confederacy was simply operating a type of flexible capitalism based on expediency. A variety of private industries ramped up wartime production for the rebel armies. This section focuses on the experiences of two important corporations and their relationship with the Confederate government: the Tredegar Iron Works of Virginia and the Shelby Iron Company of Alabama.

TREDEGAR IRON WORKS

The Richmond-based Tredegar Iron Works was founded in 1837, and by the end of the Civil War it had grown into the most important heavy industrial complex in the Confederacy. The history of the Tredegar Iron Works is inextricably linked to the career of Joseph Reid Anderson, who rose through the ranks of management to become the company's owner and president. Historian Charles B. Dew describes Anderson's meteoric rise in the iron business. As a young man, Anderson showed signs of dogged persistence and the promise of effective leadership. After twice being denied admittance to West Point, Anderson finally earned a spot as a cadet in 1832 and finished fourth in the class of 1836. Trained as an engineer, Anderson preferred fortune in his native Virginia to military fame and resigned his commission in 1837 in favor of private employment. In 1841 the aspiring engineer was hired as a commercial agent for the Tredegar Iron Works. In only seven years, Anderson had effectively managed and maneuvered to be able to buy out other controlling interests in the Tredegar.[16] Anderson paid off his creditors and possessed full control of the iron works in the 1850s, an astonishingly successful rise in the antebellum southern iron industry.

Anderson's business success was accompanied by a foray into politics. As an ardent Whig in the 1840s and early 1850s, Joseph R. Anderson supported the standard Whig policies of national internal improvements and a protective tariff. Anderson's political position was consistent with other southern industrialists because Democrats tended not to support development of the southern iron industry. However, like many other southerners, he was dragged into the bitter sectional divide over slavery and eventually sided with the southern Democrats.[17] In spite of the growing sectionalism, the Tredegar competed with and was dependent upon northern industries to continue profitable operations.

In the late 1850s Anderson wisely learned to drum up southern business contracts based on regional loyalty. It was impossible to profit solely from southern contracts, and the Tredegar remained dependent on equipment manufactured in the North.[18] Ever the politic businessman, Anderson realized that sectionalism required a two-faced approach in order to maintain profits, and he also understood that secession was a risky venture that might cut off his northern contracts and bankrupt the company. As a result, Anderson's leadership of the Tredegar through the secession crisis of 1860–1861 was a mix of enthusiastic southern nationalism and cautious conduct with respect to the firm's remaining northern business contacts.

By the time his native state of Virginia seceded in April 1861, Tredegar president Joseph R. Anderson could proudly rely on a decade of business experience as the manager of a large-scale iron manufacturing firm. In the antebellum years the business-savvy Anderson exhibited executive skills that proved valuable to the Tredegar's future wartime fortunes. Anderson's firm was consistently profitable even against the competition of larger and better-capitalized northern iron firms. By 1860 Anderson perhaps understood the daily intricacies of the iron business better than any other single person in the South. Anderson's experience gave the Tredegar a head start and a distinct advantage over other iron firms that grew during the war. As a result the Tredegar Iron Works set the proverbial gold standard for wartime southern iron production, and the firm gained immense influence as a contributor to the Confederate war effort.

Despite Anderson's capable business leadership, the secession years of 1860–1861 were financially uncertain for the Tredegar. To hedge against the potential loss of future northern contracts, Anderson pursued a "buy southern" agenda in 1860. This strategy instantly achieved results in the form of railroad contracts in August, and the Tredegar also won a munitions contract from the state of Virginia. Many southern companies struggled to maintain profits as the pending election and possible war alienated northern customers and cut access to northern markets. As noted by historian Charles Dew, Tredegar profits fell drastically in October due to payment defaults of southern railroad companies. Several bank loans floated the Tredegar through the financially difficult early months of the secession crisis in late 1860, long enough at least until new munitions orders from the fledgling Confederacy became available in 1861.[19] As Confederate delegates convened in February 1861 to create a new government, Anderson hoped to make the Tredegar profitable again under the new Confederate States of America.

The Montgomery delegates successfully crafted a relatively moderate constitution in order to attract upper southern states like the Old Dominion into the Confederate fold. For example, despite being overwhelmingly in support of free trade, rebel delegates downplayed tariff policy in order to attract Virginia protectionists, like Anderson, into joining the new nation. If the Confederacy adopted free trade policies, then the Tredegar would compete at a disadvantage with northern iron companies, so Anderson supported a protective tariff.[20] Of course this was all predicated on a southern victory and eventual independence, but the promise of a protective tariff for the southern iron industry allowed some lukewarm supporters of secession to throw in their lot with the Confederacy.

To fill the short-term revenue gaps until Confederate contracts became available, Anderson solicited the southern states for munitions contracts. By February 1861 state contracts were being arranged.[21] The rush of sovereign southern states to arm themselves for war amid the fever pitch of disunion helped sustain the Tredegar in the final months of the secession crisis, bought precious time, and generated timely profits until a unified Confederate government could be counted on for munitions contracts.

In February 1861 Anderson sent a company representative to Montgomery to lobby Secretary of War Leroy Pope Walker for a Confederate munitions contract. This resulted in the procurement of the Tredegar's first government contract on March 7th. The government ordered "$60,000 worth of ordnance,"[22] which was relatively modest compared to lucrative future Confederate contracts, but the flow of government dollars into the Tredegar's accounts had begun, along with the corresponding influence that the Tredegar eventually developed on southern industrial policy.

In April Anderson's son Archer was sent to Montgomery with an offer to sell the Tredegar to the government. This offer was a curious event in the Tredegar's history and in Anderson's management of the company. His reasoning remains unclear and historians can only speculate why this offer was made before the war got under way. Why would Joseph Anderson, after building up a profitable iron manufacturing company, want to turn ownership over to the Confederate government? Apparently, as noted by historian Charles Dew, "Anderson and his associates expected to continue to operate the Tredegar under their personal supervision," but if the Tredegar's deed were signed over to the Confederate government, Anderson and every aspect of management would then be subject to government scrutiny. Historian Raimondo Luraghi interprets this offer of sale to the Confederate government as Anderson's foresight into impending state socialism.[23] This explanation seems far-fetched. One can only speculate about Anderson's motives, but more reasonable theories can be constructed that do not rely on Anderson's uncanny prescience about upcoming socialist industrial policies.

One possibility was that, as a West Point graduate and professionally trained military officer, Joseph R. Anderson simply preferred to serve in the Confederate army instead of staying on as president of the Tredegar. If he could not run the daily company affairs then he preferred that the government utilize and manage the facility for maximum benefit to the cause. In short, Anderson perhaps believed that his services might be more valuable at the front, not as a business manager. Anderson eventually did serve on the front from the fall of 1861 to June 1862, until he was wounded at the Battle of Frayser's Farm. This prompted Anderson to resign his commission as a brigadier general and return to operational control of the Tredegar.[24]

A second possible reason Anderson offered up the Tredegar to government control in April 1861 was guaranteed profits in the midst of an uncertain future. Anderson unquestionably proved his nationalism and support for the southern cause throughout the war, but in 1861 he realized the Confederacy was desperate to obtain facilities for manufacture of war munitions and that these favorable conditions for possible sale of the Tredegar might not exist in the future. If Anderson could reap a handsome profit from selling the facility in 1861, why not query the government about a price since there was no certainty the conditions of profitable sale would be available in the future?

A third possible reason to offer sale of the Tredegar in early 1861 was to be paid for the property in stable currency. Anderson perhaps speculated that if Confederate currency depreciated over the course of war, it might be better to have payment early in 1861 with the currency on hand, the still-legal tender of U.S. dollars. If the Confederacy failed to gain its independence, Anderson would have a more secure financial future with a foundation of U.S. dollars as opposed to rebel paper currency. None of these reasons were openly discussed because the government refused to purchase the Tredegar in 1861. Anderson tried to sell the company to the government again in December 1864, but the parties could not reach an agreement.[25]

After secession, southern railroad companies suddenly found themselves cut off from competitively priced sources of northern iron that had allowed for the enormous rail expansion of the 1850s. Tredegar officials realized southern rail firms would now be requesting iron products, and since these same companies typically ignored Anderson's "buy southern" campaign before the war, there was likely a great deal of satisfaction for Tredegar's management when the southern railroad companies begged for iron products. From April to September 1861, the Tredegar produced more iron for railroad companies than for the government.[26] However, from 1862 to the end of the war, the government typically received more iron products than did private customers, and as a result southern railroad companies never acquired adequate materials to prevent infrastructure deterioration.

Sales records from 1862 and 1863 show the shift to government priority. In 1862 the Confederate government received 1,497 tons compared to private receipts of 1,323 tons; in 1863 the government received 1,350 tons compared to private receipts of 1,178 tons; and only in 1864 did private receipts outpace government sales 1,203 to 783 tons.[27] The Tredegar simply could not provide enough iron to satisfy the demands of both the government and southern railroad companies. Considering the Tredegar's close relationship with the War and Navy Departments, replete with guaranteed contracts, prices, and payment, it was only natural that government production took first priority. Southern railroad companies possessed their own unique leverage regarding the Confederate government, but from the Tredegar's perspective, southern rail companies were just another industry trying to survive in a Confederate world of limited resources and perpetual shortages.

The Confederacy's immediate need for iron products and munitions generated a large government contract for the Tredegar. A two-year contract for two million dollars was signed on October 26, 1861, and as historian Charles Dew points out, much to Anderson's pleasure, "the terms of the agreement followed the company's requests almost to the letter." Even in 1861 the Tredegar's pivotal importance to the rebel war effort meant that Anderson could leverage the government to get every contract demand. The October contract made sure that enough raw materials were available to the company. In addition, to deflect the possible ramifications of increased material costs and currency depreciation, the government "agreed to adjust future prices paid for Tredegar products."[28] Some of the contract's funds would be used to expand Tredegar facilities for increased production capacity. The Tredegar's first large-scale government contract set a precedent. The firm instantly played a preeminent role in Confederate munitions production and began a relationship in which the company possessed the upper hand and leverage in all future government contracts. The Tredegar set the standard of Confederate industrial policy, and the relationship between the company and the government in 1861 was off to an unmistakably corporatist start.

The large autumn 1861 contract positioned the Tredegar to embark upon full production and to expand it in 1862. One of the Tredegar's most important material contributions to the rebel war effort was artillery. The South began the conflict at a severe disadvantage and continued to suffer from a disparity throughout the war, but the Tredegar produced enough artillery pieces to keep rebel armies from being completely outmatched. The company manufactured field artillery—both smoothbore like the ubiquitous 12-pound Napoleon, and rifled cannon like the modern Parrot guns. A wide variety of siege and garrison artillery and seacoast guns were also produced, including many types of mortars. The Tredegar also supplied both smoothbore and rifled cannon for use by the Confederate navy's outnumbered fleet.

One of the most important Tredegar production projects in late 1861 and early 1862 was the manufacture of iron plate for the Confederacy's new fleet of ironclads. The CSS *Virginia*, moored in Norfolk's naval yard, received top production priority. The company also helped manufacture iron plate and equipment for other rebel ironclads like the *Mississippi*, the *Richmond*, and the *Arkansas*.[29] One can only speculate how this iron might have been utilized for more productive purposes by the Confederacy had it chosen not to devote limited iron resources to this new military technology. How many more cannon for rebel armies and miles of repaired railroad track could have been created with the iron set aside for the iron-clad projects?

Due to large government contracts in the fall of 1861 and spring of 1862, the Tredegar was able to expand production so that 1862 became its most productive year. For example, in 1862 the company manufactured 351 artillery pieces for rebel armies, 243 of which were field pieces, as opposed to 214 the previous year, 286 in 1863, and 213 in 1864.[30] Early in the war, the Confederate government relied on the Tredegar to close the "artillery gap" between southern and northern armies, and although rebel artillery arguably never matched the quantity and quality of Union cannon, by 1863 the company could claim that rebel armies were at least able to hold their own in artillery. In 1861 and 1862, unlike other newly founded iron companies, the Tredegar benefited from having an extant facility ready to take up large-scale government production contracts. As a result, the firm instantly became a lynchpin in the rebel war munitions network.

The Tredegar was also a seminal industry for the creation of other Confederate munitions factories across the South. Since the South lacked widespread heavy industrial capability in 1861, the Tredegar was called upon to help create iron equipment for Confederate munitions start-ups like the Augusta Powder Works. The superintendent of the gunpowder factory, George Washington Rains, secured an Ordnance Bureau contract in September 1861, and the Tredegar initiated production of the gunpowder plant's equipment. Thanks to the Tredegar's manufacturing capability, superintendent Rains received his heavy industrial equipment and began churning out vital gunpowder for Confederate armed forces. In addition to the Augusta Powder Works, as noted by historian Charles Dew, "the Tredegar works supplied various descriptions of iron to many of the government establishments, including the armories at Fayetteville and Asheville, North Carolina; the Macon, Georgia, arsenal; and the naval ordnance shops at Charlotte."[31] Without the Tredegar's industrial capacity at the start of the war, the Confederacy would have been hard pressed to create a munitions manufacturing system. In many respects, the Tredegar iron works was the sine qua non industry for the development of the South's munitions complex.

As a manufacturer of iron products, the Tredegar depended on a steady supply of pig iron, the basic raw material of iron fabrication. It was critically important for the Confederate war effort to keep the Tredegar supplied with sufficient amounts of pig iron and this necessitated, as noted by historian Charles Dew, "a dramatic shift in the government's policy toward private enterprise and brought about a revolutionary expansion of the company's activities." By 1862 the Confederate government actively sought to increase the supply of pig iron available to the Tredegar; the only question was the method to be implemented. In an excellent example of the Confederacy's corporatist preference for letting firms manage affairs in their respective economic sectors, the War Department offered to pay the Tredegar's expenses for building more furnaces.[32] This began the rapid expansion of the company's production of pig iron, which alleviated the burden of governmental supply and shifted responsibility from public to private oversight.

By removing itself from the chain of supply, the Confederate government materially assisted the Tredegar's move towards vertical integration of iron resources. In 1862 the Tredegar used government largesse to expand the company's access to the basic resources required for increased pig iron supplies. As a result, from 1862 to 1865 the amount of pig iron that the Tredegar accessed from its own network of blast furnaces outpaced the amounts received from the Confederate government. Tredegar's furnaces produced 981 tons of pig iron and 855 tons was received from the government in 1862. The following year witnessed an increase in the supply discrepancy of 3,626 to 1,737 tons, and in 1864, a similar difference, 3,127 to 1,121 tons, was registered by the company.[33] The Confederate government's actions of providing capital for increased private production of pig iron arguably stemmed from the possibility of better results achieved by private management as opposed to public ownership of the blast furnaces, but this relationship exhibited strong corporatist tendencies, in which the private firm is provided with ample public funds to support private production.

Few companies in a competitive capitalist economy can get their host government to purchase a network of facilities for the company and allow them to operate free from government interference. Despite the rebel government's generous loans to expand blast furnace capacity and increase pig iron production for the Tredegar, the company still could not produce or acquire enough raw pig iron to achieve maximum production capacity. Privately owned industries did not lack the necessary productive capacity, but instead an insurmountable shortage of raw materials, in this particular case pig iron, hampered production, and no amount of government investment or intervention could remedy the chronic shortfalls. The desperate dearth of pig iron in the Confederacy meant that Anderson's iron facility rarely operated even near optimal capacity.[34] If the South's most important heavy industrial complex could only achieve a productive capacity of 33 percent due to paucity of resources, it is a wonder that rebel armies could maintain even a basic sufficiency of war materiel.

From 1862 through the end of the war the Tredegar Iron Works benefited from highly favorable government contracts that allowed for expanded production and protected the vital firm in a relatively controlled market. On April 29, 1862, Tredegar management signed a new government contract that, according to Tredegar historian Charles Dew, "was a precedent setting document, establishing the basic pattern which the Confederate government later used to induce the expansion of other Southern iron establishments."[35] The Tredegar's corporatist relationship with the Confederacy became the standard that other iron companies aspired to emulate in their respective dealings with the government.

In the new agreement, the Tredegar promised to deliver $2 million worth of military goods each year until the end of 1864. In effect, the Tredegar had a guaranteed $2 million annual tab with the government to fill any and all munitions requests. The method of payment, which became a sticking point in other private firms' contract negotiations, appears to have been less of a concern for the Tredegar managers, who agreed that government payment to the company could be 33 percent in Confederate bonds and 66 percent in paper currency. To compensate for higher commodity costs and an increasingly inflationary environment, the government also allowed for a price increase. The main concession provided to the government was the company's vow that the government contract had priority over private iron contracts.[36] The April 1862 contract showed that while the Tredegar management might have possessed the upper hand in negotiations, the long-term effect was a symbiotic relationship between the company and the Confederate government in which each party helped to ensure the other's survival.

Joseph Anderson and the Tredegar management team requested a price increase only five months after signing the April contract. As in many disputes both parties had legitimate arguments. The company highlighted a contract clause that allowed an increase in prices to cover the cost of materials, while government officials pointed to a section of the Confederate Constitution that forbade additional compensation on government contracts.[37] This appears to be a case of "biting the hand that feeds," but it really highlights the Tredegar's strong position in forcing government compliance with its wishes and reinforces evidence of a corporatist relationship.

A growing list of plaintiffs accused the Tredegar of abusing the government's good faith by seeking exorbitant profits and amassing corporate power at the expense of the government. In late 1862 Army Ordnance Inspector Thomas Rhett initiated a bureaucratic complaint about the high prices charged to the government for munitions. He alleged that "prices have been increasing pretty steadily" and by his estimates "now yield a profit of from 30 to 50 percent," and might even be as high as "60 to 80 percent" over recent months. Rhett argued that the Tredegar exhibited the nefarious characteristics of a monopoly since "to control the Iron interests of a country is to influence all other interests, add to this the Coal, & all mechanical operations." It was clear to Rhett that munitions production in Virginia, if not the entire Confederacy, was now "subject to the will of a single Company."[38]

Tredegar's management replied to accusations of price gouging with sensible arguments that prices charged to the government were actually lower than those charged to private customers. As a result of the price conflict, Secretary of War James Seddon appointed two officials to arbitrate and set agreeable prices. After several weeks of gathering price data and looking into the dispute, arbitrators sided with the Tredegar and allowed a price increase.[39] From 1863 to the end of the war, the Tredegar requested five more price increases and despite significant opposition from powerful government officials, Tredegar management typically received a good percentage of the demanded increase each time.

At times Confederate officials likely questioned the patriotism of the company's management team. According to historian Charles Dew, "Anderson and his associates do not deserve to be dismissed merely as profiteering contractors," but they can at least be fairly criticized for allowing their instincts for "profit [to get] the better of patriotism."[40] All southern businesses struggled with skyrocketing inflation and a surge in material costs, but what separated the Tredegar from most other privately owned munitions industries was that the company could pass along most, if not all, of its increased business costs directly to the Confederate government in the form of higher prices. The Tredegar was perhaps the only firm with enough leverage to achieve this remarkable feat, and so long as the Confederacy needed ammunition, cannon, and other irreplaceable iron products, the Tredegar could maintain profitable price levels. The Tredegar's ability to maintain the upper hand in contract and price negotiations is symbolic of the Confederacy's expedient corporatist system, and a symptom of a rapidly modernizing industrial economy.

The Tredegar Iron Company was dexterously built up by Joseph Reid Anderson in the 1850s and at the outset of the war possessed great potential as a Confederate munitions provider. As one of the few southern iron companies that could compete with larger northern iron firms during the antebellum years, the Tredegar was uniquely positioned to immediately transition into wartime production. Unlike other firms that required government support before they could yield significant output, Anderson's iron works were open and ready for wartime business before rebel batteries fired on Fort Sumter. This early availability for providing war materiel gave the Tredegar leverage in contract negotiations with the government. Even when the Confederate government possessed some leverage over the company's access to resources like pig iron and specialized labor, rebel bureaucrats consistently caved-in to the demands of Tredegar management or, as in the case of pig iron, gave the company greater control. The Tredegar Iron Works set the proverbial "gold standard" of southern industrial production, and the resultant corporatist relationship with the Confederate government became a road map for aspiring firms also seeking to take advantage of government largesse.

Other private iron manufacturers continued to supply the Confederacy with products, but none ever equaled the prestige or received as much government patronage as the Tredegar Iron Works. Realizing the Tredegar's unique situation, Anderson retained control of the Tredegar throughout the war and used considerable leverage to expand facilities, increase production, and reap a handsome profit.[41] Tredegar president Joseph Reid Anderson was without question a devoted Confederate nationalist but he was also a savvy manager who showed that profits and patriotism could not only coexist but could prove immensely beneficial to both government and business. Far from being victims of arbitrary state policies, Anderson and the Tredegar illustrate the ability of select private munitions companies to influence industrial policy in an expedient corporatist environment. The Tredegar's antebellum experience and importance to the war effort helped the Confederacy to transition into the more modern industrial policy of corporatism.

SHELBY IRON COMPANY

The Shelby Iron Company, located in Shelby County, Alabama, southeast of Birmingham, was founded in 1846 by Horace Ware. This region of central Alabama eventually became a postwar industrial center for iron production; even Confederate Ordnance Bureau chief Josiah Gorgas relocated there after the war to operate an iron foundry. The 1840s witnessed the infancy of the Alabama iron industry, but the area around Shelby County remained relatively undeveloped until Jonathan Ware, Horace's father, trained his son in the iron manufacturing business. At only sixteen years old, Horace Ware learned the daily routine of running a foundry.[42] The company thrived and grew during the 1850s thanks to increased southern railroad construction, and in 1859 Ware opened Alabama's first rolling mill.

Ware's iron products garnered high praise. One client remarked that he had "been working iron for thirty years, and do not hesitate to declare yours superior to any I ever used." John Fraser, another prewar customer, declared he had "thoroughly tested the quality of the bar of Shelby iron . . . and take great pleasure in stating that I have found it equal in every respect to any I have ever used. . . . It is very compact and tenacious rendering it easy to forge, and turn, and would make the finest cast steel." Fraser declared that in his "opinion there is no better [iron] to be found in this or any other country."[43]

The onset of war in 1861 caused Ware to reconsider his options and attempt to expand his facilities. Alabama was in the process of evolving into a major center for southern iron production, and the expanded Shelby company became a significant component of this growth. On the eve of the war in 1860, Alabama's iron production was underdeveloped.[44] Larger-scale iron production was necessary, and the Confederacy desperately needed new or expanded sources of iron. Horace Ware sensed a great business opportunity to secure lucrative government contracts and in the process hopefully expand Shelby's productive capacity. The war was a boon to southern iron entrepreneurs, whether they be small-scale outfits looking to expand like Ware or established concerns ready to churn out more goods for the war effort.

In order to expand, Ware realized he needed two resources: increased capital investment and a personal contact who might assist with securing a government contract. He found access to additional capital by contacting a group of local businessmen hoping to branch into iron production. The potential profits to be made through guaranteed government contracts allowed Ware to attract southern planters and merchants to invest in Shelby's expansion. In March 1862 Ware offered equal shares of ownership to six local investors: Andrew Jones, John Kenan, James and John Lapsley, John McClanahan, and Henry Ware. These men represented a variety of backgrounds but all were interested in the profitable expansion of the iron works.[45] In fact, this new ownership arrangement was predicated upon the possibility of receiving a government contract.

The second requirement for Shelby's expansion was met when prospective owner John Lapsley used his contact with an influential member of the Confederate government. It was the probability of securing government contracts and incentives for iron production that sparked investment by the new stockholders. Lapsley informed his government contact that the prospective entrepreneurs were "men of enterprise, but . . . being cautious men, they do not wish to embark in a doubtful speculative" business unless "they had assurance of the continuance of anything like the present prices and demand."[46] Every business owner likes to mitigate risk, but the new Shelby owners could hardly be called pure entrepreneurs because they wanted to use the Confederate government to shelter them from financial loss. Without a government contract and a personal representative or liaison to arrange for Confederate largesse, these new investors likely would have balked at the iron venture. Prior to signing on as a partner with Ware, however, John Lapsley had arranged for a government contract through a Confederate ordnance purchasing agent and fellow Alabama industrialist, Colin J. McRae.

The new owners of the Shelby Iron Company greatly benefited from the services of Colin McRae. One might even say that they owed their government contracts to his initiative and instincts. McRae could be described as a patriotic industrialist. He used his background and political contacts to rapidly develop desperately needed industries around Selma, Alabama. This industrial complex eventually supplied rebel armies and naval forces with additional munitions for defense of the middle southern states. For the Shelby Iron Company, McRae was the essential human resource to pursue increased production and take advantage of the unquenchable Confederate wartime demand for iron.

The Shelby Iron Company's new ownership group used Lapsley's connection with McRae to scout out and secure a government contract in early 1862. McRae was in the preliminary stages of creating a government-owned iron manufacturing site in Selma, and understood he would need a reliable supply of cheap, high-quality iron which would hopefully be predominantly supplied by the Shelby Iron Company. On February 24, 1862, McRae telegraphed the Shelby owners from Richmond: "Foundry & Iron Matters satisfactorily arranged . . . I will be in Selma on the 14th of March with ordnance officers." To confirm the mutual plans, on March 24th Henry Ware informed John Lapsley that "McRae is anxious to get up the foundry and the government has offered him the contract as he proposed . . . he thinks it might be established at Selma and will likely go up soon to see about it." By April 27th McRae informed the owners that vital "machinery will be in the process of being taken down and on its way to Shelby" and that he had finalized plans "to go ahead with the foundry & rolling mills" on the condition that the private owners were "willing to take $15,000 for the Old Foundry property in Selma."[47] From the start Shelby's profits were directly tied to McRae's government-owned iron manufacturing project in Selma.

The Shelby Iron Company was fortunate to have Colin McRae's services. He simultaneously created a government industry to consume its iron and also looked out for the company's interests. McRae found and purchased resources for the company. Over the course of 1862 McRae, even though he was officially a government agent, purchased necessary items on behalf of the Shelby Iron Company. McRae was respectively reimbursed $63.00 on July 10th, $7,325.24 on July 26th, $176.55 on August 24th, and $621.20 on November 18th.[48] These transactions represented the symbiotic relationship between the owners of Shelby and the Confederate government through the individual action of Colin McRae. Neither could survive without the other, but eventually both parties' priorities diverged and each accused the other of attempting to abuse the agreement and gain an upper hand in the relationship.

In early 1862 the Shelby Iron Company owners negotiated a contract with the Confederate government. The owners were concerned about a number of issues prior to approval, but they were also under pressure to get production started as soon as possible. For example, Lapsley worried about the clause that stated the company was "bound to deliver iron manufactured in the most approved modern method." Self-interest is inherent in all contract negotiations, and Lapsley warned his colleagues that this phrase "might be of much importance . . . especially if the government should find . . . that they are paying more for iron than they could procure it." As a result, Lapsley feared the government "would . . . be apt to look closely into the contract and maybe require more of us than it is now their purpose to do." Lapsley suggested the phrase "neatly and properly manufactured" as a replacement and hoped this change would be "satisfactory to the government."[49]

Shelby managers also judiciously considered their lack of negotiating experience, which befitted this relatively untested group of Alabama iron executives. Lapsley confessed to his fellow directors, "if we were familiar with the subject, we would be less liable to commit an error . . . this makes it more important in so large a contract to observe great caution."[50] Shelby's board of directors did not want to be duped into a contract that held them to an unusually high standard, but neither did they want the government to think that the company would deliver an inferior product.

The most important terms of the contract were government prices, length of the contract, parity with established iron companies, and method of payment. Perhaps to sweeten the deal for the government, the Shelby owners allowed for reduced prices after the war. Since the Shelby Iron Company was a relative latecomer to full scale iron production, compared to other companies like the Tredegar in Richmond, the owners demanded equal treatment and access to resources. Even before the contract was signed, the Shelby owners wanted guaranteed parity with other iron companies and for the government to be contractually flexible.[51]

The final wish of company management was a reassurance that future payment would be made in sound currency. In early 1862 the Shelby owners could not foresee that this issue would poison their relationship with the Ordnance Department. They believed their bottom line would be sustainable "unless the currency goes to the dogs," which eventually it did. The initial contract called for payment in "current funds" but Shelby management requested a clause "making good . . . any depreciation in Confederate currency and securities, by advances in the prices to be paid." Ordnance Chief Josiah Gorgas insisted "in mortifying but not unjust terms" that Shelby's owners dispense with the issue of currency depreciation which, Gorgas believed, "reflects on the patriotism of the company." McRae, stuck in the middle of the negotiations, hoped they would accept the provision as "a personal favor" and opined that Gorgas's point, although "terribly caustic," was also "utterly just."[52] The Shelby owners won the disagreement over currency depreciation, but it ruptured the relationship between Shelby and the government.

The Shelby Iron Company's much-desired government contract was negotiated and finally approved on April 21, 1862. The agreement lasted for three years, to be concluded on April 1, 1865, and specifically designated Colin McRae as liaison with the government. To immediately expand iron production, the Shelby company was advanced $75,000. Shelby was expected to repay the government advance, which became another point of contention between the parties.[53]

In return for the government advance, the Shelby company would annually produce at least 12,000 tons of iron for the government, but hopefully more.[54] Eventually this portion of the contract was interpreted differently by government agents and company management and lay at the heart of the acrimonious relationship between the Shelby Iron Company and the Confederate government. The government hoped to hedge against any future dispersal of production by inserting the clause, "*largest quantity of iron practicable . . . and to deliver the . . . entire yield*" to the Confederate government. The biggest fear for Confederate officials, which immediately occurred after the contract was signed, was that Shelby management would quickly forget the $75,000 start-up subsidy and seek to sell its iron products to private purchasers above the established government prices.

The final important aspect of the contract and future point of dispute was the method of payment. The contract stipulated that 33 percent of government payment would be in Confederate bonds and 66 percent in paper currency.[55] Shelby owners stood to make a large profit on the 8 percent bonds, but only if the Confederacy won the war, and management was rightly concerned that the remainder of payment in Confederate currency would rapidly depreciate. The 1862 contract offered positives for both parties: the Shelby got the much-needed capital for expanded production and the government received promise of prompt iron delivery. But the contract also left both parties with legitimate disagreements about prices, resources, and payment.

In spring 1862, newly negotiated government contract in hand, Shelby management embarked upon expanded wartime production. Operators were instantly in competition for the already scarce resources in the southern states and tried to cobble together sufficient men and materiel to fulfill the contract. Government agent Colin McRae could help to a degree, but Shelby managers were relative latecomers to wartime production in comparison to other private firms. McRae warned managers that the recent conscription law would likely "deprive us of all mechanics." In July McRae recommended that Shelby management "make an application to the Secretary of War through Col. Gorgas for the detail of the men you want . . . for service in your Iron mills." McRae reminded them to "be particular" and to provide not only "the names of the privates but also the company by letter, the regiment, brigade, & division to which they belong." As a result, McRae believed there would "be no difficulty in getting the men you want."[56] McRae's advice made sure the first round of conscription did not cripple Shelby's iron production.

Shelby management was fortunate to be in an excellent coal-producing region so they rarely had to worry about coal supply, but they were concerned about reliable transportation of coal to their facility. The directors and managers performed admirably at the task of procuring materials, especially considering that the company attempted to fill most of its supply needs after one full year of war had already stretched and depleted much of the South's human and natural resources.

Only weeks after the Shelby Iron Company received its coveted government advance and contract in April 1862, company directors and government officials found reasons to reembark on negotiations to rectify disagreeable points. The prickly issue of currency depreciation reignited acrimony in the summer of 1862. Gorgas continued to insist that Shelby's owners remove the one-sided clause that promised the government would protect the company from currency depreciation. McRae opined that "the criticism of Col. Gorgas . . . is not only true but eminently just and proper." To remedy the impasse, McRae recommended that Jones convene the "stockholders together" and eliminate the objectionable "clause of the contract, to retain it will answer the suspicions of the government officials and will cause them to enforce a rigid compliance on your part of the contract."[57]

The Shelby directors were not persuaded. They promised McRae that they had "considered . . . the objections of Col. Gorgas" but argued that their "case [was] an exception." They appealed to McRae's personal relationship with management and declared that "if the gentlemen who compose this company were known to [Gorgas], as they are to you, he would not . . . be in the slightest degree disturbed by the apprehension that. . . . an unfair advantage would be taken . . . or that it would in any way be abused by the company." Citing a mixture of inexperience and pure motives, they reminded McRae that when the contract was negotiated, "these gentlemen, merchants, planters, and professional men were about to embark in a business to which they were strangers requiring a large outlay of capital," and they were worried about secure and valuable methods of payment. Back in early 1862, while the contract negotiations were underway, "recent serious public disasters, the most important of which was the loss of Nashville," caused Shelby's owners to be greatly concerned about "the marketable value of government securities" and the depreciation of Confederate currency. This prudent business concern, they argued, should not "be considered either unpatriotic or unreasonable."[58]

Shelby's directors offered a compromise. They would drop their request for guaranteed protection from currency depreciation if the government agreed to drop the 33 percent payment in bonds. Shelby management stated that while they had "every confidence in the security and intrinsic value of the bonds . . . it [was] not probable that the company can afford to hold them" until maturity. Shelby directors were "more interested in the current market value of the bonds, than in their intrinsic or ultimate value." Thus company managers attempted to use the currency guarantee clause in the contract as leverage to remove the one-third bond payment clause because they needed instantly convertible assets to keep their enterprise running, but also arguably because Shelby's directors did not have long-term confidence in Confederate victory.[59]

Government officials were clearly not pleased with further attempts by Shelby management to haggle for more secure methods of payment. After Shelby's self-interested proposal to negotiate the currency deprecia-tion clause, Gorgas decided to use his greatest leverage, withholding gov-ernment advances, to force the company's hand. McRae informed Jones he would deliver the $7,500 advance and an extra $25,000 if Shelby directors dropped their demand for more stable payment. McRae pleaded that "this objectionable clause in the contract will lead to evil results to the govern-ment and may result in great loss to your company."[60] Through their expe-riences in 1862, Shelby management realized that the issue of depreciated currency could be leveraged to negotiate a new contract with higher prices and more government advances.

Only five months after signing the first agreement, Shelby's manage-ment hounded Confederate officials for a new contract with higher prices. Ordnance chief Gorgas received a proposal in late September that re-quested the April contract be voided. If given a new contract, the Shelby directors promised to produce 1,000 tons of cold blast pig iron at 85 cents per ton, 3,000 tons of rolled iron for covering ships at 10 cents per pound, 3,000 tons of bar and rod iron at 10 cents per pound, and 1,000 charcoal blooms at 7 cents per pound. Shelby management was also willing to drop the guarantee against currency depreciation. To protect the long-term in-terests of both parties, the new contract would last for five years, and it allowed a 40 percent price reduction sixty days after the war's conclusion.[61]

The new contract proposal seemed to improve upon the deficiencies of the April contract for both parties. Gorgas confronted the contract cancel-lation request in October and replied, "if the constitutional objections to annulling contracts are removed your request will be complied with other-wise the present contract will be considered in full force." If a new contract were indeed negotiated, Gorgas informed the Shelby owners they would "be required to deliver" the promised "1000 tons of accepted gun iron . . . 3000 tons of iron plate for covering ships . . . 1000 tons of Charcoal blooms . . . [and] 3000 tons of bar bolt & red iron," and he surprisingly acquiesced to their price requests.[62] Although frustrated, Gorgas was apparently willing to let the Shelby company renegotiate its government contract, but only if management made good on its production promises. Gorgas focused on what the company could actually deliver to the government, and if that meant caving in to their demands for a new contract and higher prices, then he was willing to allow Shelby management to win this round of negotiations in this increasingly corporatist relationship.

Throughout 1862 Shelby Iron Company management continued to clash with Confederate officials over prices and delivery priorities. Due to the iron shortage, Shelby's products were sought not only by the government, but also by railroad companies and other customers who tried to cut in line ahead of government delivery. One such interloper was Flag Officer W. F. Lynch, who ordered significant amounts of plate for ironclads on the Yazoo River in Mississippi. Lynch's project symbolized the often haphazard nature of Confederate military supply, and even Gorgas initially had trouble overriding Lynch's order, as it emanated from the Navy Department, not the War Department in which Gorgas held great power.

Shelby management earned higher profits for rolling Lynch's iron plate as compared to the lower prices for government iron, and so they gave Lynch's order priority. Shelby president A. J. Jones promised that the company was doing everything possible to produce government iron, but that Lynch's order took priority. Gorgas and McRae were furious with the company's selfish decision to prioritize Lynch's order. McRae scolded Jones after Shelby's president complained about prices in the original contract. McRae declared he could not alter the prices in the contract. When Jones informed McRae about the contract to make iron plate for Lynch, the Confederate Ordnance agent demanded to "know by what authority a Flag Officer or anyone else could set aside, or relieve [the Shelby company] from your contract with the government."[63]

McRae obviously felt betrayed by Shelby management after all the professional and personal assistance he had provided the company. McRae lambasted Shelby's directors and reminded them that all the company's 1862 iron production was possible only with the government advance in the April contract. McRae warned, "you are not the proper party to decide on the necessities of the government . . . such authority rests . . . with me."

To be fair, McRae admitted that Shelby could pursue outside contracts but that the government should always be given priority. "The government is among the difficulties you have had to encounter," McRae honestly and empathetically admitted to Shelby management, "and for that reason [the government] has not demanded a rigid compliance with your contract." But after this act of bad faith, McRae insisted "that [the Shelby] shall deliver the iron as fast as it is made and that no deliveries shall be made to any other parties except from surplus iron that you may have after complying with your contract of the 21st April."[64] The sense of Shelby's ingratitude poisoned the relationship between the company and the Ordnance Bureau. Only after Shelby management's selfish actions of pursuing outside contracts to the detriment of government deliveries did the Ordnance Bureau resort to a more direct style to enforce the original contract.

Gorgas, through his agent McRae, attempted to dictate delivery priorities to Shelby management. Acquiring iron for the various munitions manufacturers might prevent work stoppages, and Gorgas took it upon himself to prioritize distribution for the Shelby Company. McRae informed Shelby "to have the order of Messrs Cooke & Brother promptly filled" and then to deliver "a car load (8 tons)" to Admiral Franklin Buchanan constructing ironclads, like the CSS *Tennessee,* for the defense of Mobile. After the first two deliveries, McRae expected delivery of the government's order, and then Shelby could complete outstanding orders.[65]

Despite the government's attempts to intimidate and prioritize iron delivery, Shelby management continued to ship iron to Flag Officer Lynch.[66] After government advances, subsidies, and guaranteed contracts, the Shelby Iron Company continued to sell iron to other customers for higher prices and greater profits.

Colin McRae likely reflected on 1862 as a year of great patriotic accomplishment. He had been instrumental in developing and expanding southern iron production and increasing manufacturing capacity in the western theater. McRae must have also been very disappointed in the selfish actions of Shelby managers. After all, he had helped along every step of their business. As 1862 came to an end, Shelby management could look back on a successful year of procuring government largesse while simultaneously pursuing independent corporate interests by seeking private customers and higher prices outside the confines of the government contract. The Shelby Iron Company's actions and experiences in 1862 epitomized the nature of a corporatist industrial policy.

With pending contract negotiations on the horizon, 1863 promised to be a year of mending the tense relationship between the Shelby Iron Company and the Confederate government. Some Shelby directors hoped to pursue a hard line and wondered what would happen if they asserted more independence. One director asked, "what would McRae do for iron? . . . he might find that he has overplayed his game."[67] In the end, cooler heads prevailed among Shelby's directors and the only major concession sought was increased prices.

The new contract was officially secured on February 17 and remedied most of the previous year's points of contention. Shelby vowed to produce at least 12,000 tons of iron for the government and received a price increase.[68] In the 1863 contract, Shelby directors secured continued government patronage while simultaneously protecting their ability to independently contract with other customers.

On April 11, 1863, the Confederate Congress authorized creation of the Nitre and Mining Bureau. The new department would operate under Gorgas's Ordnance Bureau. Its primary purpose involved increasing the production of nitre, or saltpeter, which was a vital ingredient in gunpowder production. The bureau also received responsibility for coordinating other mining resources like coal, and overseeing southern iron production.[69] The new bureau's primary tasks were increasing production of raw materials, distribution oversight, and resource allocation, for the Confederacy's various munitions manufacturers. After this bureaucratic addition, Chief of Ordnance Josiah Gorgas could now dispense with the unpleasant duties of haggling with the Shelby Iron Company. Now the head of the Nitre and Mining Bureau, Isaac M. St. John, or the bureau's local agent in Selma, William Richardson Hunt, took up the duties of contract compliance.

Some historians interpret the advent of the Nitre and Mining Bureau as the start of full-fledged government control of the Shelby Iron Company. However, events proved that Shelby's management continued to pursue an independent course. Originally a company friend, Colin McRae was phased out of dealing with Shelby's directors and eventually moved on to other government duties. From 1863 on, management was forced to deal directly with William Richardson Hunt, who employed a more intimidating and martial style in his interactions with Shelby. From 1863 to 1865, Shelby management sustained an acrimonious relationship with the Nitre and Mining Bureau. Both parties seemed intent on maintaining the upper hand, but the main difference in this era of the relationship was the government's willingness to use outright threats.[70]

Government officials now expected not only production priority but also initial repayment of the original capital advances. In this situation, the government clearly possessed the upper hand because the contract fixed iron prices and in addition, the government could deduct company debt from payments. These deductions, termed "reservations," represented a serious obstacle to Shelby's ability to maintain iron production levels. As a result, Shelby management was in a difficult situation in which the government paid fixed prices for delivered iron products but also withheld a "reservation" to pay back the advance, so even when Shelby fulfilled its contract obligations it only received partial payment. To alleviate this crippling financial situation, Shelby management asked for another price increase and a restructuring of the advance repayment.

The automatic deduction for repayment of the government advance, or "reservation," symbolized the government's attempt to dictate Shelby's policies. In 1863 the Confederate government withheld as much as 30 percent of monthly payments to Shelby.[71] Any company would justifiably complain if full production brought only 70 percent of the monthly revenues due in payment.

The Shelby directors complained to Nitre & Mining Bureau agent William Richardson Hunt that iron production was hampered by lack of capital to purchase materials. They wanted higher prices and requested that reservation payments be spread out over the next three years.[72] Shelby management also complained to Hunt about unfair treatment relative to other southern iron companies. Hunt had remarked that Shelby should be able to operate on the prices paid to the Etowah Iron Works in Georgia, but Shelby directors disagreed. However, the greatest discrepancy in pricing, and alleged proof of government favoritism, could be found with "the Tredegar Company of Richmond who have been receiving since December last, prices for their bar iron from forty to seventy five percent higher than the prices which have been allowed the Shelby Company." Despite all the previous government advances and assistance, Shelby's directors argued comparative disadvantage due to time and available resources.[73] Hunt was unsympathetic and ignored the company's plea for relief from reservations and increased prices.

Shelby's owners then appealed over Hunt's head directly to Colonel Isaac M. St. John, chief of the Nitre and Mining Bureau, asking for another price increase and easier repayment terms for the advances. Shelby directors wanted price parity with other iron firms, and they also complained to St. John that recent government actions had caused the company to acquire burdensome debt. They requested that the "reservation" of 20 percent on previous government advances be deferred, or at least spread out over time to lessen the immediate financial burden. The plight due to the reservations required solution: "in addition to the reservation of 20 percent, ten percent has been reserved on all sums . . . as security for the performance of the contract . . . These heavy deductions from the monthly earnings have so reduced [Shelby's] means as to render it necessary to borrow." To remedy the lack of capital due to reservations, Shelby management proposed to pay back one-third of the amount owed over a three-year period.[74]

Isaac St. John was more open to the complaints of Shelby management than Hunt had been, but he was still focused on maintaining consistent levels of Confederate iron production, so he negotiated a solution. St. John agreed to decrease the reservation each month from 20 to 5 percent if the company delivered 250 tons of iron. This was in effect a production incentive with significant penalties for lack of productivity. This showed that St. John sought some continued method of control and was wisely worried about holding Shelby to the contract's terms.[75]

From 1862 to 1865 the Shelby Company was periodically threatened with labor shortages in the form of conscripted workers. After the April 1862 passage of the Confederacy's first conscription act, Colin McRae successfully advised management how to "detail" crucial iron laborers out of military service and return them to the foundry. Skilled laborers in essential industries received a draft reprieve on October 11, 1862, when the Confederate Congress passed a new round of conscription exemptions. Alongside other more controversial draft exemptions like the twenty-slave clause, Congress exempted "all artisans, mechanics and employees in the establishments . . . under contracts with the government in furnishing arms, ordnance, ordnance stores, and other munitions of war." Shelby could have loosely fit under the description of "ordnance stores" but Congress also specifically exempted "all superintendents, managers, mechanics and miners employed in the production and manufacture . . . of lead and iron, and all persons engaged . . . [in] manufacture of iron . . . and all colliers engaged in making charcoal, for making pig and bar iron."[76] This provided Shelby management with official Confederate sanction to prevent conscription of its valuable skilled workforce.

Under the pseudo-direction of the Nitre & Mining Bureau, the Shelby Company received additional protection against temporary military impressment from William Richardson Hunt. He declared that company owners and their workforces would be protected by the bureau. In late 1863 Shelby's roving commissary representative, John Tillman, was drafted and only released from service after direct intervention by Hunt, who successfully argued that Tillman's importance to Shelby's iron production superseded the needs of his military service. Technically, Tillman served as secretary to the Board of Directors since March 13, 1863, and could have argued exemption as a manager under the October 1862 revisions, but apparently Confederate conscription officials deemed his frequent travels and various duties as disqualifiers and labeled him a shirker before Hunt's intercession. In another example in 1864, a local conscript officer in Talladega graciously complied with Shelby's labor needs and returned all necessary workers.[77]

Overall, the Shelby company did not experience the drastic labor shortages due to conscription that crippled other industries. At no point during the war did the draft significantly hamper productivity or appreciably denude Shelby's skilled workforce for any length of time. For the Confederacy to have drafted skilled iron workers into the armies would have been a foolish policy in which vital iron production would have been seriously curtailed for the miniscule benefit of adding several hundred men to the army's ranks. The Confederacy wisely exempted irreplaceable skilled ironworkers from military service, and the Shelby company's productivity benefited from this policy.

Unskilled white laborers were targeted for conscription, but the company replaced labor shortages in this sector by using slaves, women, and eventually children. The use of slaves in southern ironwork was commonplace long before Shelby's experience. The Tredegar Iron Works in Richmond, Virginia, pioneered large-scale usage of skilled slave labor in the industrial iron workplace.[78]

Shelby directors could have accessed industrial slave management skills learned from other firms. The board's direction that the company president maintain a viable labor supply included the authority to contract for slave labor. In 1863 the board gave a more explicit command for the president "to purchase such number of negroes suitable for the business." Shelby management discerningly decided to rent, or "hire out," most of their slave labor from masters as opposed to purchasing slaves owned by the company. This method of procuring labor allowed flexibility in expanding or contracting the workforce according to production schedules and also allowed management to return unruly, disobedient, or unproductive slaves. Shelby management typically sought one-year contracts with slave owners, which was likely viewed by cotton planters as a way to earn some profit from their slave labor force in the absence of normal market conditions. In addition, Shelby's insulated location in central Alabama was far removed from Union armies; thus some slave owners might have been enticed to hire out their hands to the iron company as a hedge against slaves self-emancipating themselves by running away to Union lines.[79]

Shelby owners also hired valuable skilled slave workers. Whether it was due to company debt, insubordination, or the desire to receive some return on investment before it was too late, on August 20, 1864, the Shelby Board of Directors decided to sell some of the small amount of slave property owned by the company, "the woman Milly and child . . . and the negro men named Fred Ware and John Howard."[80]

As in all situations in which the master class leaves most of the written accounts, it is difficult to ascertain the relationship between the management at Shelby and the slave laborers. Based upon the documents left by the directors, there did not appear to be any significant disturbance, rebellion, or sabotage by the slaves. Of course this does not mean, in a paternalistic sense, that the slaves were content in their industrial work or that they did not harbor deep animosity towards company officials, but only that they apparently did not undertake forceful actions of overt resistance. Slaves understood, like any other rational individual who kept up with wartime events, that the Confederacy was losing the war, so they avoided retaliation from rebel authorities until Union armies arrived, which they eventually did in March 1865.

Shelby management also utilized other labor sources in addition to slaves. The company also utilized over sixty adult white women and over thirty children and young adults in production.[81] This combination of hiring out slaves, both skilled and unskilled, and adding the labor of women and youth sufficed to keep Shelby's foundries in operation throughout the war.

One of the most revealing, contentious issues between the government and Shelby management was the company's insistent construction of a short railroad line. Company directors planned to build this rail line to improve access to and from the foundry, to more easily get supplies to the manufacturing site. Management also wanted a rail line to haul iron to the nearest railroad depot in the county seat of Columbiana for shipment. This was a worthwhile project for Shelby's efficiency, but the iron to be used in the rail line's construction would be deducted from other orders, namely from the government's supply, and here lay the crux of the dispute between the two parties.

Two months after signing the first government contract in 1862, Shelby's directors began discussions with the Central Railroad Company in hopes of getting a nearby depot for shipping iron. Shelby's directors planned ahead to include the legal right to construct the rail line in the 1863 contract. They made sure that technically they had the legal right to use their own iron to improve company infrastructure without breaching the government contract. Shelby management wisely stated that "it is safest to have it expressed [as] the word 'improvements' [which] would cover the railroad without naming it." Despite outspoken government opposition, Shelby's lawyer used the ongoing rail project as a reason to barter for higher prices and lower repayment of reservations.[82]

In 1863 and 1864 Hunt complained and warned Shelby management not to go forward with construction of the short railroad line. Hunt correctly argued that it would diminish the available supply of iron for the government contract, but Shelby's directors decided to continue railroad construction plans anyway. In early 1864 Shelby's board authorized negotiations with the Montevallo Coal Company for joint use and additional construction of a branch railroad line directly to the company, which further dedicated Shelby iron to local railroad improvements.[83]

In April Shelby managers informed Arkansas senator Charles Mitchell of their plans for construction of the branch rail line and their reasons for urgent completion of the project. The managers pointed out that a great amount of the iron produced in Alabama was manufactured using outdated methods utilizing charcoal. They suggested using available mineral coal for increased productivity and higher-quality iron. This, they claimed, could be easily accomplished with a new branch rail line if the objections of the Nitre and Mining Bureau were overruled. Shelby managers promised a 100 percent increase in iron production after completion of the railroad.[84]

To justify construction of the branch line, the Shelby board alleged that Hunt failed to deliver sufficient iron for the railroad. Shelby directors argued they had "acted in strict accordance with the rights of the company under the contract" and believed the rail spur necessary due to the "considerable number of mules [that] have been lost" while hauling the iron by wagon. Shelby management expressed "regret" for "any temporary inconvenience which may have been caused the government by the appropriation of this iron for the rail road." The board asserted that construction of the railroad was initiated with the "interest of the government" in mind.[85]

Shelby's railroad line symbolized an obstinate insistence to put the long-term interests of the company ahead of immediate government priorities. Despite threats from government officials and under extremely difficult circumstances with regard to available resources, the branch rail line was finished in January 1865.[86] The railroad dispute highlighted the substantial leverage possessed by Shelby's directors in the face of government cajoling, threats, and attempts to dictate company policy. In the end, the Shelby Iron Company got its railroad and the Confederacy received less iron as a result.

The tense relationship between the Shelby Iron Company and the Confederate government reached a pinnacle in 1864. In addition to the heated disagreement over railroad construction, Shelby's management continued to push for higher prices and access to additional government support, some of which was rightly owed the company. By the summer of 1864 Hunt was furious and threatened "to report" company president A. J. Jones for military duty unless Shelby delivered as agreed in the contract and complied with the government's demands.[87]

Shelby's directors defiantly came to the defense of their president and laid out a lengthy argument against Major Hunt's breach of contract allegations. The Shelby owners boldly asserted, "we know not how to construe your threat to report [Jones] to the enrolling officer," and as a result, they felt it was "no longer necessary to carry out the contract." To personally threaten President Andrew Jones was useless, they argued, because he only carried out the wishes of the Board of Directors. Shelby management awaited the decision of Colonel Isaac St. John, head of the Nitre and Mining Bureau, who was considering the dispute between Hunt and Shelby management. Contrary to Hunt's breach of contract accusations, the Shelby Board of Directors claimed that "the company had been previously injured and impeded in their efforts to perform their part of the contract." The alleged impediment to production, according to company management, was the reservations, or repayment of advances, that cost the company $50,000 in revenues. The board argued that repayment crippled the company's ability to pay other bills.[88] In short, Shelby management blamed the Confederate government for its inability to meet expenses, despite the fact that without generous advances and constant patronage the company likely would have never expanded production in the first place.

Major Hunt appealed to his superior in the Nitre and Mining Bureau. Obviously frustrated, Hunt complained that the Shelby company's "leading idea seems to be, to build their establishment up during the war and have it in good running order after peace is declared." He confessed that although Shelby directors were pursuing "a cold hard selfish policy in which self-interest predominates . . . on that policy [the government] will be forced to meet them."[89] By fall 1864 Shelby management had somewhat mended its relationship with Hunt and the Nitre and Mining Bureau, and production for the government contract resumed in a less confrontational mode.

From the outset of their business enterprise, Shelby owners found themselves in a difficult relationship with the Confederacy, dependent upon government largesse but also seeking to maintain essential aspects of corporate autonomy. The Shelby Iron Company could not have jump-started expansion or maintained full production without government advances and patronage, but that same addiction to supplying the Confederacy also hampered the company's ability to sell its iron products on the open market. If the government then refused to fully honor the contract or was unwilling to increase prices apace with other foundries, then the company, they argued, was placed at the whim and mercy of government

agents. Shelby's directors lamented, "there is . . . no legal liability on governments . . . they can not be sued [so] you have to rely on their . . . sense
of justice." [90] Complaints by Shelby's directors about the government not
upholding its end of the contract, however, are dubious and one-sided.

An objective observer might conclude that the government's main priority, like any cost-wise customer, was to secure as much iron production
as possible at the lowest price. Confederate agents believed they had a right
to claim Shelby iron at a reasonable and fair price, because the government
had provided capital advances for expanded production. When Shelby directors attempted to sell iron to other customers at a higher price, Confederate agents intervened, demanded delivery at the fixed prices agreed to
in the contract, and demanded remission of capital advances. In the face
of these government demands, Shelby management continued on a semi-
independent course in an attempt to sustain profitability through a mixture
of continued government patronage and sales to outside parties.

The actions of the Shelby Iron Company were similar to the self-
interested experiences of the Tredegar. Both firms used the leverage of
their vital products to secure subsidies from the Confederate government
and to increase profits. Due to the relatively late expansion of its iron production facilities when compared to other firms, however, the Shelby Iron
Company did not so much help to create Confederate industrial policy as
it was created by government assistance. Private firms that produced essential materiel for the war effort exercised considerable influence over
Confederate industrial policy, and what at first looked like a public-private
partnership eventually developed the characteristics of a corporatist relationship. It was perhaps inevitable, given the rapid modernization caused
by the war, that companies like the Shelby would simultaneously depend
on government largesse and also hold the upper hand in contract negotiations and production priority.

CONCLUSION

Private munitions industries played a key role in the Confederate war effort, and their contributions and experiences represent the operations of a
corporatist state. The government allowed powerful private interest blocs,
in this case munitions manufacturers, to provide leadership in policy for-

mation and implementation in return for production priority. Many historians focus on the Confederate government's regulation of private industry as a top-down "statist" or "command" economy in which the regime forced compliance through fixed prices and control of the labor supply. However, important private industries possessed great leverage in dealing with Confederate authorities, and some even influenced policy creation for their economic sectors.

The term *patriotism for profit* used by historian Mary DeCredico to describe Georgia's wartime urban entrepreneurs might also be applied to larger private interest blocs that arguably placed profits before patriotism.[91] The relationship between the state and these private interest blocs was symbiotic, in which both parties received benefits from the other and depended on one another for survival. This relationship was meant to assure Confederate leaders of sufficient manufacturing production. In exchange, select private industries received government subsidies and patronage, protection from competition, and occasionally a direct role in formation of Confederate industrial policy. Private munitions companies' relationship with the Confederate government is an excellent example of how government-industry cooperation evolved into a corporatist system.

Corporatism can be defined as a system of interrelated sources of power that connect government and private enterprise.[92] Important munitions firms were well represented to sources of political power by the likes of Joseph R. Anderson, on behalf of the Tredegar Iron Works, and Colin J. McRae, on behalf of the Shelby Iron Company. Another potential avenue to political protection was through the highly respected Ordnance Department, but this depended on faithful fulfillment of government contracts. The desperate need for munitions meant that some private firms greatly influenced government policy. Private firms like the Tredegar and the Shelby possessed such great leverage that they created their own sphere of influence within the Confederate economy, and private power within this economic sector characterized corporatism in the Confederacy.

3

✤

CORPORATIST INDUSTRIAL POLICY IN THE CONFEDERACY, PART TWO

State-Owned Munitions Industries

✤

Necessity teaches all things.
—German proverb

At the outset of the Civil War, the southern states had a severely insufficient industrial base for munitions production, and there was no history of government ownership in heavy industries. Both of these circumstances would be completely overturned by the desperate necessity of the war effort, and so the Confederacy embarked upon an unprecedented program of state ownership in the vital munitions sector. Some historians view this state ownership as an example of socialism.[1] State ownership of industries, however, did not fit with traditional southern conservatism and notions of individual property rights. The wartime development of state industrial ownership was not an example of state socialism, but instead an expedient cornerstone of the Confederacy's corporatist industrial policy.

Former federal arsenals captured by the state governments after secession and later turned over to the Confederate government were among the first government-owned facilities. In 1861 the captured federal arsenals were of little use to the fledgling Confederate war effort because production capability was inadequate.[2] Although in need of serious augmentation, these minimal industrial concerns were placed under the direct control of the Ordnance Bureau, headed by Josiah Gorgas, a flexible, disciplined, and highly effective organizational leader.

The Confederacy began the conflict woefully deficient in heavy industries capable of artillery and armament production. Most importantly, the Confederacy possessed no large-scale capacity for manufacturing gunpowder, but Josiah Gorgas was determined to remedy this critically important industrial disadvantage. Josiah Gorgas was born in the town of Running Pumps, Pennsylvania, on July 1, 1818. Young Josiah received a commission to West Point and graduated sixth in the class of 1841, after which he chose the Ordnance branch of army service. Gorgas was assigned to the Watervliet Arsenal in Troy, New York, and quickly learned the trade of armaments producer. Gorgas supplemented his regional knowledge by touring Europe to review arms factories in 1845–1846. After capable but undistinguished service in the war against Mexico, Gorgas served at a variety of arsenals around the country in New York City, Pittsburgh, Fortress Monroe, and Mount Vernon, Alabama. At the Mount Vernon post, Amelia Gayle, daughter of a prominent Alabama family, caught Gorgas's eye and the two were married, which cemented Josiah's personal attachment to the South. From 1856 to 1860 Gorgas commanded arsenals at Kennebec, Maine, Charleston, South Carolina, Fortress Monroe again, and finally the Frankford Arsenal in Philadelphia. In early 1861, Gorgas initially spurned Confederate offers but, after what amounted to a demotion in the U.S. Ordnance service, Gorgas eventually decided to cast his lot with the rebels on April 3rd and was appointed the chief of ordnance.[3]

Gorgas's abilities were immediately put to the test. As the war expanded his role and duties, Gorgas exhibited the highest standards of bureaucratic leadership. One of his main managerial strengths was his uncanny ability to select the correct subordinate for the required task at hand. Throughout his Confederate career, he deftly managed state-owned facilities and shrewdly bargained with, or cajoled, managers of private firms into maintaining a sufficient supply of munitions. There is little historical doubt that Josiah Gorgas was the most effective and innovative bureaucrat in the Confederate hierarchy, accomplishing a great deal with severely limited means. Gorgas positively influenced subordinates with his unshakeable determination to achieve production goals and his unqualified patriotism. He was always ready to remind the owners of private firms about their patriotic duty during contract negotiations and price disputes. In terms of war materiel production, Gorgas's plan, organization, and implementation yielded impressive results. They represent a remarkable success story in the annals of the Confederate war effort. Assessing the situation in 1861, Josiah Gorgas instantly realized that nationally owned facilities would be needed to bolster existing southern industries, but only to fill specific gaps in the Confederate munitions production network.

Two primary circumstances dictated the need for Confederate state ownership: first, absence of previous availability. This circumstance sparked government investment, construction, and eventually production. Second, the Confederacy required the purchase of private firms that produced quality munitions but were unable to operate for profit in the wartime economy. One type of nationalized industry, in which Gorgas and the Confederate government created an enterprise where private industry was insufficient, is best represented by the Augusta Powder Works, which proved the viability and potential productivity of Confederate state ownership. Another type, in which a private firm was purchased by the government and then converted for expanded munitions production, will be described in discussion of the Selma Foundry.

THE AUGUSTA POWDER WORKS

From the start of the conflict, one of the primary concerns for Gorgas and Confederate armies was the supply of gunpowder. The southern states no longer had access to private manufacturing firms like the Hazard Powder Company in Connecticut or the E. I. DuPont Company of Delaware, and could not expect to import enough from outside sources to sustain the war effort. Unless Gorgas could quickly create a Confederate manufacturing foundation for gunpowder, the fledgling nation was doomed to a hasty demise. As historian Frank Vandiver pointed out, "when the war began, the supply of gunpowder in the whole Confederacy could not be counted on to last more than a month," and unlike the Union, "the Confederacy entered the conflict with no powder mills of consequence—two in Tennessee and two in South Carolina being little more than local suppliers."[4] To remedy this potentially disastrous situation, Gorgas embarked upon an unprecedented mission to construct a state-owned facility.

Perhaps Gorgas's greatest choice of subordinates was the selection of George Washington Rains to head the project. Rains was a native North

Carolinian and graduate of the West Point class of '42. Rains's greatest asset was adaptability, and this penchant for flexibility produced fruitful results for Gorgas and the Confederate war effort. Rains was appointed head of the gunpowder factory with "a *carte blanche* being given." Aside from determination, the always resourceful Rains created the Augusta Powder Works based on the experience of a man named "Wright . . . who had seen gunpowder made . . . [and] had been a workman at the Waltham Abbey Government Works, in England." In addition, Rains had access to "an invaluable pamphlet by Major Bradley, the Superintendent of the Waltham Abbey Works"; however, this pamphlet contained only a description of the process and did not provide detailed drawings, working plans, or descriptions of the buildings or required machinery.[5]

The creation of a large-scale gunpowder plant would have been an impressive feat in and of itself, but Rains eventually oversaw the creation of an immense state-owned industrial complex in Augusta, Georgia, which also included the Augusta Arsenal, "a Machine and Foundry establishment," a gun-carriage department, and various buildings for "preparation of small arm cartridges, and other purposes." Although the rapid industrial expansion in Augusta was entirely a result of government impetus, Rains viewed the coexistence and cooperation of state-owned and private industries as a normal circumstance. After the war he remarked, "It is the custom of the different nations in addition to the private factories of gunpowder, to have erected at different points national works to supply the demand for war," and the Confederacy was no different.[6]

Rains could not have achieved this impressive industrial growth without the complete support of Josiah Gorgas, Chief of Ordnance. Throughout the war, it was Gorgas who gave Rains the greatest chance for success with government finances, bureaucratic acumen, and sometimes just plain encouragement. In September 1861 Gorgas reassured Rains "that you are doing all you can to rush the mill" and reminded his subordinate that "patience, patience, and yet again patience" was needed.[7]

Rains recalled the difficult circumstances of creating a gunpowder plant in the resource-deficient Confederacy of 1861 and early 1862: "I immediately left Richmond to begin the work not waiting even for my commission. . . . Day and night for several months I almost lived on railroad cars; devising plans, examining the country for a location, hunting up material, engaging workmen, making contracts, and employing more or less every available machine shop and foundry from Virginia to Louisiana."[8]

It was decided to create the factory in a single, safe location. Although "no nation possessed such a single complete manufactory, each distributed its work among separate establishments erected in different places for safety and convenience," Rains reasoned; "the Confederacy could not afford to divide its resources," so government resources were devoted to the principal Confederate gunpowder plant in Augusta.[9] Against all odds, by the spring of 1862 Rains, with Gorgas's unmatched bureaucratic influence, succeeded in creating a large-scale gunpowder factory in Augusta. Without the impressive efforts of both men, rebel armies would have been unable to fight the Civil War from 1862 onward.

From September 1861 to April 1862, the gunpowder factory was under various stages of construction. Rains oversaw the purchase and delivery of equipment along with recruitment of skilled laborers to commence production after the factory's completion. The construction project got underway in September 1861. It was completely financed by the Ordnance Department, and George Washington Rains quickly went to work to get the factory established. Rains paid John R. Grant $40.00 for surveying the property on September 18th and M. B. Grant $120.00 for "engineering" two days later. Rains himself withdrew $5,300 from accounts and expensed another $5,000 to Captain W. G. Gill to apparently repay funds previously sent to Rains at Nashville. In materials, Rains paid $0.06 each for 2,000 new bricks and in October purchased 114,500 used bricks for $5.50 per thousand, for a total outlay of $629.75, one of the first examples of wise use of available resources at the site.[10]

Initial labor needs for construction combined both free and slave labor. In October Rains hired a slave named Henry for twenty-seven days at a daily rate of $1.25. Rains also hired four other men, presumably white laborers since there was since no mention of slave status, for four days at a daily rate of $1.00. Either the slave laborer Henry was performing some specialized work that warranted a higher daily rate, or his master who hired him out was a better wage negotiator than the white laborers were.[11]

It is important to point out that the Augusta project was not Rains's only concern in the fall of 1861 and early 1862. While he arranged for the construction of the Augusta powder plant, Rains was also deeply involved in attempting to get the Sycamore powder plant in Nashville running at full capacity along with another potential project in Manchester, Tennessee. Rains also traveled to New Orleans to meet with General Mansfield Lovell to discuss saltpeter supplies. Only after the disastrous month of February 1862, when Ulysses S. Grant captured Forts Henry and Donelson and later occupied Nashville, did Rains fully devote his entire energies to the Augusta project.[12]

Technically, production at the Augusta Powder Works began in April 1862. As with any new manufacturing facility, there would be equipment adjustments and supply interruptions that hamstrung full productivity until management better understood how to anticipate the needs of operations. In May 1862 the factory shipped a measly 16,350 pounds of gunpowder. By June production was reaching impressive levels. In July shipments of gunpowder had increased to 48,841 pounds. Shipments actually decreased until the breakout month of December, in which 144,775 pounds was shipped to munitions facilities across the Confederacy. After a sluggish start in the spring of 1862, it seemed as if the Augusta Powder Works had achieved a repeatable standard of high production by the end of 1862.[13]

In 1863 the powder factory increased the amount of powder shipped. In January the amount dropped to 97,026 pounds but in April almost doubled to 184,429 pounds. August 1863 was the pinnacle of output for the powder factory, with 214,728.5 pounds of gunpowder shipped to the armories and arsenals of the Confederacy. After a dip in October and November, the amount shipped bounced back above 100,000 pounds in December.[14]

In 1864 production levels remained consistently high. In January 132,485 pounds of powder was shipped and the amount peaked in June, with 148,774.7 pounds delivered to rebel facilities. Only when Sherman's armies threatened the facility in November and December did the powder factory lose production days and thus see the amount of powder shipped drop in the last two months of the year. Even in the truncated year of 1865, the powder factory shipped out 71,200 pounds in January and managed to ship 7,234 pounds in April. The total amount of gunpowder sent to Confederate munitions factories to be manufactured into ammunition was an impressive 3,378,118 pounds. At the start of the war many southerners would not have believed it possible that a state-owned facility could be constructed, produce so much vital war materiel, or that government management could achieve such an extraordinary feat.[15]

Finding adequate labor was a problem for the Augusta Powder Works throughout the war. William Pendleton, superintendent of the powder works, kept a daily log in which he recorded the number of laborers and later more specific information about types of work performed. From November 1862 to November 1863, Pendleton jotted down the total number of workers in the powder factory. All workers, whether black or white, free or slave, were simply listed as "Labourers." Security and oversight of the workers was performed by "watchmen," later described as "guards" from late 1863 on. The average daily number of workers at the powder factory during full-scale production from November 1862 to November 1863 was as follows:

November 1862	60.4
December 1862	60.6
January 1863	70.2
February 1863	63.4
March 1863	66.5
April 1863	67.1
May 1863	71.9
June 1863	69.3
July 1863	72.2
August 1863	82.5
September 1863	74.6
October 1863	88.4
November 1863	100.5

On some days, Pendleton noted that only a few workers were present for repairs or refitting, and these limited workdays were not included in the averages. For example, the days needed to repair equipment in January 1863 were January 11th "on steam pipe," January 18th "repairing steam and water pipe," and January 25th "on cooling wheel in saltpeter room, on water [barrels] in mills." The Sabbath was also observed when possible, as for example on May 3, 1863, when there was "no work today (Sunday)." The months of October and November 1863 must have been productive for the powder factory because there was no mention of stoppage for repairs. The total number of daily workers topped one hundred for the first time on October 20th, and in November the average of daily workers topped one hundred. All of this labor was managed by government officers and paid directly from government coffers.[16]

In late 1863 Superintendent Pendleton began to include more specific information about the laborers and their daily assignments. For example, on December 7, 1863, the ninety-eight employees were assigned the following tasks:

Machinists	1
Engineers	3
Firemen	8
Blacksmiths	1
Carpenters	6
Coopers	2
Painters	2
White Labor	3
Black Labor	37
Guards	32
Clerks/Storekeepers	3

Pendleton then broke down the tasks of the "White Labor" and "Black Labor" categories. The white workers were typically assigned duties of "engines cleaning & firing, lead furnace, dry house, kettles, stables, and office log." The black workers were assigned the tasks of "repairing slip cylinders, jobbing, splitting wood, burning charcoal, hurling wood in furnaces," and would have worked alongside white laborers at the "lead furnace, dry house, kettles, stable, [and] office log."[17]

Slaves and free black men made up the "Black laborers" category. Slave workmen were not owned by the factory but instead hired out. Initially the powder works used around thirty slaves and by the end of 1864, the number of slave workmen had increased to around one hundred. The cost to hire out these industrial slave workers averaged $12 per slave each month. Superintendent Pendleton mentioned that at least twenty-nine "Free Negroes" worked at the powder factory and listed the home counties of twelve of them, "5 from [Burke] County Ga, 5 from Augusta, Ga, [and] 2 from Edgefield District So[uth] Ca[rolina]."[18]

The amount of labor used for operations at the powder factory increased from December 1863 through April 1865. The average number of workers needed per day each month was as follows:

December 1863	91.0
January 1864	82.1
February 1864	132.2
April 1864	107.0
August 1864	134.4
September 1864	139.2
October 1864	150.3
November 1864	149.4
December 1864	121.7
January 1865	110.4
February 1865	115.4
March 1865	125.4
April 1865	125.0

The average daily labor requirements increased throughout 1864, peaked in October and November, and still maintained impressive levels in April 1865.[19]

Just as in other industries, skilled laborers were hard to acquire and difficult to retain. The Confederacy experienced chronic manpower shortages throughout the war, but the critical competition for manpower, between industries and the army, became acute in 1864. In January Gorgas predicted that "the danger now seems to be a too eager disposition to sacrifice everything to putting men in the field at the expense of the industrial interests."[20] By fall 1864 the labor shortage threatened to hamper production, but rebel armies were also desperate for men. Workers realized that munitions industries were no longer guaranteed safe havens from conscription. "Mechanics [skilled workers] will not work and soldier both," Gorgas declared, and he pointed to "the desertion of 114 men" from Richmond facilities since May 1st as proof that skilled workers should be completely exempt from military duty. But where to find a supply of skilled labor for the vital munitions facilities around Augusta?[21]

Gorgas suggested two possibilities to overcome the labor shortage. The first idea was to encourage skilled foreign workers to come to the Confederacy by promoting a new law "exempting all mechanics coming to this country . . . from military duty." This was fantasy. Even if foreign workers were willing to emigrate, there was no guarantee they could pass the blockade and it would take months, if not years, for such a plan to produce results. Gorgas's next suggestion for Rains was to recruit "foreign mechanics" among Union prisoners of war. "After a while they may swear allegiance and become citizens," Gorgas hoped, but he admitted they "should be kept under surveillance until they prove their new faith by their good works."[22] The Augusta powder factory and other munitions plants throughout the Confederacy were lucky to keep the skilled workers they had and prevent them from being conscripted into the army.

On January 30, 1865, Superintendent Pendleton listed at least some of the workers at the powder plant who had been exempted from military service. Of the twenty-five men listed, one was a "chemist exempt by professorship in Franklin College, Athens, Ga," six other men were "detailed conscript[s]," and eighteen men were "detailed soldier[s]."[23] This was hardly a vast reserve of manpower being withheld from the front, and despite pleas from officers who would have put these men in the ranks, the Ordnance Department wisely kept them protected for the important industrial duties on behalf of the Confederacy.

In late 1864 when William Tecumseh Sherman embarked upon his famous "March to the Sea" from Atlanta to Savannah, the Augusta Powder Factory was threatened with destruction. On November 21st, Gorgas believed "the troops of the enemy will combine on Augusta." Rains ordered the powder works dismantled and moved to Columbia, South Carolina, losing valuable production time. Superintendent Pendleton did not make ledger labor entries from November 23st to December 5th or from December 8th through December 11th, presumably due to the deconstruction and then reassembly of the machinery.[24] Fortunately for the Confederacy, Sherman's forces did not target the vital rebel facilities as anticipated. Instead, Sherman's army headed straight for Savannah to link up with Union naval forces.

In 1865, as Sherman moved north through the Carolinas, Gorgas and Rains again worried that Union forces might make a foray to Augusta and destroy the powder factory. At this stage communication was unreliable, but Gorgas advised Rains to relocate to Athens, Georgia, should circumstances require. Gorgas also contemplated other possible sites for the government powder mill safely out of range of Union armies, like Lynchburg, Virginia. When Sherman moved into North Carolina in March, Gorgas felt secure enough to request the return of the powder mill from Athens back to Augusta, but in fact it had never left. Gorgas admitted that the Confederacy appeared "to be on the brink of despair and ruin" but he mistakenly hoped "ill fortune has nearly run herself out against us." By mid-March, Gorgas told Rains, "the storm of war has swept by you, and you will be left comparatively undisturbed, in fact . . . Augusta, Athens, and Washington [Georgia] are now about the safest places for operation and for [military] stores in the Confederacy."[25] As the events of April 1865 unfolded, Rains kept the powder mill running, but by the end of the month there were no Confederate munitions facilities to accept delivery because the nation had ceased to exist. Over the course of three years, the state-owned Augusta Powder factory managed to deliver over three million pounds of gunpowder that allowed for the manufacture of much of the Confederacy's ammunition from 1862 to 1865. The Augusta Powder Works highlighted the potential of government ownership and management in munitions production.

George Washington Rains's record with the Augusta powder plant was very impressive, but his prestige was greatly enhanced by the numerous other duties he undertook for the Confederacy. Throughout the war Rains was tasked with other duties in addition to getting the powder mill up and running. In February 1862 Gorgas stated that since "the national powder mill [is] well underway, it devolves on you to establish a national foundry" in Augusta, "if the location suits you." Rains ended up becoming a regional industrial inspector of sorts for the Ordnance Department, and was assigned additional duties of helping to found arsenals, iron works, and munitions manufacturing facilities around Georgia.[26]

Due to his West Point training, Rains was also distracted by local defense duties. The Augusta site was selected for its security, but the possibility of a Union amphibious raid up the Savannah River remained a possibility. Rains had to develop a makeshift defense plan for this now-important

Confederate munitions hub. In May 1862 former senator James H. Hammond, a local planter and national political icon of "King Cotton" fame, offered his assistance in helping Rains better understand local geography. From his nearby Redcliffe Plantation, Hammond voluntarily provided Rains with a detailed description of defensible points and recommended the Augusta Bluff as opposed to the Shell Bluff, "from which there is no retreat." Hammond decried the absence of manpower and armaments for local defense and blamed the "imbecile administration" for taking away local troops, "their arms and munitions, their energy and courage to defend the homes of others." Rains apparently did not heed Hammond's advice, because defenses were constructed at Shell Bluff. Rains eventually commanded a local defense force comprised of ten companies from Augusta and surrounding areas, replete with cavalry and artillery, but he was never forced to lead them in defense of the city.[27]

George Washington Rains's Civil War colleagues appreciated his industrial service to the Confederacy. Benjamin Huger, chief of the Ordnance Bureau in the Trans-Mississippi, transferred from combat in the eastern theater after the Seven Days Campaign in Virginia, declared that "getting those [powder] works in such order has been of the greatest benefit to us, and you have been of value to us at least equal to the generals." A Georgia Ordnance Department officer took time to "congratulate [Rains] upon the success of your operation" and hoped "that the untiring energy and devotion to the work . . . will meet with adequate reward."[28] Many more famous individuals, particularly combat generals, performed admirable service for the Confederacy, but perhaps none played a more critical role in keeping Confederate armies in the field with such little acclaim as did George Washington Rains.

Rains's feat at the Augusta Powder Works was unparalleled and unprecedented in the Confederate war effort. In an industrial sector that was virtually nonexistent before the war, the government filled the vacuum of investment and management to construct and operate a highly productive gunpowder manufacturing facility. Sheer necessity caused this development, because no private facility could have been expanded quickly enough to meet the consumptive demands of Confederate armed forces. With the possible exception of Joseph R. Anderson at the Tredegar Iron Works, no single person oversaw such a vital facility that kept rebel armies supplied with enough ammunition to prosecute the war than did George Washington Rains.

The Augusta Powder Works was arguably the most successful government-owned facility in the Confederacy. Under the bureaucratic guidance of Josiah Gorgas and the determined management of George Washington Rains, the powder works made it possible for rebel armies to be supplied with ample amounts of gunpowder in defense of the embattled Confederacy. The construction, operation, and productivity of the powder plant was a remarkable feat for a relatively nonindustrial region, and credit for the facility's success should be given to the partnership between Gorgas and Rains. The Augusta Powder Works was financed entirely by government resources. Rains never had to worry about profit margins or running out of capital as privately owned businesses did because his sole customer and his sole investor were the same entity, the Confederate government. The Augusta Powder Works was so vital to the Confederate war effort that it occupied its own economic niche. Although it was constructed and owned by the government, the powder works was not an example of state socialism, but instead it was one of the most powerful examples of the *expedient* aspect in the Confederacy's flexible capitalist industrial policy.

THE SELMA FOUNDRY

In some instances, the Confederate government purchased an extant facility to bolster munitions production. This process was typically aided by an individual with direct ties to both the manufacturing site and the government. Not all state-owned industries were created from scratch like the Augusta Powder Works. In several cases, government officials had to carefully determine which private industries were worthy of purchase and expanded production. Although Josiah Gorgas, and other high-ranking members of the War and Navy Departments, officially possessed responsibility for final decisions of state ownership, government authorities also relied on subordinates. For example, it was Gorgas's superintendent of armories James H. Burton who assessed the potential and practicability of national ownership.

There was no consistent or uniform policy for state ownership of firms, but an ad hoc determination based on circumstances and factors that included priority of manufactures, effectiveness of private management, and productivity. Historian and Gorgas biographer Frank Vandiver explained one example of how this process worked: "The pistol factory operated by Messrs. Spiller & Burr in Atlanta was purchased in January, 1864, and its machinery transferred to the Macon Armory," but when "the Red Mountain Iron and Coal Company . . . inquired if the government would bail them out . . . [superintendent] Burton reported the plant as unsatisfactory, incomplete, and thoroughly inferior . . . [and] refused to recommend its acquisition."[29] Iron was certainly a priority commodity for the Confederate war effort, but Burton refused to advise the facility's purchase due to poor private management and low productivity. State ownership apparently required immediate promise of productivity or at least filling of a gap not already covered by the growing war industries.

An excellent example of government purchase of an extant manufacturing facility was the Selma Manufacturing Company, founded in the 1850s, which became known as the Selma Foundry. The company's owners looked to sell their business to the government, so they contacted their provisional congressman and one of the most successful facilitators of Confederate industrial development, Colin J. McRae.

Colin John McRae was born in North Carolina in 1812 but moved with his family to Mississippi at a young age. McRae's father died in 1835, so at age twenty-three, McRae continued in the family mercantile business. Young Colin apparently possessed a keen business mind and in 1840, he moved his business interests into the bustling port of Mobile, Alabama, where he broadened investments into slaves, railroads, and cotton trading.[30]

Profits from his partnership in the Boykin & McRae Company afforded Colin an opportunity to parlay his business success into political opportunities. In February 1861, being recognized as a staunch supporter of secession, he was selected to represent Alabama as a delegate at the Confederacy's formation in Montgomery. However, McRae's true love was business, not politics. He abandoned political service after 1861, but he contributed his influential business connections and acumen to the war effort. Colin McRae was a rare and indispensable Confederate commodity. He possessed established business contacts overseas through his experiences in the cotton trade but also assisted the Confederate war effort through industrial expansion in Alabama.

In February 1861 McRae was contacted by several entrepreneurs about the possible government purchase of the Selma Manufacturing Company. The owners proposed that the site might be easily expanded into an "armory for the manufacture of arms and ordnance," and although the facility had "been put up at a cost of near $75,000" the owners would be amenable to sell "to the Confederacy for the sum of $40,000." Apparently the owners were already actively seeking buyers, but by selling to the Confederacy they might show their patriotism and be relieved of their investment. The proposition included a persuasive geographical argument since the facility was already "connected by railroad and river" and also "most fortunately situated with regard to the means of manufacturing in iron."[31] McRae agreed with the proposition and through his connections to Confederate political elites, advocated the use of government funds for industrial development around Selma.

Early in 1862 McRae actively sought government backing for development of a state-owned facility in Selma. McRae believed the Selma manufacturing facility might be converted into a productive munitions manufacturing center and bolster vital supplies of finished iron products like cannon, plating for warships, and even railroad equipment. On February 4, 1862, McRae requested that President Jefferson Davis consider government development of a Selma facility. McRae supplied a "description of a Foundry property at Selma . . . [which] belongs to some gentlemen, not mechanics or machinists, who undertook to have the . . . business carried on by hired Superintendents and workmen."[32] Playing to Davis's ingrained affinity for the southern planter class, McRae assured the president that the sellers were gentlemen who had ventured into the iron business.

McRae provided a detailed description of the area to entice the president's support. "The grounds . . . are ample and . . . well located with regard to the River and Rail Roads," McRae boasted, and he assured Davis that "an abundance of Iron of the very best quality . . . can be had by Cart load from I. Kelly Co (Wares Mines)." The location was ideal since "coal also of superior quality can be had by Rail from the Shelby Coal Mine," and the city of Selma was "accessible by the Alabama and Coosa Rivers to the Mines." Besides the bountiful natural industrial resources surrounding Selma, McRae also pointed out to the president that "Selma is far enough . . . inland to render it secure from an invading foe." Selma fulfilled all of the requirements for uninterrupted industrial production: readily available material supply, excellent access to transportation networks, and geographical isolation that minimized the threat of destruction by Union armies. "For these reasons," McRae advocated, Selma was "highly favorable for the establishment of a National Foundry & Armory," and he further declared that "no other point in the Southern part of the Confederacy can offer superior or equal advantages for that purpose."[33]

Colin McRae was not just a well-placed friend of the project with access to Jefferson Davis, but he was also given power to negotiate between the owners and government officials. McRae informed Davis that the existing facility cost $70,000, and he offered to expedite the process since he was "authorized by the owners to make a sale of the property . . . [or] enter into the necessary arrangements with the proper departments of the government."[34] Davis was not overtly opposed to the idea, but he referred McRae's plan to the heads of the War and Navy Departments, Judah Benjamin and Stephen Mallory.

As Davis requested, McRae contacted Benjamin and Mallory. McRae was left to deal with the department heads with the president's endorsement. Bureaucratic delays forced McRae to press the subject and tell the department heads, "The President informs me that he thought well of the proposition, that he had turned the papers over to your departments for consideration . . . but not having heard from you I infer that your time has been occupied with more pressing engagements." The decision to purchase the extant Selma facility or allow it to remain under private ownership was left up to the secretaries. McRae offered to personally purchase the works if the government was not interested but still hoped he might be considered for government financial assistance in making the foundry operational. McRae's gesture hardly qualified as a pure example of entrepreneurial risk, but one might argue that he patriotically believed a government facility at Selma was indeed the wisest possible choice. On February 24th McRae made a final plea to Davis about the "absolute necessity of putting" a government-owned foundry "in the interior of the southern portion of the Confederacy in operation *immediately*," but the plan for immediate government purchase and expansion of a foundry in Selma was apparently not coming to fruition.[35]

Government purchase seemed remote but McRae still believed that the

Confederacy needed a regional foundry. In another attempt to obtain government support, Gorgas's trusted subordinate George W. Rains inspected the Selma facility and "thought it would not do for a national foundry." McRae then turned to groups of private investors, including the group at the Shelby Iron Company who declared "that the government ought to have a foundry in the Gulf States" but demanded that the site be moved from Selma and closer to their facilities. After being rebuffed by the government and the overly demanding investors in Shelby County, McRae decided to use his extensive business connections to cobble together a group of private investors from around Alabama, himself included, to purchase the Selma manufacturing site. If the government would not invest in the facility, then it still might assist private owners by placing orders. McRae proved extremely useful in arranging these hoped-for government contracts with the Ordnance Department. George Minor, chief of ordnance for the navy, informed McRae that "both [the War and Navy] departments are now ready to execute the contract" and that he was impressed by McRae's typical "zeal in establishing a foundry near Selma for the fabrication of guns, boiler plate, & plates . . . for covering ships." McRae intended to make the Selma Foundry a regional hub for manufacturing iron plating for a gulf fleet of ironclads. McRae's foresight was pivotal because it indeed became Confederate "policy to plate every vessel that will carry a gun."[36]

Although the Selma Foundry never produced iron plating for naval vessels, the ironclads were armored and equipped at the naval facility in Selma, the CSS *Tennessee* being perhaps the site's major contribution to the war effort. The importance of the company's manufactured products increased throughout 1862, and in the meantime, if McRae and his fellow investors reaped a profit from government contracts then so much the better, but McRae was still convinced that Confederate officials should play a more active role in managing southern munitions production.

The 1862 government contract for the Selma Foundry was negotiated between McRae and the Confederate secretaries of war and the navy. The foundry was to produce "all such guns, mortars, shot, shells, bar, bolt and boiler iron, and iron plates for covering vessels as . . . may be used by the Army and Navy of the Confederate States." The contract specified the types of guns and other materiel and a schedule of prices but did not establish a minimum production quota. In fact, the onus of minimum support was placed upon the government. The contract stipulated that the government was required to purchase at least $600,000 worth of products in 1862, and at least $800,000 worth in both 1863 and 1864. McRae obtained a three-year promise of revenues from government contracts at fixed prices to offset competition. In addition, the contract called for a $75,000 government advance "to be refunded by deductions on deliveries . . . [and] re-imbursed" by January 1, 1864. In case of higher material costs, then the Selma Foundry was to receive an increase in prices equivalent to that of the Tredegar Iron Works. The Selma Foundry's 1862 contract offered another example of private owners who possessed the upper hand during negotiations. In a quintessential corporatist style, McRae secured government subsidies, promises of future contracts, and government revenues, and ensured the Selma Foundry would have some modicum of economic parity with the South's premier iron factory.[37] McRae's visionary achievements in 1861 and 1862 were indeed astounding, and he helped to personally develop the institutional and structural support for Alabama's growing wartime industrial centers.

The notion that traditional agricultural capitalist planters could rapidly and successfully reallocate investments into heavy industrial manufacturing facilities and effectively manage production was doubted by contemporaries in the early 1860s, and has been ever since by historians. Colin McRae, however, was determined to combine the capital of local investors with government subsidies and government demand for war materiel into a workable relationship. If former planters could not sustain a productive munitions manufacturing facility then perhaps an amalgam of local profit motive and government patronage could help meet the insatiable munitions needs of Confederate armed forces. Government subsidies were necessary if southern planters expected to erect productive heavy manufacturing plants. McRae understood this and facilitated the connection.

Amidst the booming antebellum cotton economy of Alabama, planters typically reinvested profits in additional acreage and slave labor. However, as pointed out by historian Jonathan Weiner, Alabama's "planters never opposed industry *per se*" but instead "favored limited industrial development . . . to the extent that it served their own interests and occurred under their own auspices."[38] Alabama's wartime industrial expansion did not occur solely due to the leadership of the planter class but also required significant assistance from the Confederate government—an institution comprised of leaders familiar with and sympathetic to the traditions of planter capitalism and cognizant of the frustrations inherent in the rapid industrial transition to a wartime economy. Colin McRae was one of the few individuals capable of assembling these economic and political institutions together for the benefit of both the investors and the Confederate war effort.

McRae's indefatigable efforts and ultimate success in the private sector made him an excellent choice to oversee government production in the region. On May 14, 1862, Josiah Gorgas appointed McRae to be an Ordnance Bureau officer charged with purchasing iron for the government. McRae was given full authority to negotiate contracts and enforce their terms, which meant McRae began oversight of the Shelby Iron Company contract.[39] This new office meant that McRae was not only part owner of the Selma Foundry project but also responsible for the government receipts attached to this and other facilities. Government duties diminished his ability to get the Selma Foundry up and running for full production in 1862.

In an effort to obtain additional investment, McRae contacted Alabama governor John Gill Shorter in November but was turned down. In December 1862 the state of Alabama provided a state charter of incorporation for the Selma Iron Foundry Company, but McRae would not be around to see the facility he worked so hard to develop churn out war materiel for the southern cause. In early 1863 McRae was asked to alter his government service and go abroad to investigate the Confederacy's foreign financial problems. McRae accepted the overseas assignment only on the "condition that he should be relieved of his works and contract at Selma without pecuniary loss to himself."[40] McRae agreed to perform his patriotic duty but also wanted to make sure he did not take a loss on the industry he had worked so hard to promote and get under way.

On February 12, 1863, the Selma Foundry was purchased by the Confederate government. The War Department and Navy Department temporarily used the facility jointly until June, when the Navy took total responsibility for production. Under government ownership and management, the Selma Foundry produced, as noted by preeminent Confederate naval historian William Still, "over a hundred large naval guns" and a variety of artillery pieces and mortars for land forces. In sum, the Selma Foundry, expanded by the efforts of Colin McRae and later purchased by the Navy Department, "produced nearly two hundred guns, second only to the famous Tredegar Iron Works," which was an impressive achievement given the lack of capability in 1861.[41]

The wartime history of the Selma Foundry provides an excellent example of how a privately held factory was assessed, developed, and eventually purchased by the Confederate government to augment military production. Colin McRae represented the indispensable human element in the process. He used his extensive political and business connections to join the interests of entrepreneurs and government officials to develop the Selma Foundry. Given his profit motive, unquestionable patriotism, and flexibility in cobbling together investors and government contracts, McRae, in many respects, personified the public-private partnership at the core of the Confederacy's expedient industrial policy. He tirelessly worked to create a much-needed foundry for the Confederacy's central region but at the same time sought profit opportunities for himself and other Alabama industrialists. McRae's wartime endeavors could be described as Confederate political economy in microcosm because he was willing to experiment with all manner of unprecedented arrangements between the public and private sectors to achieve his primary goal of southern independence.

CONCLUSION

On April 8, 1864, Josiah Gorgas reflected on his three years as head of the Ordnance Bureau and proudly noted that "I have succeeded beyond my utmost expectations." Boasting of his organizational accomplishments, Gorgas listed the numerous state-owned facilities that had been created with limited resources and were now supplying the Confederate armies with sufficient war equipment and munitions.[42] Gorgas succeeded thanks to excellent judgment and the wise selection of subordinates. He was flexible enough to pursue state ownership, but he prevented unnecessary nationalization of other southern industries.

Two main circumstances dictated the necessity of Confederate state ownership. The first was that the industry simply did not exist, or was pitifully small. This situation required creation of industrial facilities from the ground up, a process completely financed and managed by the government, and was best symbolized by the Augusta Powder Works. The second circumstance required the conversion or expansion of potentially productive munitions facilities. Private owners were bought out by the government and the facilities were refitted to meet the government's needs. An excellent example of this process was the conversion of the Selma Foundry into a government facility. Another example of opportunistic state ownership was the Etowah Iron Works.

Mark Anthony Cooper owned the Etowah Iron Works in northern Georgia. In early 1861 Cooper hoped his foundry would benefit from Confederate contracts. He solicited Secretary of War Leroy Pope Walker for a contract in March but was temporarily denied. On April 24th Cooper successfully obtained a government contract, but in July he requested a sixty-day extension to deliver the armaments. Cooper blamed lack of capital for the delay after a crucial investor fell ill, and in September he admitted the government's order could not be filled. Cooper requested an additional $250,000, on top of the $350,000 he had already invested, to complete the contract. In January 1862 Cooper was offered a government contract for sheet iron but turned it down because "the manufacture of bar iron and nails were too profitable." He knew that Confederate agents were looking to purchase facilities like the Etowah Iron Works but doubted that it "could be purchased on favorable terms." Gorgas sent his two industrial experts in the region, J. G. Minor and G. W. Rains, to inspect Etowah's potential, and the men recommended that the Confederate government purchase the facility. Cooper sold to a group of private owners on July 19, 1862, but the Etowah Iron Works were eventually purchased by the government on August 26 for $400,000 in Confederate bonds.[43] In effect, the government could not get the Etowah Iron Works to produce exactly what it needed, so it arranged to buy the facility, remove the inefficient or uncooperative management, and fulfill its munitions priorities.

None of these types of state ownership, however, are examples of state socialism. In each case it was necessity and state survival that forced the Confederacy to embark on this unprecedented use of government ownership.[44] The notion that men like George Washington Rains and Colin McRae were intent on national ownership of industries because of an ideological drive for a socialist political economy is utterly wrong. These types of industrial leaders were motivated by patriotism to the southern cause and the opportunity to make a profit.

State ownership was a new method of ensuring munitions production. Government intervention into the munitions market did not necessarily undercut private profits, but in reality, the Confederacy's only choice was to create a limited system of state-owned facilities if it expected to meet the needs of its armies. The ad hoc policy of state ownership best suited Gorgas and his subordinates to their primary task: provision of Confederate armed forces with war munitions in the immediate future. If the purchase of a productive private firm would further this goal, then the Confederate government added that specific industrial operation to the growing constellation of state-owned factories. However, there was no preplanned blueprint for the creation of a vast state-owned industrial network. Nationalized Confederate industries represented an expedient policy in an otherwise corporatist industrial system, which was implemented solely to fill gaps in military production. Capitalism remained the inherent economic paradigm of the Confederacy.

A brief comparison with northern wartime economic organization is useful to better comprehend the qualities of Confederate economic and industrial policy. Charles and Mary Beard laid the foundation for most economic interpretations of the North during the Civil War with their interpretation of the sectional conflict as a "Second American Revolution." This interpretation focuses on how "the capitalists, laborers, and farmers of the North and West drove from power in the national government the planting aristocracy of the South" and replaced the dominant political economy of slavery with more modern economic institutions like widespread wage-labor, industrialization, and financial capitalism. Preeminent economic historian of the Civil War era Roger Ransom noted that the Beard thesis was updated in the 1940s by historian Louis Hacker. The Hacker-Beard thesis argues "that there was a rapid acceleration in the growth of GNP during and after the Civil War that was a direct result of changes brought about by the Northern victory in the Civil War."[45] This notion that the Civil War provided an upsurge in national production seemed unquestionable. Northern wartime economic performance was even more impressive when one considered the deterioration of economic conditions in the southern half of the country.

The Hacker-Beard thesis was contested by the first generation of quantitative economic historians, or cliometricians, in the early 1960s. Based on long-term Gross National Product (GNP) figures in the nineteenth century compiled by Robert Gallman, historian Thomas Cochran argued there was no drastic increase in GNP during the Civil War era, and GNP might have actually been slightly lower relative to other decades. Cochran's challenge to the Hacker-Beard thesis was bolstered by highly respected quantitative historian Stanley Engerman, who agreed that the statistical data proved the underlying assumption of the Hacker-Beard thesis was not supported by the evidence. Whether there was a national economic boom of revolutionary proportions in the 1860s, as implied by the Hacker-Beard thesis, or simply the continuation of steady GNP growth during a costly Civil War, the central point of both interpretations remains valid: The North's political economy proved to be the more resilient and dominant economic system and continued to expand despite the serious drag of a devastating war. In the context of long-range changes in national political economy, northern victory in the Civil War was a watershed moment of immense importance. Historian James McPherson analyzed the Beardian notion of the Civil War as a "Second American Revolution" and described the conflict as "the last time, perhaps, aggrieved Americans rose in the name of Jeffersonian republicanism in a counterrevolution against the second American revolution of free-labor capitalism."[46]

The scholarly consensus about wartime Union economic policy tends to be positive. Many historians agree that the North did an admirable job of financing the war through a good balance of direct taxation, bond issuance, and monetary policy. In conjunction with the "Second American Revolution" thesis, the Republican-dominated Thirty-Seventh Congress, now freed from the obstacles of southern Democrat obstructionists, was free to implement a flood of new legislation to propel northern capitalism into a more modern phase.[47]

What specific aspects of northern industrial policy assisted with ultimate Union victory and how did these policies compare to Confederate corporatist industrial policy? Historian Mark R. Wilson describes the North's "mixed military economy" as being predicated on the government's decision to either "make or buy" necessary supplies. As Wilson points out, the U.S. government "bought more than it made," which caused contractors and purchasing agents to consider "the ethics of procurement and the flow of military dollars." The Confederacy was not burdened with such abstract notions because it simply did not have enough private industrial capacity to produce sufficient war materiel. There is no doubt that U. S. government spending and production increased during the war, but the long-term effects of this expansion, according to Wilson, were citizens' interactions with "a truly massive national state, which featured a robust administrative bureaucracy and large scale public enterprises," and the creation of "a giant public procurement machine capable of bypassing some mercantile intermediaries and . . . highlighting economic inequalities." Wilson interprets the northern Civil War economy as an important era that "evidently amplified the producerist critiques of commercial capitalism that had long been part of the popular political economy in America, while suggesting that the national state might play a larger role in administering and regulating the economy than had previously been imagined."[48] If one agrees with Wilson's interpretation of northern industrial policy, then there is a drastic difference between the two wartime systems of the Union and Confederacy. If, as Wilson implies, Union industrial policy provided the latent foundation for increased government involvement in the twentieth century, particularly during the Progressive and New Deal eras, then Confederate industrial policy was a polar opposite. The Confederacy's expedient corporatist industrial system combined the mutual interests of the national government and business leaders to create a system that was designed solely for national survival.

What role did the mixture of private and state-owned industries play in the overall Confederate economy and war effort? The standard economic interpretation of the Confederacy typically highlights a failed monetary policy that caused rampant inflation, and also points out the impressive wartime industrial growth despite serious resource deficiencies. For example, James McPherson summed up the Confederate economy's overall performance and stated, "under the pressures of blockade, invasion, and a flood of paper money, the South's unbalanced agrarian economy simply could not produce both guns and butter without shortages and inflation." This tone of respect for an ultimately doomed system pervades many economic interpretations of the Confederacy. Another major theme of Confederate economic analysis can be found in Emory Thomas's *The Confederacy as a Revolutionary Experience* (1971). Thomas explored the relationship between the government and industry and argued wartime expansion "constituted nothing less than an economic revolution . . . characterized by the decline of agriculture, the rise of industrialism, and the rise of urbanization."[49] Thomas's work advanced the idea that Confederate industrialization was a modern form of economic organization. These foundational economic interpretations fostered scholarly discussion about the pivotal relationship between the Confederate government and southern industries, but deeper investigation was required into the unprecedented public-private relationship inherent in Confederate industrial policy.

The unusual mixture of nationalized and privately owned industries symbolized the flexible nature of Confederate capitalism, but was the corporatist industrial system beneficial to the Confederate economy and the rebel war effort? One must first remove the negative stain of Confederate defeat from the equation before making an objective assessment. The fact that the South ultimately lost the war does not necessarily mean that Confederate political economy was doomed to the dustbin of history. Many other governments have voluntarily implemented corporatist industrial systems since 1865. It is also abundantly clear that the Confederacy could not have maintained viable armed forces without drastic action and experimentation. For example, without a government-owned gunpowder factory it is possible that southern armies could not have conducted major campaigns after 1862. Likewise, without firms like the Tredegar Iron Works, rebel armies would have been severely hampered by lack of artillery and ammunition. Most historians discuss Confederate industrialization with some degree of admiration. This interpretation is justified and perhaps should be amplified. Confederate industrial policy was one of the essential ingredients in southern nationalism. If, as historian Gary Gallagher asserts, General Robert E. Lee's Army of Northern Virginia was the most important symbol of Confederate nationalism, then the industrial policy that kept all rebel armed forces equipped was the backbone of the southern nation.[50] Necessity sparked the government-business cooperation required for national survival, and Confederate leaders unintentionally created a corporatist industrial policy that became a precursor for other modern nations.

4

———— ✤ ————

THE CONFEDERATE SYSTEM

———— ✤ ————

The man of system . . . is apt to be very wise in his own conceit.
. . . he seems to imagine that he can arrange the different members of a
great society with as much ease as the hand arranges the different pieces
upon a chess board; he does not consider that the pieces upon the chess
board have no other principle of motion besides that which the hand
impresses upon them . . . but that, in the great chess board of human
society, every single piece has a principle of motion of its own
altogether different from that which the legislature might choose
to impress upon it. . . . to insist . . . upon establishing all at
once and in spite of all opposition . . . must often be
the highest degree of arrogance.

—Adam Smith, *The Theory of Moral Sentiments*

Thomas S. Bocock understood the bitter antagonisms of prewar party politics because of his experiences as a stalwart southern Democrat in the U.S. House of Representatives from 1847 to 1861. He personally participated as a candidate in the bitterly contested 1859 speakership contest against Republican John Sherman. This sectional fight was eventually resolved only after the forty-fourth ballot, when the position was awarded to compromise candidate William Pennington. Since he had been an uncompromising antebellum southern Democrat, Thomas Bocock knew firsthand the potentially crippling power of partisan politics. Bocock's fellow Confederate representatives unanimously elected him Speaker of the House on February 18, 1862, and he addressed the Assembly about the importance of unity in the upcoming struggle. He pleaded with the members to "hush every murmur of discontent, and banish every feeling of personal grief." Bocock also realized that some leaders might "grow restive under the enforcement of those rules which you make for your own government" but reminded his peers that "submission to authority is the primary necessity in all communities." Bocock then declared that the Confederacy was a "new system . . . founded on a different system of political philosophy . . . sustained by a peculiar and more conservative state of society."[1] Bocock could not predict specific Confederate policies, but he understood that personal sacrifices and submission to authority would eventually be necessary to secure Confederate independence. Bocock anticipated legislators would likely have to construct controversial policies that might subordinate individual rights. Perpetuation of the Confederate system was the paramount goal of all policy and trumped any ideological or constitutional considerations. Bocock presciently described this new system as conservative and although he did not name the political philosophy, the resultant policies exhibited the qualities of an expedient corporatist state.

"The Confederate system" is a phrase used to describe policies implemented by the government. These policies were directly influenced by political culture, but this section deals with the actual governance of the Confederate states, the intersection of policy with southern citizens, and the corporatist nature of railroad policy. The evolution of Confederate policies and the relationship of political leaders to the people, or the friction of governance, alongside the government's relationship with the railroad sector, allow an understanding of the Confederate system in operation and highlight the actions of the expedient corporatist state. Examination of these topics provides insight into the debate between consent and coercion, the corporatist state in action, and the nature of Confederate nationalism.

CONSCRIPTION

Arguably no other Confederate policy exemplified the power of the expedient corporatist state like conscription. The continual necessity of maintaining a standing army forced Confederate leaders to enact and expand conscription laws. Three waves of conscription, followed by exemptions, occurred in April 1862, September and October 1862, and February 1864. Conscription provided the Confederate government with unprecedented power not only to control the size of its military, but also to directly control labor access through exemptions. As the war progressed, fewer draft exemptions were allowed and some were subjects of popular dissent like the "twenty-slave clause" passed in the fall of 1862. Despite considerable popular resistance, Confederate leaders were compelled by circumstances to continue mobilizing through conscription as an expedient necessary for national survival.

If civil liberties had to be temporarily set aside then Confederate leaders proved willing to pursue the interests of the government over individual rights. This does not mean that Jefferson Davis and other Confederate leaders conspired to foist an undemocratic plot on the southern people and force them to participate in a devastating war. Confederate policy was dictated by necessity and the will to survive, and used policies like conscription only as temporary expedients. However, conscription represented the logical policy outcome of an authoritarian Confederate political culture. With respect to extensive military mobilization of society, the Confederacy shared a characteristic with twentieth-century corporatist regimes.

The original call for 100,000 twelve-month volunteers in March 1861 was clearly insufficient to fight a protracted war. Congress bolstered and extended recruitment on August 8, 1861, when it called for 400,000 more volunteers who would be required to serve for between twelve and thirty-six months. This was a stopgap measure to make sure the Confederacy would have enough troops through 1862, but even this measure was not enough. On December 11, 1861, Congress tried to promote extended service among the 1861 volunteers with a reenlistment bonus, or bounty. This enticement included a $50 bounty and a paid sixty-day furlough in exchange for agreement to serve for three years or the duration of the war.[2] After the crushing defeats at Fort Donelson and Shiloh, Confederate leaders realized immediate action was required. Half-measures or further requests for volunteers would not meet the emergency.

A state-level precedent provided some guidance for Confederate conscription. Just as it had taken the lead in secession, South Carolina first implemented compulsory military service and foreshadowed the Confederacy's national draft system. A drastic 1862 shift in South Carolina's governance allowed for conscription to be essentially decreed by state authorities. South Carolina had created an Executive Council during the secession crisis to serve as a cabinet for Governor Francis Pickens that consisted of the lieutenant governor and five members of the secession convention. In 1862 this advisory group was turned into a governing body in response to the Union occupation of Port Royal and to counter growing dissatisfaction with Governor Francis Pickens. The state convention, acting in secret session, created a refurbished Executive Council by a vote of 96 to 23, empowering it with sweeping and largely unchecked powers. The new governing body was comprised of five members including governor Francis Pickens, lieutenant governor W. W. Harlee, and three elected members from the state's secession convention, James Chesnut, Isaac Hayne, and William Gist.[3]

The Executive Council decreed statewide conscription on March 6, 1862. This law forced white males between 18 and 45 years of age to enroll for possible military service. Local enrollment was assisted and enforced by sheriffs and local tax collectors. Information about volunteers already in military service was recorded to facilitate reenlistment. Exemptions were allowed for numerous professions, which was almost identical to later Confederate exemption policy.[4] This was not necessarily a blueprint for Confederate conscription, but South Carolina did anticipate national draft policy. When Confederate authorities created their own conscription system, the Executive Council could simply hand over its enrollment information to the Confederate authorities overseeing nationwide conscription. Another influence from South Carolina on the Confederate government was the head of the Palmetto State's conscription system, John S. Preston, who carried his institutional knowledge into the national system. In an ironic form of state sovereignty, it was the centralized state government of South Carolina, under the Executive Council, that created a working model showing the Confederate government how to implement a system of conscription across the southern states.

On April 16, 1862, the Confederate Congress passed "An Act to further provide for the Public Defence," which created the conscription system. The law authorized the president to call out all eligible white males from 18 to 35 years of age for service of three years or until the war's end. Current soldiers' enlistments were continued for three years from the date of their enrollment, which meant that the rebel volunteers of 1861 would at least serve until 1864. To amend for breaching the original enlistment contract with 1861 volunteers, the act allowed for up to sixty days of paid furlough and travel expenses. For those veterans who had already reenlisted and been furloughed back home, the government promised "in lieu of a furlough the commutation value in money of the transportation" costs granted to furlough recipients. The Confederate government wisely attempted to lessen the impact of the law's authoritarian and coercive nature with paid leave or equivalent compensation.[5]

How could the Confederacy entice white men to serve? The purpose of the April 1862 draft law was not to coerce men to serve in Confederate armies, but instead to strongly encourage voluntary service. The Confederacy did not have sufficient human resources to manage a system like the one in the northern states, which possessed an empowered and ubiquitous Provost Department. Union draft officers, backed by armed soldiers, fanned out across northern congressional districts to enforce the law and enroll Union draftees. The Confederacy could not afford the luxury of posting large numbers of soldiers across southern congressional districts to enforce the law. As a consequence, Confederate draft legislation depended on cooperation between the state and national governments. State militia officers were used to enroll eligible conscripts. Quotas of volunteers were established for each congressional district, and if this number was not met then state militia officers began the process of drafting local men.

Southern governors typically complied and helped to administer national conscription policy. "It shall be lawful," declared the draft act, "for the President, with the consent of the Governors of the respective States, to employ State officers, and on failure to obtain such consent, he shall employ Confederate officers, charged with the duty of making such enrollment." Much historical debate has concerned the resistance of southern governors, but very little attention has been paid to the acquiescence of most states.

Those draftees who did not immediately go to active units were held in reserve without pay. If reserves who were called up for duty "shall willfully refuse to obey said call, each of them shall be" treated by the government as "a deserter and punished as such." The Confederacy asked conscripts to bring their own weapons, and the government was willing to purchase them or to pay $1.00 per month to each soldier who provided his own weapon.[6] The April 16th law was the foundation of the Confederate conscription system and gave the national government unprecedented power over the lives of eligible white men.

The first controversial exemption policy passed Congress on April 21, 1862. Politicians naturally exempted themselves and government officials at both the national and state levels. The law then allowed for a rather liberal number of service exceptions. All postmen, pilots (harbor and river guides), workers engaged in river or railroad transport, ministers with extant congregations, iron workers, coal miners, newspaper printers, and teachers with at least twenty students were not required to enlist. Professors, nurses, managers of textile factories, and pharmacists "now established . . . [and] a practical druggist" were also allowed to sit out the war for now.[7]

The first set of exemptions left too many loopholes. Some eligible men abused the exemption system, and one controversial exemption was for justices of the peace. These officially held state government jobs combined elements of low-level judicial duties and other civil functions. Some citizens felt that exemptions for justices of the peace allowed for otherwise capable young men to shirk their military duties. In August 1862 a citizen named D. W. Hill from Cumberland County, North Carolina, advised his congressman to close the exemption loophole for justices of the peace. Hill knew that the pending draft expansion increased the upper limit of service to 45 years of age and he commented "with regard to justices of the peace we have quite a sufficient number over forty-five to . . . [conduct] all the business in all the counties of this state, or any other state in the Confederacy." To leave this abused exemption untouched, Hill argued, "calculated to engender hard feelings among the soldiers" already enlisted in military service. Another concerned observer wanted his congressman to enlist the younger officials because there were "enough old magistrates to hold all the courts, [and] try all the warrants, [and] marry all that want to get married."[8]

The policy of substitution was also controversial and remains a staple of historians who allege class conflict was a primary weakness in Confederate nationalism. A wealthy draftee could hire a substitute for his military service. The rate for hiring substitutes was based entirely on a market system and was negotiated between the parties. There was no government manipulation like the North's commutation fee where an individual could pay $300 and skip a draft cycle. Southern men were left to their own bargaining skills, and the cost of hiring substitutes could be as high as $3,000, which was a significant sum considering the lowly pay of enlisted rebel soldiers. This paid-for replacement only got the conscript out of one draft, but substitution caused such a political uproar that it was eliminated in December 1863.

Confederate substitution policy was a corollary of conscription and highlights important aspects of southern society at war. The symbolism of substitution was, in many respects, more important than its actual effect on the southern war effort. An estimated 50,000 men, or principals, hired substitutes, a significant source of potential reinforcement for rebel armies. Many historians discuss substitution in terms of the "Rich Man's War, Poor Man's Fight" thesis, which argues that national policies eroded the morale and support of lower-class whites. However, the evidence of class tension based upon Confederate substitution policy was more complicated than implied by the facile slogan "Rich Man's War, Poor Man's Fight."[9]

In the summer of 1862 some southerners realized another draft would be necessary. The Seven Days Campaign saved the Confederate capital from capture but cost the Army of Northern Virginia dearly in precious manpower. Even before the bloodlettings of Second Manassas and Antietam, Ordnance Department head Josiah Gorgas thought that if "volunteers are not forthcoming by the 15th of August then a draft is to be made." This was necessary, according to Gorgas, because "a great tendency has been shown to avoid duty."[10]

On September 27, 1862, the Confederate Congress passed a second round of conscription. This act raised the upper limit of the draft from 35 to 45 years of age. This should have been a concerning sign of troubled times ahead for rebel armies. Some 45-year-old men doubtless made good soldiers, or at least could serve in less demanding departments, replacing younger men sent off to the main armies. In reality, however, most 45-year-old men were simply incapable of the rigorous physical demands of active Civil War campaigns. The second draft assigned the new conscripts to any incomplete state regiments created after the April act and only after those units were full were new regiments to be created.[11]

The second round of exemptions passed on October 11, 1862. Some of the exemptions were state militia troops, essential railroad and telegraph company employees, and one newspaper editor along with essential labor for publication. Congress specifically exempted conscientious objectors from several religious sects like the Quakers, Dunkards, Nazarenes, and

Mennonites, but all eligible males had to either "furnish substitutes or pay a tax of five hundred dollars." Skilled laborers like millers, shoemakers, and blacksmiths had to provide evidence of their productive capabilities, and the government required the exempted artisans to sell their products to the government at 75 percent of cost. After abuse under the first conscription act, one pharmacist "in good standing who is a practical apothecary" could be exempted. Vital munitions factory employees were exempted and to be verified by the Ordnance Department. Miners, salt manufacturers who produced a minimum of twenty bushels a day, and all ironworkers were also allowed to defer service. The most controversial exemption was the twenty-slave clause, which stated that "one person as agent, owner or over-seer on each plantation of twenty negroes" could be exempted in order "to secure the proper police of the country." One exemption, the oldest eligible male, was also allowed for any two plantations within five miles of each other with an aggregate slave population of twenty or higher.[12] The second round of conscription exemptions was a detailed attempt to prevent earlier abuses and to scour the southern states for available manpower without hampering the productive capabilities of the wartime economy.

The twenty-slave exemption was highly controversial and symbolic of the potential class conflicts inside the Confederacy, although the idea of retaining military-age white males on plantations to offset the potential for slave revolts was not a new concept. After the existential crisis of the Stono Rebellion in 1739, the colony of South Carolina passed a law that required "one white man to be present for every ten blacks on a plantation." In March 1862 it was South Carolina again that took the lead in exempting one overseer for every plantation with fifteen or more slaves when state-wide conscription went into effect. The first Confederate conscription law did not exempt overseers, so influential South Carolina politician James Chesnut Jr. lobbied Secretary of War George Wythe Randolph to include an exemption for "one of the most important classes of our people." Chesnut argued that "if the overseers should now be taken, the agricultural indus-try of the State must be immeasurably damaged and diminished."[13] South Carolina took the lead in Confederate conscription policy and set the prec-edent for nationwide exemption of overseers, although the Confederate government temporarily set the minimum number of slaves at twenty as compared to fifteen in the Palmetto State.

On May 1, 1863, the Confederate Congress amended the twenty slave exemption to lessen the implications for class conflict. The exemption for combined plantations within five miles of each other was dropped. To prevent abuse, the law also disallowed exemption for "any farm or plantation on which the negroes have been placed by division" since October 1862 to meet the exemption requirements. In addition, each large-scale slave owner who utilized the exemption was required to pay $500 annually to the government.[14]

In the third round of conscription in February 1864, the twenty-slave minimum was dropped to fifteen. As of January 1, 1864, if a plantation had fifteen or more slaves between 16 and 50 years of age, then one owner or overseer could be exempted. However, this round of exemption required proof of productive slave management in the form of an annual 100-pound delivery of bacon, pork, or beef to the government for each working slave from 16 to 50 years of age. The Confederate government would pay below-market fixed prices for the meat, and if the exempted plantation managers could not furnish the minimum amount of meat, then two-thirds of available grain could be purchased at fixed prices.[15] Therefore each plantation owner or overseer who was exempted in 1864 under the modified fifteen-slave clause would have to prove that his presence on the home front was being put to good use in the form of foodstuff productivity. Class arguments aside, if each exempted large plantation owner or overseer furnished a minimum of 1,500 pounds of meat each year to hungry rebel armies, then these exemptions were of far greater value to the war effort than if he had been conscripted into the infantry.

A valid economic and security argument could be made for retention of the twenty/fifteen–slave exemption, but this particular avenue of conscription evasion still smacked of elitism and continued to elicit cries of a "Rich Man's War, Poor Man's Fight." The total number of service exemptions under the twenty-slave clause was not as important as what the loophole represented for class dialogue.[16]

By January 1863 the Confederate government decided it needed a national organization to oversee the massive task of drafting soldiers, so a Bureau of Conscription was established as a branch of the War Department. The ubiquitous Richmond clerk John Beauchamp Jones was asked to help out with setting up the bureau. Jones pointed out an important fact about the "new bureau"—that it was "created by the military authorities, not by law." The officers put in charge of the new bureau were Brigadier General Gabriel J. Rains and Lieutenant Colonel George W. Lay. Jones noted that Rains was "a most affable officer" but Lay did most of the work. Rains, brother of George Washington Rains at the Augusta Powder Factory, distracted himself with explosive science experiments and became famous, or infamous, for inventing the land mine. Lay worked on conscription issues, and because he was the son-in-law of highly influential War Department scion John D. Campbell, some believed that Campbell directed the Bureau of Conscription through his in-law proxy.[17]

In May 1863 the ineffective Rains was replaced by General Charles Field, who had been seriously wounded at the Battle of Second Manassas. Field temporarily served in the bureau until his return to frontline service. On July 30, 1863, Field was replaced by Colonel John S. Preston, an experienced conscription bureaucrat from South Carolina. It appears that the early months of the Bureau of Conscription from January to July 1863, were largely ineffectual; the bureau was a temporary assignment for officers with no post.

Thanks to his statewide experience with the draft, John S. Preston had been appointed in 1862 to head up Confederate draft implementation in South Carolina. Preston had to reconcile the differences between the state and Confederate laws and their exemption policies, but these were minor obstacles. In each case the governor and Executive Council of South Carolina complied with Preston's requests for troops. In November 1862 Preston informed his superior in Richmond that South Carolina's "authorities most earnestly and promptly tender all reasonable aid in the prosecution of the enrollment." By July 1863 Preston had proved himself as one of the most productive conscription officers and was moved to Richmond to take overall command of the Bureau of Conscription. John S. Preston was eventually commissioned as a brigadier general on June 10, 1864, and during his twenty months of service the Bureau of Conscription had capable leadership and operated more effectively to fill the ranks of rebel armies.[18]

In late 1863 and into early 1864, the Conscription Bureau began to assert itself as a legitimate organizational arm of the War Department. It clarified policy for state officials, and if necessary held them accountable to government enforcement. By 1863 conscription policy was being more comprehensively implemented and the results were substantial. Josiah Gorgas commented that "conscription is rigidly enforced, and stragglers are pretty generally bro't back to their companies . . . [the] system is being established in this vast army of 400,000 men, and it is getting to be manageable."[19]

Despite two rounds of conscription in April and October 1862, disastrous battles in 1863 meant that the Confederacy would be required to sweep the home front for more manpower in 1864. On February 17, 1864, the Confederate Congress passed the third conscription law with updated exemptions. To prepare for the future, Confederate leaders realized that the age limits needed to be expanded and exemptions severely restricted. Eligible males between the ages of 17 and 50 years of age were now required to enroll for military service for the "duration of the war." Dropping the lower limit to 17-year-olds was a depressing admission that the Confederacy was willing to sacrifice its future leaders in exchange for temporary survival. Forty-five-to fifty-year-old conscripts were intended to serve as replacements within the internal security apparatus and release younger men for frontline duty. The pending enrollment of men ages 45 to 50 did not sit well with some. Josiah Gorgas labeled this "unnecessary" and said that middle-aged men should "stay at home to support the fighting portion— supplying all the food, and material of war."[20] Confederate leaders used national power to scour the southern landscape for all available able-bodied white males in a last-ditch attempt to reverse the momentum of the Union war effort in 1864.

The February 1864 conscription law did contain some positive attributes. For example, all noncommissioned officers and privates were promised a $100 bounty to be paid on October 1st, but in 6 percent Confederate bonds. This probably did not inspire many would-be volunteers who, if they were lucky enough to survive until October, were going to be compensated in government bonds. Another positive change was the dissolution of the substitution loophole, which had been eliminated by Congress in December 1863. Religious dissenters were not required to enroll, but they had to pay a fee to avoid conscription.[21]

Confederate nationalists were heartened by the law's crackdown on exemptions. Only the most influential and essential eligible males qualified for exemption in 1864. Many of the October 1862 exemptions were reaffirmed and conditions were restated. For example, medical doctors could be exempted only if they were over 30 years of age, could prove they had been in continual practice for seven years, and were not actually dentists pretending to be physicians. Eligible males in the commissary, quartermaster, ordnance, and navy departments were also targeted for enlistment and replacement with enrollees who had been deemed unfit for frontline service. Railroad employees involved in the essential daily operations of transport, repair, and management were also exempted.[22] The Confederacy faced the difficult task of denuding its human resources to extreme limits without causing a complete breakdown of Confederate society. The February 1864 conscription law and bare necessity exemptions epitomized the Confederate system in survival mode. By 1864 Confederate conscription symbolized how a once ad hoc national policy could mature into a more effective mobilization tool by eliminating superfluous exemptions and combining the strengths of local enforcement with national power. The evolution of conscription policy from 1862 to 1864 is a powerful example of modernization in the Confederate government.[23]

What motivated conscripts and later enlistees to finally join rebel ranks? Was it outright government coercion or a mixture of reward and punishment that compelled less enthusiastic soldiers to finally serve? The motivations of Civil War soldiers have become the object of a cottage industry among some scholars who argue about why young men took up arms. However, until recently the motivations of southern conscripts have remained relatively obscure. The words "later enlistment" and "conscription" do not necessarily carry the same connotation, but they are inextricably linked by their motivations, or lack thereof, to support the rebel war effort. About 120,000 men eventually were conscripted into rebel armies. Some late enlistees accepted the inducement of government bounties to enroll, others hired substitutes, and some reasoned it was better to sign up than to be forced into the army, but ultimately these alleged shirkers based their late decision to support the Confederate war effort on a range of factors.[24] If Confederate conscripts and later enlistees can be faulted with anything, it is that they were too old for hard campaigning and the rigors of a grinding war, and like many other soldiers after the realities of war set in, would rather have stayed at home if given the choice.

Confederate armies could not devote substantial amounts of manpower to conscription enforcement. State governments, despite oft-quoted gubernatorial objections, helped enroll eligible men who were then passed along to the oversight of the Conscription Bureau and sent to military camps for training.

There is one central question concerning the nature of Confederate conscription that historians need to address. Did the draft represent authoritarian government coercion of unwilling participants, or were draftees simply less patriotic than volunteers, merely needing the government nudge of compulsory service? The best answer probably lies somewhere in between these two poles. There is no doubt the Confederacy intended to utilize all eligible white manpower to fill the army's ranks and eventually even authorized enrollment of African American slaves in 1865. To achieve this goal a centralized bureaucracy was required that emanated from the Bureau of Conscription in Richmond down to the individual states. This top-down system was not particularly effective until 1863, but by the end of the war the Confederate government had created an imposing institutional structure in the attempt to provide rebel armies with sufficient manpower.

There is also proof that conscription could not have been carried out without the compliance of the southern states. Contrary to the notorious grievances from southern governors, there appears to have been a general willingness on the part of state leaders to use their own apparatuses to enroll and enforce the law at the local level. To be sure, there were disagreements over specific aspects of the system like exemptions, and there were hyperbolic howls about assaults on state sovereignty, but the Confederate conscription system continued to perform its designed task throughout the war. Local compliance was far more prevalent than the topic's historiography conveys. The conflicts caused by Confederate conscription have received a superordinate share of historical attention, likely because they are simply more interesting than the mundane process of enrolling, drafting, and training of rebel conscripts. More importantly, alleged class conflict over conscription is central to some historians' arguments that the Confederacy was plagued with divisions and lost the war "behind the lines" rather than on the battlefield.[25]

Conscription policy is one of the lynchpins of a top-down and centralized historical interpretation of Confederate political economy. Some economic historians see conscription as the origin of a *command economy* in which the Confederate government indirectly controlled the labor availability of southern industries through a stranglehold on exemption policies. However, the notion of Confederate conscription as an all-encompassing, absolute, centralized power is an oversimplification. The Confederate government may have been moving towards this type of system, but national conscription still required state support and local enforcement. The Confederate government could not enforce the law in all areas of the South, and some pockets of outliers and deserters defied not only national authority but also the local home guard troops sent to uphold the legitimacy of the conscription system.

Union conscription policy, much like its Confederate counterpart, was designed to spur voluntary enrollment, but due to large numbers of draft dodgers and the policies of substitution and commutation, Union conscription was not a highly effective mobilization tool. As historian James McPherson correctly questions, "What kind of conscription was this, in which only 7 percent of the men whose names were drawn actually served? The answer: it was not conscription at all, but a clumsy carrot and stick device to stimulate volunteering." Historian James W. Geary assessed the historiography of northern conscription and made several important analytical points that might also be considered when assessing Confederate conscription. Geary notes that "evasion, resistance, and general discontent with the draft might be attributed more to a sense of isolation from the national destiny than as a response to class distinctions." As a result, Geary argues, "the belief that the Civil War was 'a rich man's war and a poor man's fight' should no longer be accepted at face value."[26] The argument that northern conscription generated excessive class conflict is dubious given the total number of draftees who actually served in the military.

Abundant circumstantial evidence highlights the similarities of Confederate conscription to other modern draft policies, but the rebel conscription system was created entirely as an expedient for survival. In the late nineteenth and early twentieth centuries other corporatist governments utilized peacetime conscription to prepare for imminent war or initiated a draft policy when profligate wars lasted longer than expected. The Confederacy was forced to create a rudimentary conscription system that operated more effectively as bureaucratic experience increased, but it was still an expedient necessity that never fully developed into an efficient draft system like its more modern counterparts. However, Confederate conscription did set an important precedent in American history for how a corporatist state might implement a draft, a lesson that would not be lost on future American leaders in wartime.

The Confederacy developed and managed a complex domestic passport system to regulate internal transportation. The original purpose of the passport system was to ensure that troops stayed with their commands at the front, but the Provost Department simultaneously developed a domestic passport network to oversee civilian travel. The task of creating a domestic passport system to regulate internal transportation was an ambitious undertaking. Over the course of the war, many Confederate citizens became upset with this system, but in important ways the South was well prepared to create an internal pass system due to its long experience with slavery.

Across the antebellum South, slaves were usually required to obtain their master's written permission to travel even short distances and often to have a brief declaration of purpose. This slave control system remained intact in the Confederacy as witnessed by the large number of passport requests from masters listed as "Negroes" in the Richmond Passport Office files.[27] Confederate cities continued the antebellum regulation of slave travel through passport systems even as the peculiar institution eroded in less controllable areas. The desire to keep track of the comings and goings of slaves, especially when in close proximity to Union lines, continued as a wartime necessity, but the Confederate government also established a passport system to oversee the travel of white citizens, which caused remonstrance from some southern civilians.

The government bureaucracy that regulated the domestic passport system was the multitasked Provost Department. As a division of the War Department, the provost section was both an executive and military entity that evolved into a regulatory agency over civilian travel. The original task of the Provost Department was to make sure that rebel soldiers did not take unauthorized leave from their respective armies. Confederate soldiers were always required to obtain permission to be away from their commands, whether it be a thirty-day furlough or a brief visit to a nearby city, but inevitably some troops took "French leave" and traveled without authorization. This nonsanctioned travel weakened armies and proved particularly vexing in cities near the front lines like Richmond, where provost officers almost daily rounded up rebel soldiers hoping to temporarily enjoy the temptations of the capital city. Thus a primary function of the Provost Department was to arrest and rejoin soldiers with their units at the front. The provosts performed a pivotal enforcement role in the attempt to maintain frontline manpower by making sure that all enlisted soldiers reported back to their commands. Regulating the travel of soldiers was a legitimate function of the War Department, and the provost marshal's enforcement powers were usually not questioned by army officers.[28]

In addition to the military system to control soldier movements, the Provost Department also developed a domestic passport network to oversee civilian travel. One might assume that the domestic passport system was implemented late in the war to enforce conscription and prevent desertion, but it was actually created in July 1861 in response to citizens' requests to visit family members at the front. A passport officer recalled that in 1861, "applications to the then Secretary of War, [Leroy Pope] Walker, were frequently made by officers and citizens, having relatives in the army, for passports . . . and it was common, also, for citizens, desirous of going to different sections of the Confederacy, to ask for passports to facilitate traveling [and] passing pickets."[29] Early in the war passports were voluntarily sought by prospective travelers, but eventually the pass network evolved into an interconnected grid of checkpoints to monitor the southern home front.

The domestic passport system was initially implemented in regions threatened by Union armies along the Confederate periphery and later spread to the southern home front. No centralized plan emanated from Richmond bureaucrats; in fact, the capital city symbolized just another important security concern along the outer edge of Confederate control. Local commanders developed their own passport offices in a "grass roots" manner with only limited advisement from Richmond. It was not until 1864 that the War Department eventually attempted development of a coherent nationwide passport policy.

On October 28, 1861, General Benjamin Huger, commander of the strategically important region around Norfolk, Virginia, sought clarification from the War Department on what to do with disloyal citizens. Huger asked, "who is to determine who are our enemies . . . and who is to arrest them and how are they to be punished?" Secretary of War Judah P. Benjamin responded, "Put them all in prison as prisoners of war and . . . send the men [to Richmond] as such. Write to same effect to passport clerk." On March 6, 1862, the Norfolk area passport system became fully operational. Provost Marshal W. A. Parham declared that after "10 o'clock p.m. sentinels will begin to challenge all passers. All persons of every degree without a countersign or a written pass, signed by the provost-marshal . . . will be arrested and carried before the captain of the guard for examination." Given the proximity of Union blockaders and the constant threat of amphibious assault, military authorities required "persons desiring to leave the district . . . will be required to give one day's notice to the provost-marshal," and officials reminded potential civilian travelers that "sentinels around the cities and district will suffer none to pass upon any pretext, and will arrest any attempting to go without the written passport of the provost-marshal."[30]

Creation of a passport system under such circumstances was tolerated by loyal Confederate civilians and represented a common sense solution to prevent espionage. Thus it was no surprise that the domestic passport system evolved on the outer rim of the Confederacy under the aegis of nervous military department commanders wary of Yankee attacks. Early in the conflict the War Department was more concerned with assisting local commanders with pressing protective duties than implementing a "top-down" hierarchy of rules for passport offices. The basic philosophy of leaders in Richmond seemed to be to arrest all overtly disloyal people, and a more comprehensive passport policy could be developed later.

Other department commanders under imminent threat of Union attack also instituted passport systems and appointed provosts to substantiate citizen loyalty. In March 1862 General Mansfield Lovell created a provost network in New Orleans and the surrounding parishes of Jefferson, Saint Bernard, and Plaquemines. He ordered "a system of registry and passport" to be created and declared that no one would "be permitted to sojourn in the . . . parishes without satisfying the provost marshals of their loyalty." In addition to Louisianans bearing the burden of proof for their own loyalty, Lovell asked "all good citizens . . . to report to those [provost] officers all who are suspected of hostility to the government." In a theme that became familiar throughout the Confederacy, provost officials were not simply confirming loyalty among travel applicants; they also encouraged loyal Confederates to become informants against those who might betray the nation. In remote areas like the Trans-Mississippi, passport systems were more dependent on local judgment and knowledge. In May 1862 Colonel George Flournoy requested advice on the status of disloyal persons. Brigadier General Paul Octave Hebert responded from his Houston, Texas headquarters in a blunt fashion: "Passport system not yet established. You can arrest, place in confinement or turn back any person you deem suspicious."[31] The impetus for a domestic passport system was spurred by the immediate necessities of military department commanders and only later evolved into a more expansive bureaucratic network based in Richmond.

As with so many other Confederate systems that were eventually implemented, there was very little planning or prior thought given to domestic passports. In fact, War Department clerk J. B. Jones recalled "that the origin of the passport office consisted merely in a verbal order from the first Secretary of War [Leroy Pope Walker]" and that he "was requested to take charge of the office . . . in August 1861." Jones remarked on the lax standards in the early months of the war and stated that "up to the time of the declaration of martial law [in March 1862], the passport system was not compulsory, [and] a very large proportion of citizens voluntarily applied for and received passports." At the outset, no written orders or regulations were provided to the passport office clerks. This absence of standard written procedure caused some citizens and politicians to cry foul about the arbitrary abuse of civil rights by government officials, but also allowed for plausible deniability by the War Department in the event of harsh criticism. Jones remained in service at the passport office and was later ordered by the new Secretary of War Judah P. Benjamin "to act under the instructions of Brigadier General [John] Winder,"[32] head of the Provost Department. It was Winder's leadership that turned the passport office into an effective regulatory tool over Richmond travelers and later over civilians throughout the Confederacy.

In March 1862 the Provost Department assumed responsibility over the passport system. Brigadier General John H. Winder commanded the Confederacy's Provost Department, but in 1861 he only served as the head of law enforcement in the rebel capital. Winder eventually oversaw the various provost offices throughout the South and the notorious Confederate prison system in 1864, which made him one of the most controversial characters of the Civil War. A native of Maryland, Winder spent most of his adult life in the military. He taught tactics at West Point in the 1820s and later served with distinction in the Mexican War. After the Civil War broke out, Winder resigned from the U.S. Army and was commissioned as a brigadier general in the Confederacy, assigned to head the Provost Department in Richmond. [33]

Due to his internal policing duties, Winder became one of the most vilified government officials in the South, and as the war progressed, Winder was accused of favoritism and corruption. After Jefferson Davis declared martial law in Richmond on March 1, 1862, Winder instituted a more stringent military-style process for passport applicants. The main targets of Winder's provost marshals were army deserters, but he could also detain alleged civilian criminals. [34] In the early months, civilians and government officials viewed Winder's department as a necessary addition to the policing apparatus of the Confederate capital.

The Provost Department established a Richmond passport office to begin its duties. War Department clerk J. B. Jones temporarily assisted with operations and noticed that "Winder has established a guard with fixed bayonets at the door of the passport office." Richmond citizens were required to apply in person at the often overcrowded facility. Jones observed that guards "let in only a few at a time, and these, when they get their passports, pass out by the rear door, it being impossible for them to return through the crowd." This horde of one-way traffic suggests that detectives only lightly inspected individual applicants. On March 12, 1862, the passport office was relocated to the corner of Ninth and Broad Streets. Jones described the building as "filthy" and the office "was inhabited . . . by [Winder's] rowdy clerks." According to Jones, four provost clerks, all Maryland natives, filled out the forms, which then required Jones's approval. [35] It could hardly be expected that such a limited and overworked staff could successfully identify disloyal elements among the throng of passport applicants. For example, Union spy Elizabeth Van Lew secured a passport in early 1862 and used her travel permission to collect information. However, this seemingly confused mass of personal information being collected daily by provost departments across the South was essential for the transition of the domestic passport system from a local monitoring system into a national internal policing apparatus.

One of the fundamental purposes of the passport system was to make a basic judgment about an applicant's loyalty to the Confederacy. This visceral decision by the detectives at the passport office might mean the difference between permission to travel, or arrest. To be sure, passport officials did not have sufficient time or manpower to scrutinize every request, but at least military authorities could look passport applicants in the eye and make a quick decision about a traveler's intent.

Across the Confederacy passport officers and provost guards continually assessed loyalty. Passport applications frequently contained proclamations and attestations of allegiance to the southern cause. For example, Richmond citizen Lewis P. Chamberlayne penned a passport application on behalf of "Mrs. Virginia Pendleton (wife of James Pendleton) of this city, a loyal citizen," and sought to gain travel permission "for herself and three children and a servant girl." Chamberlayne confirmed that "Mrs. P has been a resident of Richmond for several years and is unquestionably loyal to the Confederacy."[36] Influential citizens of confirmed loyalty could greatly enhance an applicant's chances for securing a travel permit.

Domestic passports contained prewritten loyalty oaths that theoretically bound the traveler to patriotic behavior. H. C. Price, provost marshal for Lynchburg, Virginia, signed a pass on December 13, 1864, for "Dr. W. Waugh to visit Richmond." The attestation of loyalty on Dr. Waugh's pass was similar to others issued throughout the Confederacy. The standard pledge stated:

> By authority of the Secretary of War, permission is hereby granted to _____ to visit _____ upon honor not to communicate in writing or verbally, for publication, any fact ascertained, which, if known to the enemy, might be injurious to the Confederate States of America. (subject to the discretion of the military authorities)

Passports issued from Richmond contained the same oath, and on the reverse side an additional supporting statement of loyalty had to be signed by the traveler and cosigned by the issuing passport officer. This oath stated:

I _____, do solemnly swear or affirm, that I will bear true faith and yield obedience to the Confederate States of America, and that I will serve them honestly and faithfully against their enemies.[37]

At the very least the mandatory loyalty oath forced travelers to continually reaffirm their patriotism, but on a more functional level the oath allowed provosts to arrest anyone suspected of breaching that oath and served as a powerful warning to anyone considering aiding the enemy.

Well-known institutions in Richmond could use their considerable reputations to smooth the passport process at the Richmond office. The Tredegar Iron Works frequently requested passes for business purposes. For example, company representative W. P. Woodroof requested a pass for "R. L. Wilkerson to visit Lexington, Va," in which Woodroof served as proxy for influential company owner Joseph Anderson. Family connections apparently had more privileges. On the same day that middle manager Woodroof supported Wilkerson's pass, Anderson took the time to pen a passport request for his "daughter Ellen and son Joseph R. Anderson Jr., to go to Rockbridge County." Other reputable establishments like the Ballard House and the Spotswood Hotels catered to their guests' inconvenient but required interaction with the Richmond passport office. In 1864 both the Spotswood and Ballard House Hotels, along with the Tredegar Iron Works, printed their own blank passports with open spaces for name, destination, and the signature of management, to expedite the process at the Richmond passport office. By 1864 the passport clerks were able to instantly recognize the recommendations of powerful local institutions and frequent travelers who had been previously verified.[38]

Southerners without influential connections who hoped to avoid the bureaucratic inconvenience of the local passport office appealed directly to the secretary of war. In July 1864 Maryland native Albert Tolson requested permission to return home. Tolson had dropped out of school at age 16, joined the Beauregard Rifles in April 1861, and then transferred to the 1st Maryland Artillery. Tolson was "severely and dangerously wounded at Chancellorsville" and was hospitalized for a long period, after which he "applied for light duty." In the spring of 1864 Tolson returned to his command, "where he was placed on the lightest duty possible," but now he "experienced considerable pain and uneasiness . . . the wounded parts breaking out into sores every few weeks." The young Marylander doubted his ability "to perform military duty" and requested "to return home in order to go again to school to complete his education." Tolson reminded officials that he was "entitled to his discharge from the service by reason of the expiration of the period for which he enlisted—3 years" and furthermore swore that he was "loyal to the Confederate cause and [would] not . . . communicate" with the enemy. The supplicant attached a corroborating document from the "Clerks of the Second Auditors Office, Treasury Dept" signed by C. S. Kuch, which confirmed the young man's loyalty and service and supported his passport application.[39]

On rare occasions, passport permission descended the chain of command from the secretary of war to the Passport Office. In January 1865 Major Isaac H. Carrington, provost marshal in Richmond, ordered pickets to allow passage for "Susan Marshal & her daughter Mary . . . to proceed by Charles City Road to their homes with the object of removing their effects." Carrington gave instructions that "the Sec. of War directs me to refer their application to the officer commanding the pickets on that road [and] if their statement be correct, they will be allowed to pass for the object alleged." After minor skepticism and apparently without serious investigation, the women were allowed to bypass the normal application process and successfully appealed directly to the secretary of war.[40]

Some rebel officers apparently believed the passport system did not apply to their movements and were rudely reminded by the Provost Department that travel permission was required by everyone. In early 1864 a rebel officer named Pegram received a scathing rebuke after testing the resolve of Major Elias Griswold in the Richmond passport office. This exchange showed the supreme authority of the provost officers and the source of power from which that authority emanated. Griswold lectured Pegram that he "received distinct and plain orders some time ago . . . that no persons were to pass out of the City without a passport signed in the original hand of the President, the Secretary of War, Brig. Gen. Winder, or one from the passport office under my charge." Griswold explained that to prevent forged passes, "the original signatures of these officials are kept here and distinct orders given to Detective Officers to recognize no others." Griswold obstinately declared that passport officials would continue to "refuse to let persons pass upon permits signed by the Adjutant and Aid[e]s," and if the plaintiff disagreed, then he should have "this question be definitely decided by written order."[41] Obviously Major Griswold was a seasoned veteran when facing an entitled officer who thought he might circumvent the passport process. Griswold had no problem sending this complaint up the chain of command because he knew it would be decided in his favor.

Investigation of the day-to-day operations at the Richmond passport office gives one a glimpse into the method and mindset of the Confederate bureaucracy. Major Isaac H. Carrington headed the Richmond Provost Department, which included direction of the capital city's passport office, where he oversaw a small group of detectives and clerks. Carrington reported directly to Brigadier General John Winder, head of all Confederate provost marshals. Carrington and his subordinates at the Richmond passport office were a direct source of intelligence. Major Carrington and the passport clerks provided Winder and the War Department with personal information about the comings and goings of citizens in the Confederacy's most important urban area. By forcing citizens to obtain passports, Carrington's office could collect and assess information on the frequency and purpose of travel and could also make queries into loyalty.

The passport office was provided with a finite number of permits each day to distribute to applicants. The number of applications was set, or at least approved, by General Winder, and implemented through the office of Major Carrington, head provost of the Richmond area. It is likely that Carrington originated the daily quota and merely got Winder's approval on a periodic basis to conform with travel expectations. A sample of the pass quotas allowed by the Richmond passport office from March 1862 and March 1864 provides an excellent glimpse into the inner workings of the system, and reveals how the Richmond passport system changed over the course of the war.

An examination of the five-day period from March 8th to March 12th in 1862 indicates that passes were divided among several categories so that the passport clerks could record who was traveling on particular routes: railroads, turnpikes, or riverboat. For example, on Saturday, March 8th, the pass quota sheet resembled a simple list with limited travel modes, which combined for a relatively low total number of passes available (Table1).

TABLE 1. Quota of Travel Passes,
Richmond, March 8, 1862

Turnpikes	150
York River RR	50
Packet Boat	100
Total	300

On Sunday, March 9th, a more comprehensive list of travel routes was available to passport applicants and the number of possible travelers also increased (Table 2).

TABLE 2. Quota of Travel Passes,
Richmond, March 9, 1862

Central RR	200
Petersburg RR	300
Danville RR	200
Fredericksburg RR	50
York River	50
Packet Boat	50
Turnpike	50
Total	900

Over the next three days the routes for travel options were roughly the same, but there was no listing for "Packet Boat" for Monday, March 10th, when a total of 950 passes were allowed. On March 11th, 1,325 passes were available, followed by an increase to 2,125 on March 12th.[42] Over this five-day period, from Saturday to Wednesday, a total of 5,600 travel permits were allotted by the Richmond passport office, an average of 1,120 per day. It is important to point out that records for this period only show the number of obtainable passports, not the actual number issued, but given the multitude of applicants and the chaotic conditions in the passport office reported by interim clerk J. B. Jones, in-depth scrutiny was unlikely and so travel permits were probably casually granted to applicants. Since Richmond's population was about 38,000 in 1860 and growing with an influx of refugees and government employees in 1862, it seemed to be relatively easy to acquire a passport in the rebel capital during the first two years of the war.

By March 1864 the Richmond passport system had evolved into a more detail-oriented bureaucracy more capable of screening applicants and selectively issuing travel permits. Circumstances in the Confederate capital had changed since 1862. In addition to the influx of southern refugees and wartime workers, the swelling population of Union prisoners of war meant that Richmond was overcrowded with strangers, which correspondingly increased the importance of the passport system. Union prisoners on Belle Isle and in Libby Prison posed a potential internal threat, as witnessed by a prisoner escape from Libby Prison in February 1864. To alleviate the menace of prison breaks and to lessen the amount of food imports into the city, thousands of Union prisoners on Belle Isle were ordered to be transported to a new facility in southwestern Georgia called Camp Sumter, later known as the infamous prison Andersonville. In addition to this possible internal threat, Confederates had recently turned back the notorious Dahlgren Raid of late February and early March, which sought to release Union prisoners, burn Richmond, and allegedly assassinate rebel leaders. The desperate and dangerous times of 1864 witnessed a bureaucratic shift to stricter security measures in and around Richmond by Carrington's Provost Department. In 1864 every applicant was a possible spy, escaped Union prisoner, or Confederate deserter, and all persons moving around the capital deserved intense scrutiny before being permitted to travel.

By March 1864 the Richmond passport office operated a more detailed permit system. The first major change was the periodic addition of a heading alongside the possible routes, but the new column of "Ladies" described the type of traveler and not the route. Another column titled "Negroes" also described the traveler instead of the route and was added by 1865. The motivation for adding these two specific categories is unclear. Were women and slaves viewed as more or less of a security threat? The new categories were likely created for functional reasons. "Ladies" passports allowed for widows and female visitors to gain access to the capital city and then return to their homes while the "Negroes" column acknowledged the fact that slaves needed to travel in and around Richmond to conduct important business on behalf of their owners. Richmond's passport records are filled with slave owners' requests, typically on small scraps of paper, to allow their "Negroes" to travel for business purposes. The addition of these two passport columns does not prove that rebel authorities viewed travel by these groups as bearing less scrutiny, but officials simply recognized the fact that daily duties in the Confederate capital required travel by women and African American slaves.

On January 12, 1864, Virginia representative Muscoe R. H. Garnett offered a resolution in the House of Representatives that requested more information about domestic passport operations. Members of the lower chamber unanimously asked President Davis "to communicate any orders or regulations establishing a domestic passport system for citizens," and more importantly for the prerogatives of the legislative branch, "the authority under which such order or regulations are made." The House also sought detailed information about "the number and compensation of the officers and men employed in administering and enforcing such system of domestic passports."[43] Congressman Garnett died of typhoid in February before the final report was delivered to the House, but his colleagues eventually read a report filled with plausible deniability and the accretion of power by the War Department.

The chain of reports compiled by President Davis in late January began with Secretary of War James Seddon. Consistent with early implementation of passport systems, Seddon told Davis that "no orders . . . are to be found establishing or regulating the system of passports now in use." Seddon showed a remarkable lack of knowledge about such a large and important bureaucratic network in his department. He promised to seek further information from Provost Department chief Brigadier General Winder, but for now Seddon could only give his best guess about the origins of the domestic passport system. Information about the Richmond pass system was readily available, but "in other cities and towns of the Confederacy," Seddon remarked, the domestic passport network "has been under the control and direction of the military authorities, and its supervision has been. . . . entrusted to provost marshals." Seddon either would not or could not provide information about the creation of the system. He speculated that "its development through the country was probably due to the proclamations for the suspension of the writ of habeas corpus, and the necessity . . . to restrain stragglers and deserters . . . and to detect spies." Despite his alleged lack of information about the system's evolution, Seddon admitted that "the habit of requiring all persons to obtain passports became general, and, with all its inconveniences, has been productive of beneficial consequences." In effect, Seddon claimed ignorance of the domestic passport system's implementation and passed responsibility down the chain of command in case Congress needed a scapegoat.[44]

Head of the Provost Department John Winder ordered a report from Major Elias Griswold, Richmond's provost marshal. Griswold delivered a brief history but confessed he "had no personal knowledge of the orders or regulations establishing a domestic passport system." Griswold had begun his duties in May 1862, so he sought and received information from J. B. Jones about the early months of the system's operation. Jones told Griswold the initial orders for establishment were "verbal, and that, up to the time of the declaration of martial law, the passport system was not compulsory" and "citizens voluntarily applied." Griswold reaffirmed the March 1862 orders requiring passports in the Richmond area, but he could not provide details on "what ways the system originated in other parts of the Confederacy . . . other than it followed the declaration of martial law." Griswold declared that his office had "no control of the system beyond the limits of the Department."[45] Griswold did not mention Brigadier General John Winder's capabilities as head of the Provost Department for the entire Confederacy, although Winder could access the various local provost officers for information, issue orders, and impose regulations.

Major Griswold provided the most detailed explanation of the domestic passport system's internal operations for the edification of the House of Representatives. The domestic passport network typically consisted of a contingent provost "guard, not more than five at any one train, with a non-commissioned officer . . . at the depots of the different railroads to inspect passports, and prevent any one leaving who [does] not [have] a passport." Griswold estimated there were "issued from the passport office, daily, an average of one thousand three hundred and fifty passports [but] at times it reaches a number much larger." The accounting process was very precise, and each passport required receipt confirmation from the clerks. The permits were "signed by a clerk," cosigned by Griswold, and "then delivered to a commissioned officer in charge of the clerks . . . who receipts for them and distributes them to the clerks taking their receipts." At each step of the internal distribution process the passports were carefully accounted for to prevent fraud. Griswold explained the strict oversight process and stated that even "when the clerks are relieved from duty by others, they account for all passports issued and cancelled, and return those not issued, a report of which is daily made to me, and daily compared with the receipts."[46] This orderly process discouraged clerks from being careless with travel permits and held them accountable for any discrepancies.

Major Griswold also described the day-to-day operations of the Richmond passport office. To maximize accumulated knowledge among clerks, Griswold decided "to assign one clerk to each of the main roads." To accommodate permit seekers, "there [were] office hours named [but] the office [was] never closed in the day nor at night, as long as any applicant remains in the vicinity of the office desiring a passport." However, the passport office closed at the end of posted hours if no one was waiting for a permit. Former artillery officer Captain John J. Ancell assumed leadership of office operations on November 17, 1863, and he reported directly to Major Isaac H. Carrington of the Provost Department. Other officers assigned to the passport office in 1863 included William T. Kelly, who was responsible for signing passports. Major Carrington noted that "Kelly . . . signs my name to passports . . . his signature of my name has been sent to all the Provost Marshals in the Confederate States." After Kelly signed the passports, "he delivers [them] . . . to Capt. Ancell . . . taking his receipt," after which "Capt. Ancell delivers them to the squads and reports daily the number used." Two other former artillery officers and fellow Virginians, Captain C. T. Huckstess and Lieutenant T. U. Smith, assisted with oversight of the clerks and office management. The clerks interacted with applicants and were the face of the system to southern citizens. In 1864 the Richmond passport office employed sixteen clerks, four hailing from Maryland, ten from Virginia, one from Louisiana, and one from Spain. The widespread rumor that the passport office was filled with Marylanders shirking their military duties was statistically a myth. Clerks received a salary of $250 per month and worked in shifts to allow for continuity and to accommodate peak hours of requests. Major Carrington described the office's labor organization:

> The clerks are divided into two squads of eight each. Capt. Huckstess and Lt. Smith each being in command of a squad. Squad No. 1 goes on

duty at 2 ½ pm, remains on duty until 9 pm—again from 6 to 7am and from 8am to 2 ½ pm. Squad No. 2 goes on duty at 2 ½ pm and remains on duty for the same periods for the succeeding 24 hours.

These daily routines resulted in thousands of passports being issued each week, and every single pass needed to be accounted for, so "at the expiration of each week, the account of Capt. Ancell is settled, the number of passports on hand counted, and the register of passes examined." Despite the allegations of politicians and popular rumors, the Richmond passport office appeared to have been a well-organized and well-managed bureaucracy.[47]

By 1864 the major change in Richmond's passport policy reflected an increase in denied requests. The 1862 records had only shown the number of daily passports allowed, presumably issued under relatively lax standards. More detailed records emerged for 1864–1865, showing not only the passports available each day, but also indicating the exact number issued, the number denied, and the unissued passes returned to the Provost Department. For example, Chief of the Richmond passport office John Ancell filed a detailed ledger-like "week ending" report to Major Griswold of the Provost Department on March 14, 1864 (Table 3).

TABLE 3. Breakdown of Number of Passes, Richmond, March 14, 1864

Passes Received		8200
Passes Issued	6301	
Passed Canceled	118	
Total Out	6419	6419
On Hand This Day		1781
Returned to W. T. Kelly per Receipt		1781

A strict daily and weekly accounting of all passes issued, canceled, and returned was common practice by 1864, and more oversight of passport issuance became the norm. When a miscalculation occurred, inquiry from the Provost Department was inevitable. On March 22, 1864, Major Carrington notified the passport office that "there is an error in the column of ladies passports—the discrepancy on the Danville route must be explained so as to show who is chargeable with the deficit & the reason." A reply on the same notification was returned to Carrington "with the explanation [that] the three short in the Danville [rail] road was the result of miscounting" and duly corrected by the passport clerks.[48] Every single travel permit among the several thousand issued each week had to be accounted for, including the increasing number of cancelled or denied passes that also counted towards the weekly totals.

The daily records of the passport office in March 1864 reflected a more detailed process for recording travel permits. A look at the records from Saturday, March 12th, through Monday, March 14th, provides a glimpse into the daily operations of the Richmond passport office. For example, the daily record for Sunday, March 13th, showed an expanded list (Table 4).

TABLE 4. Breakdown of Number of Passes, Richmond, March 13, 1864

Route	Rec'd	Signatures	Issued	Marked	On Hand	Totals	Remarks
Ladies	35		4	0	31	35	
Petersburg RR	10		10	0	0	10	
Central RR	20		15	0	5	20	
Danville RR	30		24	0	6	30	
Fredericksburg RR	20		12	0	8	20	
York River RR	10		3	0	7	10	
Turnpikes	20		11	0	9	20	
Packets	10		6	0	4	10	

Of the 155 passports available on March 13th, only 85 were issued to applicants, so only about 55 percent of the possible permits were given to citizens. The column of "Marked" passes indicated requests that were denied or canceled by officers, and although no one was refused a permit on March 13th, the number of "marked" passes counted towards the daily allowance totals. That meant that if a pass was denied it was not recombined with the per diem passes allowed and was counted as part of the daily allotment.

The figures for the three-day period from Saturday, March 12, through Monday, March 14, provide a broader look at operations (Table 5).

TABLE 5. Breakdown of Number of Passes, Richmond, Totals for March 12–14, 1864

Route	Rec'd	Signatures	Issued	Marked	On Hand	Totals	Remarks
Ladies	260		178	6	76	260	
Petersburg RR	335		310	8	17	335	
Central RR	220		208	2	10	220	
Danville RR	205		195	3	7	205	
Fredericksburg RR	145		144	1	0	145	
York River RR	50		42	1	7	50	
Turnpikes	150		115	2	33	150	
Packet Boats	100		31	1	68	100	

Over this three-day period, of the 1,465 passes available, 83.48 percent were issued to travelers, 1.63 percent were marked or denied, and 14.88 percent were left "on hand" or unused.[49] At first glance, the office's denial rate of 1.63 percent does not indicate an overly strict scrutiny, but if one considers that some of the unused passes represented citizens who did not even try to obtain passports due to questionable loyalty or previous elimination, then one gets a better sense of the system's effectiveness. Even if only 1 percent of applicants was suspected, questioned, and denied each week, over three years a comprehensive list of forbidden travelers could be accumulated. Over the course of the war, passport officers faced a constant influx of new faces of refugees, workers, and soldiers heading to and from the front, but given enough time they could eventually sort through them and categorize travelers as either eligible or ineligible. By 1864 passport offices had collected enough information on suspect individuals to deny them immediately. Conversely, some of the 83.48 percent of applicants issued passes were frequent travelers whose loyalty and intentions had already been validated. Over time the passport officers' duties of confirmation or denial of applications became simplified through experience. The Confederate domestic passport system might be described as a rudimentary version of modern data collection systems that differentiate modern travelers between "frequent fliers" and the "no-fly" list. Although Confederate methods were tedious and painstaking, the goals were identical to present-day collection of travel data in order to ascertain motive and to be more capable of distinguishing between potential threats and the regular travels of loyal citizens.

To prevent impostor fraud among applicants, each travel permit listed several physical features about the prospective traveler. Provost guards across the Confederacy listed the applicant's age, eye color, hair color, complexion, and height, and some offices added place of birth and current residence. For example, domestic passport "No. 36,410" issued by the Atlanta Provost department to "Rev. E. Lewiston" in September 1863 noted his destination of "Wilmington, N.C.," followed by the customary loyalty oath, and then the physical description. In Lewiston's case, the thirty-two-year-old minister had "hazel" eyes, "dark" hair, a "Lt" (light) complexion, and was six feet tall. Reverend Lewiston's land of nativity was "Ireland" but he currently resided in "Yo[u]ngsboro, Ala."[50] Domestic passports issued in the Richmond office also contained such personal physical descriptions. Passport clerks could authenticate travelers with previous descriptions as long as they were able to match the names and physical descriptions. In an age before widespread photographic evidence of identity, this was a painstaking way to make sure the applicants actually were who they claimed to be. It was required that southern travelers match the physical description written down by the originating passport clerk. If not, the individual was open to immediate arrest by provost guards at any point in the transportation network. Although it was never completely organized and implemented, the Confederate Provost Department compiled a vast amount of personal data about citizens to be used for purposes of rooting out disloyalty. This systematized method of information collection, though never reaching its full potential, was a powerful symbol of the Confederate government's nascent modernism.

Members of Congress debated the efficacy of the domestic passport system. The unapproved implementation of the network offended the political sensibilities of some congressmen because the legislative branch had not been properly consulted, aside from the perfunctory request for War Department appropriations. Some congressional members expected preferential treatment when traveling or at least not having to be submitted to the indignities of asking permission. In early August 1862 when Texas representative Franklin Sexton traveled to Richmond, he noted he had been "stopped at the lines by a guard [and] only got through by whispering in the ears of the officer that [he] was 'M.C.,'" apparently code for being a member of Congress. Another Texas congressman, Williamson Oldham, complained that he "was not allowed to go from here to North Carolina without going to the Provost Marshal's office and getting a pass like a free Negro." Oldham was disturbed that internal transportation had been subjected to military oversight and "thought the provost marshals should be abolished."[51]

It was doubtful if Congress even possessed the power to dismantle the domestic passport system, and this only further frustrated congressional critics. On August 25, 1862, Mississippi senator Albert Gallatin Brown complained that the Richmond provost marshal had the "power to burst open the trunks of respectable gentlemen," and when the senator attempted to visit the provost's office, a "blackguard told him he did not care who or what he was, but that if he did not go off he would run his bayonet through him." In October 1862 Georgia senator John W. Lewis, appointed by ardent states' rights governor Joseph Brown, wanted the "Judiciary Committee to inquire into the extent of the legal right which the military authorities have in putting restrictions upon . . . citizens of the Confederate States in traveling from one section to another." Lewis excoriated the passport system and provided a detailed description of the intimidating bureaucratic web that Confederate citizens were required to navigate in order to travel:

> When Congress shall adjourn I wish to go home, but before I can be permitted to do so I must get someone who can identify me to go along with me to the Provost Marshal's office to enable me to get a pass. At the Provost's I shall be met at the door by a soldier with a bayonet. After getting the pass, I shall again be met at the cars by other soldiers with bayonets, who will demand to see my pass. The conductor must then see my pass. At other towns along my route I must be confronted by other armed men, and be obliged to obtain other passes and undergo other examinations.

Lewis further criticized the passport system for "the expense," and he worried that military regulation of civilian mobility was "having the effect of alienating . . . the Government [from] the affections of the people." Senator Lewis touched upon a larger issue when he stated that some southerners "are beginning to doubt whether they are really gaining much by this revolution." Lewis reminded his colleagues, "All I have is embarked in this great contest . . . [and] my two sons are either in the army or in their graves; and it does not seem to me either just or proper that I cannot be permitted to go from this city to my home without obtaining a pass like a negro."[52] Part of this congressional protest came from a sense of entitlement in which legislators believed themselves above such petty harassment, but there was also genuine outrage against the passport system. Congressmen ultimately heard constituents and were asked to reform or remove the system, but this was unlikely since the network of provosts was directed by the War Department.

Another reason for congressional disapproval was jealousy of power. The entire system was created outside the realm of congressional approval and represented a potential threat to the powers of the Confederate legislative branch. Personal egos aside, the domestic passport system symbolized a crucial step towards government centralization under the auspices of the executive branch. Congressmen did little more than register vocal complaints about the system. The domestic passport system was proof that the executive branch could implement civil liberty restrictions despite the pusillanimous objections of a Congress that was only needed for purposes of tacit assent.

Perhaps to allay the complaints of both congressmen and local citizens, President Davis and Richmond mayor Joseph Mayo both dutifully sought passports on August 20, 1863. Although "the passport office was besieged . . . by large crowds of persons soliciting permissions to leave the city," the two political leaders requested and obtained travel passes to Chesterfield County alongside fellow Richmonders.[53] This symbolic gesture showed that no individual, no matter how powerful, could skip passport requirements. After this symbolic episode, President Davis could advise disgruntled congressmen to swallow their pride and accept the travel provisions of the Provost Department or be labeled unpatriotic elitists who demanded special traveling privileges. Southern citizens who heard about Davis's humble act of visiting the passport office likely felt a sense of common inconvenience, and cynical southerners, including Davis-haters in Congress, probably dismissed his passport application as a political stunt.

One logical complaint against the domestic passport system was that it used up valuable manpower that might be used at the front, and late in the war this became a consistent argument against the network. In October 1862 a Texas senator complained that "whilst every able bodied citizen was being taken and put into the army, there were at least ten thousand men and five thousand Provost Marshals along the railroads interfering with and annoying our citizens, who should be in the field to meet the enemy." Some southerners regarded provost duty as an unofficial exemption from combat and resented the slightest harassment from bayonet-wielding men they viewed as shirkers. In July 1863 Georgia governor Joseph E. Brown hypocritically appealed to class-conscious Georgians by encouraging "the Secretary of War . . . [to] compel the thousands of persons in Confederate service, who, on account of the wealth of parents or political influence . . . are now keeping out of the reach of danger, as passport agents." On October 17, 1864, Brown and five other southern governors met in Augusta and issued a joint statement that claimed the passport system denied precious manpower to rebel armies. The governors requested "that the Confederate authorities will send to the field every able-bodied man . . . whose places can be filled by either disabled officer and soldiers, senior reserves, or negroes, and dispense with the use of the of all provost and post guard[s] . . . and with all passport agents upon railroads not in the immediate vicinity of the armies, as we consider these agents an unnecessary annoyance to good citizens."[54] The governors not only argued that the passport system was an unwise use of available manpower, but also denigrated the service of provost guards by implying that the feeble, aged, and African Americans could handle these simple duties. Even the idea that "negroes" would be considered for internal police tasks was proof of the acute manpower shortage in 1864 and the desperate remedies southern officials might consider.

This time the Confederate government responded to critics of the domestic passport system. One week after the governors' request, Assistant Inspector General William Levy asked generals in the Deep South to scour their military departments for "post commanders, adjutants, officers of guards, passport officers" and send them to Confederate armies, because in addition to "the pernicious influence which is exerted by these innumerable hiding places from active service, the expense of keeping them up is a matter worthy of serious consideration."[55] Levy believed passport agents were not only unpatriotically avoiding frontline duty, but they also received undeserved Confederate pay and ate southern food without sharing in the sacrifice of their brothers-in-arms on the front lines. The argument that the passport network was an unwise use of human resources transcended mere personal annoyance or civil liberty infringement, but was acted upon too late in the war to diminish the system or appreciably bolster rebel armies.

Some southerners believed the strict passport system undermined Confederate nationalism. In February 1864 a citizen, J. J. Sloan, informed Secretary of War James Seddon that recent Union meetings held around Greensboro, North Carolina, were instigated by the heavy hand of the Provost Department. Sloan complained that when local citizens visited Richmond they were "hunted about the city by spies—low rowdies from Baltimore—under the control of General Winder and one Griswold." In the process of conducting "legitimate business," several civilians were "arrested by these detectives and carried before Winder and subjected to the most insulting treatment and profanely abused." According to Sloan, "disaffection . . . [was] now largely on the increase" in his region, and he believed the best corrective method was for the secretary of war to "abolish the detective feature, dispense with the passport system, and let every citizen who travels be required to exhibit a certificate from his county clerk." Sloan did not criticize the Provost Department's strict regulation of soldiers traveling to and from the home front, but he was convinced that if the "arrest and imprisonment of our best citizens on mere suspicion" would stop, he gave his "best assurance . . . that we shall have no more Union meetings here."[56]

In a widespread network dependent on human interaction like the domestic passport system, an opportunity for corruption and bribery crept into the process. Evidence of illegal activity is typically more difficult to prove since historical actors purposefully tried to conceal their actions, but some southerners accused the Provost Department of malfeasance. One would not typically expect money to change hands when applying for a passport, but early in the war the passport office accepted monetary donations for the war effort. War Department clerk John B. Jones recalled "registering 'patriotic contributions' in the passport office," and he "estimated" that the "value of voluntary contributions registered in 1861-'62 amounted to more than $1,500,000."[57] This revenue stream would have been a very tempting target for any dishonest passport official.

Implications of dishonesty were also leveled against War Department employees above the passport office level. J. B. Jones periodically wondered about the passes issued to mysterious characters by Assistant Secretary of War John A. Campbell. Jones's remarks, at times anti-Semitic, cast suspicion upon Campbell's motives and willingness to bypass official passport regulations for business that required traveling inside the Confederacy and also crossing into enemy territory. Campbell understood that unofficial channels could benefit the Confederate cause and reportedly "said openly that [General] Winder's brown paper passes could be had for a hundred dollars apiece" or negotiated at a lower price for those who knew where to inquire.[58] Many of the allegations of corruption with regard to passports can probably be explained away as rumor, but the motive and means for corruption were inherent in the passport system and possibly abused on some occasions.

The ability of southerners to access domestic passports was directly affected by wartime exigencies. In times of peace no domestic pass system would have been necessary, but the enormous pressures of war meant that the War Department assumed responsibility over granting permission for domestic travel.

The domestic passport system evolved as an expedient policy that started along the Confederate periphery and eventually reached deep into the southern home front. The system began as a local institution, a response to the urgent requirements of desperate Confederate officers under imminent threat of Union attack in places like Norfolk, New Orleans, and Richmond. In the early years of the war, rebel officers implemented local passport systems with limited guidance and routine approval from the War Department, much in keeping with a corporatist, albeit militaristic style, and only later in 1864 did the Confederacy develop a more centralized bureaucratic approach to the domestic passport system.

The domestic passport system grew into its own fiefdom of military power over civilian life. Military police consistently regulated travel around vital rail transportation hubs, and Winder's men could hold anyone without charge, including congressmen who voiced outrage at being treated like ordinary citizens. When questioned by a unanimous House of Representatives in 1864, the secretary of war pursued a course of plausible deniability about the origins of the domestic passport system, but in reality Winder and the southern provost network provided an unpleasant but extremely valuable service to the War Department. The system's martial nature offended many civilians and haughty politicians, but the domestic passport network was an omnipresent reminder that the national military effort took precedence over all other considerations, even civil liberties.

The domestic passport system's influence on home front morale is difficult to gauge, but one might argue that the Provost Department stemmed the tide of Confederate desertions in the waning months of the war. Major Elias Griswold in the Richmond Provost Department believed the domestic passport system was indispensable in thwarting desertion. Griswold sadly acknowledged that "many well-born and bred, who would once have shrunk from the least moral delinquency, boldly barter all in the alteration or forgery of an official paper to get away from the army." Griswold warned against eliminating the system and declared that if people in "citizen's dress" were allowed "to travel uninterrupted, there is no calculating the extent of desertion which would ensue." Griswold could think of "no other check than the passport system for this evil," and despite the fact that many southerners were "sincerely desirous . . . to be rid of the system," Griswold's "experience and judgment oppose its abolishment." Finally Griswold appealed to the patriotism of southerners and pointed out "how little this one sacrifice of personal liberty is . . . compared with the terrible privations, exposure, and toils of our brave soldiers."[59]

If a domestic passport system was required to keep soldiers in the field and disloyal southerners in check, then one has to question the extent of Confederate nationalism, and whether this nationalism was not partially a result of government coercion. Loyal southerners viewed the system as necessary but legal. The hassle of applying for travel permits, combined with giving detailed personal information to government authorities, was regarded as yet another sacrifice in the interest of independence. Preventing desertion in exchange for civilian travel permission was an acceptable trade-off for loyal Confederates hoping to sustain the rebel war effort.

Historian Mark Neely briefly analyzed the domestic passport system as an example of how the Confederacy denied civil liberties to its citizens. Neely states that "the domestic passport system in place in much of the Confederacy during the war required the issuance of a government document each time a citizen wished to travel . . . [and] affected all railroad travel for most of the war and imposed restrictions on other modes of travel in places far from the military front."[60] A detailed look at the evolution of the domestic passport process shows that the system was by no means uniform throughout the war. Neely overstates the alleged ubiquitous nature of the system. All travel did not require a domestic passport. Civilians could still typically travel from town to town, across regions, and even into other states without encountering provost guards demanding passports, provided the route did not traverse a major city or transportation nexus. Although it had originated in areas threatened by Union military forces, by 1864 the domestic passport system, as Neely points out, had spread to interior transportation hubs. However, by this phase of the war one might argue that what remained of the Confederacy should have been treated essentially like the military front; certainly that was the case in cities like Richmond and Atlanta. In 1864 the domestic passport system's major functions of affirming loyalty and preventing desertion were obvious, but the system also was an additional layer of security against tens of thousands of Union prisoners of war being held across the South and often transported on the railroad network. It would have been foolish for the Confederacy not to have a domestic passport system to verify the identity and surmise the purposes of railroad passengers in 1864–1865.

The Lincoln administration did not find it necessary to create a domestic passport system in the northern states. In August 1861 Secretary of State William Seward devised a system of checking individuals entering or leaving the United States. Passport agents operated in ports like Boston and New York and also other heavily traveled access points into the northern states. Seward's wartime passport system was terminated in June 1865, but it proved that the Lincoln administration was also concerned about keeping tabs on travelers.[61] One can only speculate why the North did not develop a domestic passport system like the Confederacy. There are several possible explanations. The simplest reason is the North did not need a domestic passport system because desertion and serious internal military threats were not existential problems like they were in the Confederacy. Also, treasonous and disloyal elements in the North were effectively suppressed by civil and military courts, so there was little need to assess the loyalty of everyday travelers.[62] Even if the Lincoln administration wanted to create a domestic passport system, doing so played right into the hands of Democratic critics of the administration's already controversial record on civil liberties. If the North was losing the war in 1864 and not the South, one can only wonder if the Lincoln administration would have created a domestic passport system as well.

Critics of the Confederate domestic passport system argued that this was not merely an inconvenience but a serious threat to individual liberties. For critics, the domestic passport system symbolized a centralized and intrusive force into daily life, the very reason that some rebels seceded from the old Union. However, patriotic southerners tolerated the system and understood it was a necessary evil. The domestic passport system was not a source of serious public grievance. Many Confederate citizens, along with most members of Congress, tacitly understood the purpose and necessity of the system to the war effort. Confederate leaders recognized that a domestic passport system was required for a variety of reasons, among them the reaffirmation of national loyalty, but the mere existence of the system does not necessarily prove there was rampant disloyalty in the Confederacy.

Modern history has since showed us that governments rarely collect vast amounts of personal information for idle reasons, and some southerners likely speculated that the Confederacy might use the records for nefarious purposes in the future. Despite the domestic passport system's negative standing in public opinion, Confederate leaders felt it was necessary to retain military control over travel not only in the war zones like Richmond but throughout the southern transportation network.

CONFEDERATE RAILROAD POLICY

John Moody arguably understood the railroad business better than any other person in the world at the turn of the twentieth century. As founder of the Moody Bond Rating Service, he possessed immense power over railroad companies' ability to attract capital through bond sales. In his book *The Railroad Builders* (1919), Moody analyzed the endemic conflicts of emerging railroad industries. He could have been describing the vexing problems facing the Confederacy when he pointed out that "many of the railroad evils were inherent in the situation; they were explained by the fact that both managers and public were dealing with a new agency whose laws they did not completely understand."[63] In the absence of any national experience in railroad management, the Confederacy used a corporatist method of allowing the railroad companies to take the lead in developing policy.

Wartime stresses and lack of technical knowledge about the railroad industry hampered Confederate leaders' ability to articulate a consistent policy. Railroad company managers eagerly filled the vacuum of inexperience and lack of government leadership in railroad policy. Southern railroad corporations were vital to the southern war effort. In this particular economic sector, private firms directly formulated state policy in a corporatist manner and successfully practiced their policies to the eventual detriment of the Confederate war effort.

During the antebellum period southern railroad companies enjoyed a close relationship with the individual states in which they operated. Georgia and North Carolina owned or operated railroads ostensibly as objects of social benefit. Despite the resistance of planters and Democratic Party leaders, southern railroad construction boomed in the 1850s. Competent railroad management would be an important factor in the Confederate war effort, especially for utilizing interior lines of defense and ensuring proper supply of armies. Due to this importance one might expect the Confederate government to have implemented a centralized plan for state management of the rail network. Some historians argue that there was no Confederate railroad policy.[64]

There was a Confederate railroad policy but it consisted of an ad hoc approach designed and submitted by the managers of private rail companies. Instead of mimicking the antebellum precedent of southern states in close cooperation with private rail companies, the Confederate government opted for a relatively hands-off policy.[65] Due to the primacy of private business concerns in the development of public policy, Confederate railroad policy represented one of the best examples of expedient corporatism in operation.

By contrast, the Lincoln administration acted to ensure official coordination of the northern rail network and implemented a uniform railroad policy. Union policy threatened government takeover of the railroads if the president deemed it a wartime necessity. The mere threat of government takeover was sufficient to keep northern rail companies in line and allowed Union leaders more effective coordination of the transportation network.[66]

Confederate leaders also considered state control of the railroad network. In August 1861 the Confederate Congress debated granting these same powers to Jefferson Davis. On August 21, 1861, William Porcher

Miles, member of the powerful House Committee on Military Affairs, endorsed a railroad bill that would allow "the President to regulate and take control of railroads in certain cases." Section Two of the bill declared that "in case the managers of any railroad company shall refuse to observe & execute such regulations as may be made by the President . . . then the President is authorized and empowered to take military possession of such railroads, and place the same under the control & management of the War Department." Section Three of the bill called for conflict arbitration between the government and railroad companies by creating a board composed of "three Presidents of railroad companies independent of and unconnected" with the railroad company undergoing "adjudication & settlement." The railroad board was allegedly impartial with "one [member] to be selected by the R[ail]road, one by the Sec. of War and the third by the two first selected" members."[67]

There were several reasons why the bill did not become law. Congressmen had to allay concerns about executive overreach. One representative was satisfied and endorsed the bill, stating, "there may arise cases when it would be proper for the Pres[iden]t to have this power and the bill is sufficiently guarded to prevent its application to any other than cases of necessity." Another reason the August 1861 railroad bill stalled in the House was that other issues seemed more important at the time. In 1861 the railroad network operated fairly well. The severe infrastructure deterioration and stresses of full-scale war still lay in the future. The desperation of later years was not felt in the summer of 1861 and so railroad policy was not a top congressional priority. The bill to authorize the president to take control of the southern railroad network failed to become law in August 1861, and by default, railroad companies initiated policy in a corporatist manner.[68]

Why did Congress balk at giving power to President Davis and control of the railroad network to Confederate bureaucrats? It is possible that issues of states' and property rights played important roles, but the basic reason for refusal to implement state control over the railroads was lack of experience in this vital economic sector.[69] Due to inexperience, Confederate leaders left railroad operations and policy formulation in the control of private railroad managers, a stark example of corporatism in action.

Railroad owners and managers exhibited a robust patriotism in 1861. Many on both sides believed the war might be a short affair, but true patriotism required endurance and willingness to repeatedly sacrifice private interest for public good. Southern railroad executives sincerely wanted to help the Confederate war effort, but only on their own terms, not within a system of direct government intervention. Several rail lines offered free transport for government business in early 1861. Southern railroad managers foresaw that competitive rate cuts would be detrimental to their mutual interests, and they came together to institute profitable uniform rates.[70]

The zenith of patriotic action by southern railroad companies occurred in the first months of the war. As the prospects for private contracts constricted with the loss of northern freight, railroad company managers sought a unified, noncompetitive contract with the Confederate government from which all firms would profit. On April 26, 1861, the heads of thirty-three railroad companies met in Montgomery, Alabama, to craft a national railroad policy acceptable to both the government and railroad companies. Railroad executives agreed to the government request for freight rates. On May 1, 1861, the agreement was applied to all southern railroad companies whether or not they were represented at the Montgomery convention. Railroad managers agreed to transport passengers, soldiers, and others on government business, at the rate of two cents per mile. For cargo such as munitions, foodstuffs, and any other commodity associated with the war effort, the convention agreed to charge the government half the going local rate. These rates symbolized a patriotic gesture by railroad companies that would later be trumped by the profit motive. Since cash was scarce, railroad executives agreed to accept payment in government bonds.[71]

Leaders of southern rail companies called another convention on October 4, 1861, in Chattanooga, Tennessee, to amend freight rates and revise the uniform policy. This series of so-called "Chattanooga rates" symbolized a decline in the patriotic generosity of railroad companies displayed in the April 1861 agreement. The Chattanooga delegates refused the requests of Quartermaster General Abraham Myers and thereby reversed the roles of policy development, completely switching control from the public to the private sector. Railroad executives established four categories of uniform freight rates for government cargo to ensure profits. The Chattanooga rates were approved by Quartermaster General Myers, and he recommended that all southern railroads adopt the new set of prices.[72]

By the end of 1861 railroad company managers had assumed control over policy and received government sanction. Railroad executives were directed only by a loose strategic agenda and left to their own devices and technical expertise to accomplish the government's goals. The operational details of freight rates, schedules, and resource allocation were left almost entirely in the hands of railroad managers and dictated by their judgment. The initial stages of Confederate railroad operation clearly reflected a powerful private sector interest group creating policy on its own terms, a prime characteristic of a nascent corporatist system.

In 1862 some Confederate officials called for government control to replace the Chattanooga convention. Lieutenant Colonel Larkin Smith of the War Department audited payment to railroad companies and argued that the Chattanooga rates overcharged the government. Up until the Chattanooga convention, Smith pointed out that railroad companies "have charged the government only one half of the local rates or one half the rates paid by individuals" but, Smith added, "the Chattanooga plan pays the roads much more than they have been receiving." Smith crafted a detailed argument that the government was now paying higher rates than individuals for all classes of freight.[73] Prominent Confederate leaders were also concerned that continued private control would disrupt the war effort. General Robert E. Lee sought to alleviate the lack of railroad coordination and recommended that "the movements of railroad trains should be under one undivided control." Conflicts between military commanders seeking emergency powers over rail traffic and private railroad managers soon threatened to undo corporatist policy. In July 1862 Josiah Gorgas remarked that "the railroads are badly conducted," but he blamed the "great struggle in which we are engaged [that] disorganizes everything which is not energetically supervised."[74] High-ranking military and government leaders now called for centralized government management of the southern railroad network to more capably support the war effort.

Early in 1862 the House of Representatives reconsidered a government takeover of the railroads. On March 11, 1862, the Committee on Military Affairs began deliberations on a new railroad bill. The initial goal was to "give increased efficiency to our interior lines of railroads," but on March 19th Texas congressman Peter Gray asked the committee to consider nationalizing the entire railroad system. On April 17th a comprehensive railroad bill was brought to the House floor. The lengthy bill created the position of a "military chief of railroad transportation" with enforcement powers over recalcitrant railroad companies. Representatives watered down the bill with amendments, and it eventually passed by a vote of 39 to 33.[75] The Senate did not seriously consider the bill before adjournment, so again a railroad bill did not become law and corporatist railroad policy continued through 1862.

Due to military necessity, Quartermaster General Myers agreed to adopt uniform control, but in the absence of a legally binding government policy that uniformity came from the private sector. In fall 1862 Myers explained that he was "opposed to taking military possession of the roads" because the rail workers "would promptly resign rather than be subject to the orders of officers of the Army . . . wholly ignorant of railroads and their management." Instead of military control, Myers recommended "the appointment of an able, methodical, and energetic person as chief of transportation, to have entire control over and power to regulate all matters pertaining to transportation . . . and after conference or correspondence with the several railroad presidents and superintendents to bring into harmonious action the different roads in the Confederacy."[76] Myers's plan essentially sustained corporatist railroad policy but with a government figurehead to ostensibly keep companies in line.

Confederate politicians sided with Quartermaster General Myers and allowed continued corporatist management of the rail network. Myers had first attempted government-led railroad coordination in 1861 by employing the services of William Shepperd Ashe, former North Carolina congressman and ex-president of the Wilmington and Weldon Railroad. Ashe recommended network improvements but was constantly rebuffed by railroad managers, so he resigned in April 1862. After Congress agreed to Myers's fall 1862 request, William M. Wadley was appointed railroad supervisor in December 1862. Myers did not select Wadley. The new supervisor of Confederate rail traffic was selected based on his previous experience as president of the Vicksburg and Shreveport Railroad. Wadley came highly recommended through a letter of introduction to President Jefferson Davis from Charles T. Pollard, president of the Alabama and Florida Railroad Company. Pollard praised Wadley "as one of the most energetic and reliable men connected with railroad service in the Confederate States." Although his experience for improving Confederate rail coordination was encouraging, Wadley did not possess the power to coerce railroad companies.[77]

William Wadley's reform efforts were typical of his private sector background. He called another railroad meeting in Augusta, Georgia, on December 15, 1862. Forty-one railroad companies sent delegates to discuss schedules, elimination of supply bottlenecks, and more efficient use of rolling stock. However, railroad presidents were less concerned with these issues than with freight rates and government payments. Wadley's request for a pool of interchangeable cars failed, and instead the convention decided to increase rates for all passengers and government freight.[78]

Wadley reported the convention's proceedings to Inspector General Samuel Cooper on December 31, 1862. He described how "a resolution was introduced expressing an earnest desire to co-operate with me in carrying on Government transportation, but failing to agree upon any definite plan of action [Wadley] regarded the resolution as of no value beyond the expression of the good wishes of the convention." Convention delegates also opposed uniform rates and sought to address "the disregard many army officers have for the private property of railroad companies." The practice of "impressing cars and engines" caused disruptions and "the demoralization of railroad employees." The December 1862 meeting only further entrenched the power of railroad companies over Confederate railroad policy, and their recommendations were duly adopted by the government. Wadley later admitted to Secretary of War James Seddon that the only foolproof way to guarantee coordination of rail transportation was for the Confederate Congress to allow government control.[79] Wadley approached the problem of rail coordination in a corporatist manner and arguably put the interests of the railroad companies before the interests of the war effort despite his role as a government official.

Secretary of War Seddon decided to reconvene the railroad managers in Richmond on April 20, 1863. Wadley presented government requests and the railroad managers asked for more government support. Government officials sought better coordination of rail traffic, and railroad managers wanted more government subsidies for infrastructure improvements. The Richmond convention finally agreed upon several resolutions that acknowledged the power of Wadley's Railroad Bureau, but only in order to better coordinate and distribute government aid to the companies. The most important resolution "provided that the Government was to abstain from direct control of railway operations." The Richmond convention did not achieve the government's wish for better rail coordination and actually reaffirmed the corporatist system of private control over the South's railroad network.[80]

A faction in Congress sought to establish government control over the railroads. Senator Louis Wigfall of Texas introduced a bill "to facilitate transportation for the Government." Bill S. 112 cleared the Committee on Military Affairs and the Senate awaited the results of Seddon's railroad convention before voting, in order to adjust the bill based on the secretary of war's recommendations. Seddon reported to Congress that the convention was a failure since the railroad companies had exhibited "the selfish interests inherent in money-making corporations." Seddon's recommendation to Congress was that the "power of regulation should be vested in a single agent of the Government . . . and if his directives were willfully disobeyed, the Executive should possess specific authority to seize the offending carrier."[81]

The railroad bill passed the Senate and the House and was finally signed into law on May 1, 1863. The law allowed President Davis to seize rail lines and other company property if the government's demands were not met. Government officials now possessed the legal standing to coerce railroad companies into compliance through threat of government seizure. This law could have stemmed the corporatist arrangement between railroad companies and the Confederate government, but Wadley and the government did not implement the law. It is unclear why the Confederate government did not use the May 1863 law to seize, or at least cajole, the railroad companies into a more compliant position. One might speculate on any number of reasons, for example; William Wadley's nomination as head of the Railroad Bureau was rejected by the Senate on May 1, 1863, the exact same day the government railroad bill was signed into law.[82] Whatever the reason for Wadley's dismissal, the fact remains that the government removed a capable railroad administrator before he had a chance to use the newly established government powers. For almost two more years the government failed to enact control over the railroad network, probably because Confederate leaders did not have sufficient knowledge or experience to oversee the rail system in conjunction with hostile private management.

On June 4, 1863, William Wadley was replaced by Captain Frederick W. Sims. It immediately became clear that Sims represented the concerns of the rail companies. Sims blamed the government for the imminent collapse of the rail system and declared that "the roads have no means . . . for keeping their machinery in proper repair. . . . It is utterly impossible to continue in the present destructive course. . . . What the roads ask, and what they must have, is iron ore, permission for foundries and rolling-mills to work for them, and a liberal system of detailing machinists from the Army. . . . Nothing else will do."[83] Sims voiced rail company grievances and believed only more government subsidies and resource allocation could stave off inevitable collapse. This was an example of the corporatist rationale at work, in which private companies continued to request government assistance but maintained resistance to any type of oppressive government intervention in their affairs.

Sims followed Wadley's precedent and called another railroad convention in Macon, Georgia, in November 1863. R. R. Cuyler, president of the Georgia Central Railroad, served as chairman over nineteen railroad company representatives who accounted for most of the main rail lines in the ever-shrinking Confederacy. Cuyler informed his fellow railroad delegates that the goal of this gathering was to increase "the present rates paid by the Government for transportation." To convey this request, a five-man committee was created to cooperate and "consult" with government Railroad Bureau chief Major Frederick W. Sims.[84]

The convention decided on new government rates for human and material cargo. Railroads charged four cents per mile if carrying less than one hundred men, but over that only "two and one-half cents per man per mile." Furloughed soldiers traveling to and from their loved ones back home would be charged four cents per mile and "for the bodies of soldiers that are killed in battle or die in service, each [railroad company] shall adopt its own rules and rates of charge." This was a very unpatriotic policy by railroad managers, who appeared indifferent to the suffering and sacrifices of the average rebel soldier and his grieving family. Railroad managers did not like government officials abusing travel privileges, so government business travelers would be "charged full local fare." The Macon convention delegates also created six classes of freight for material objects that also increased government rates.[85] Given the spiraling inflation, railroad companies could legitimately request rate increases, but they could have at least attempted to do so in a more patriotic way.

After unilaterally raising freight rates, the delegates had the audacity to demand faster payment from the government. Railroad managers asked government Railroad Bureau head Major F. W. Sims to "represent to the [War] Department that as the railroads in this Confederacy are principally occupied with government transportation, it is a matter of importance to them that their bills for this service should be promptly paid." All the rate changes and new railroad policies went into effect on December 10, 1863, only two weeks after the convention.[86]

Major Sims was overwhelmed by the collective demands of railroad managers. Sims was an ineffective government representative at the Macon convention and served as little more than a messenger to inform the government that the railroad companies were increasing rates. Sims had no negotiating position, so he could only vocally protest the one-sided railroad policy. Sims watched as the attending railroad companies adjusted Confederate railroad policy to conform to their specific needs.[87]

Confederate leaders knew that 1864 would prove to be a pivotal year for national survival, so government policies reflected this desperate nature, but the Confederacy continued to operate a corporatist railroad policy throughout 1864. Some were hopeful that improved railroad management might bolster rebel armies in the upcoming campaigns. Josiah Gorgas believed that "with proper energy in the use of the railroads there is no doubt food can be bro't forward from the South and troops and capital fed." Gorgas's hope for improved management was mistaken. In April 1864 even General Lee had to argue for military priority on the deteriorating rail system. He begged Secretary of War James Seddon not to "allow private interests . . . to interfere with the use of all the facilities for transportation . . . until the wants of the army are provided for."[88] Despite the pleas of generals and wishful thinking of government officials, the corporatist system of private control of the railroad network remained in place throughout 1864.

The power of the railroad companies and their influence over government policy was on full display in the third conscription act of February 1864. The Confederate Congress closed many draft loopholes and exemptions to more fully utilize manpower, but railroad companies continued to garner special favor from the government. Railroads that conducted government business could exempt the company "president, treasurer, auditor, and superintendent" and other employees "indispensable to the operation" of the company.[89] This amounted to a virtual carte blanche for railroad presidents to declare a reasonable number of employees exempt from military service. Considering the many clashes between military officers and railroad presidents over control of the southern rail network up to 1864, this aspect of the February 1864 draft law proved that the government sided with railroad management over the demands of rebel officers. This was a quintessential example of corporatist policy at work, in which the particular economic sector not only influenced government policy, but was also granted the power to conduct its business without interference from other government entities.

On April 13, 1864, railroad managers met at yet another convention in Columbia, South Carolina. The main complaint at this meeting was taxation. Railroad executives felt unfairly taxed by a February 17, 1864, law. They protested to Congress about the "unjust bearing and oppressive operation" of the new tax system and claimed that the "objectionable feature is inequality." Claiming that depreciated currency caused the new tax policy to discriminate against "shareholders in railroad operations," the delegates argued they were now "subject to a tax five to ten times greater than the mass of their fellow citizens, who have suffered less heretofore." Destitute families of frontline soldiers would have certainly been offended by these remarks, but the railroad managers carried their specious argument even further. They claimed that the new tax law was "class legislation" and represented "ruinous oppression" to the shareholders, who the delegates claimed were "the weakest and most helpless in the community . . . women and children, trusts, estates of deceased persons; literary, religious and charitable institutions." Railroad mangers requested that shareholders be placed on an "equal footing" and detailed their sacrifices on behalf of the Confederacy. Despite dominating Confederate railroad policy, the companies declared that they had "made no net profits for the last three years," and instead recommended a "uniform ad valorem tax" based upon 1860 assessed values. The audacity of railroad managers to complain to Congress about a tax law passed on February 17, 1864, the same day railroad companies were given the most liberal conscription exemptions in the Confederacy, irked many politicians who now viewed railroad managers as ingrates. The fact that convention delegates sent this protest to Congress proved that by 1864 railroad companies were confident they could get the Confederate government to fulfill practically any demand. Corporatist railroad policy had clearly run afoul, securing private interest to the detriment of the war effort.[90]

The corporatist pattern of private sector formulation of railroad policy continued throughout 1864, but the Confederate government finally implemented centralized control over the rail system in February 1865. As the Confederacy teetered on the brink of collapse, Congress finally approved full government control over the railroads. This tardy effort at railroad reform, as described by historian Charles Ramsdell, allowed "the Secretary of War to place any railroad . . . under such officers as he should designate, to place the regular railroad officials, agents, and employees . . . on the same footing as soldiers in the field, and to maintain any road in repair or to give it any necessary aid."[91] This law proved too little and too late. By 1865 the endemic problems of the southern rail network were too immense to overcome. One might argue that earlier state control of rail resources could have provided Confederate armies with a greater chance of ultimate victory. Instead, the Confederacy opted for a corporatist railroad policy that left control in the hands of private railroad companies.

Why did the Confederacy wait until 1865 to implement centralized control over the railroads? Union leaders benefited from early coordination of the northern rail system. According to railroad historian George Edgar Turner, "the most significant event of 1862, if not of the entire war" with regard to railroad policy on either side "was the act of the United States Congress authorizing the President to take possession of the railroads if and when, in his judgment, the welfare and the safety of the country demanded it." The Confederate Congress contemplated similar legislation on August 21, 1861, but the bill did not pass. Perhaps at this early stage the Confederate Congress was apprehensive about giving the executive powers of property confiscation. By May 1, 1863, Congress understood the importance of centralized railroad coordination and provided President Davis with the coercive legal tools to force compliance upon recalcitrant railroad companies. Why Davis did not go forward with state control at this point is a mystery, and unfortunately this study can only add to the historical speculation.

Railroad managers possessed great influence in Richmond. When the Confederate Congress opened the possibility of state control, the railroad managers hoped that Davis would not implement the law. It appears as though state confiscation and coordination of railroads was a policy that neither the Confederate Congress nor President Davis wanted to implement out of concern for the relationship between the government and private property. Historian Charles Ramsdell argued that "imbued as the Southern people were with laissez-faire ideas, their government was slow to take a hand in the operation of the roads, and when finally compelled by force of circumstances to interfere, it came only by degrees to any assumption of control." Ramsdell's assertion of a state laissez-faire attitude towards railroads might better be expressed as lack of will to implement government control. Both the government and the railroads sought control over specific aspects of the wartime economy, hardly the characteristic of a laissez-faire system. As political scientist Graham K. Wilson points out, "corporatist systems are not laissez-faire systems; on the contrary, they are systems in which governments play an active part not only in the macroeconomic management of the economy, but in microeconomic policies affecting individual . . . industries."[92] In the case of railroads the Confederate government did not exhibit a tendency to intervene. A constant in corporatist relationships is a struggle between the government and influential power blocs for control over policy formulation, and in some instances, such as management of the southern railroad network, the power blocs ultimately define the limits of their own power.

One reason railroad managers might not wholeheartedly devote their machines and infrastructure to the Confederate war effort was that, unlike the impact of the complete loss of property for slaveholders, Union victory would not necessarily destroy the railroads. If the Confederacy lost the war, the assets of southern railroad companies would suffer inevitable damage to rail-lines, cars, locomotives, and human resources, but these losses could be eventually recovered. A victorious Union army would require a southern rail network during Reconstruction. Perhaps this aspect of long-term self-interest explains the railroad managers' conditional support for the Confederate war effort, but it does not explain why Jefferson Davis did not simply coerce or nationalize the southern rail system for more effective supply and transportation.

To be fair, Davis and other Richmond bureaucrats continually had to prioritize Confederate policies based on circumstances. The Confederacy struggled to produce sufficient munitions. To also provide enough resources to keep southern railroads operating at optimal capacity was simply an impossible task. In addition to the lack of available resources and industrial capacity necessary for adequate repairs, "the Confederates committed two major sins," according to historian Robert C. Black. First, Black argues, "railroad owners, managers, and even employees were unwilling to make serious sacrifice of their personal interests" in exchange for more centralized organization of the rail network. Also, and even more importantly, "the Confederate Government was loath to enforce the kind of transportation policy the war effort demanded . . . [and] without either wholehearted public cooperation, or government coercion," the evolution of a corporatist railroad policy put the private interests of railroad companies ahead of national survival.[93]

A brief comparison with Union wartime railroad policy will allow a better understanding of Confederate railroad policy. Historian Robert G. Angevine notes that the Lincoln administration could have pursued any of "three potential models of military-industrial relations." Union leaders did not select the "policy of minimal government intervention in railroad affairs implemented by the Confederacy," but instead used a combination of "direct military control . . . to supervise and operate the Southern railroads during the war," and a more "cooperative approach . . . with Northern railroads." The cooperation of northern railroads, however, was backed by an explicit threat of government takeover, embodied in the Railroad Act of 1862, should the companies disappoint northern leaders. Regarding Confederate railroad policy, Angevine argues, "the Confederacy's principal problem was an inability to devise a satisfactory organization for controlling and coordinating railroad operations."[94] This correctly summarizes the Confederate railroad experience, although Angevine does not attempt to label the Confederate system. Angevine asserts that after the war, southern railroads were eventually subsumed into the Union's new cooperative policy, thus implying an abrupt end to the organizational style of Confederate railroad policy, essentially condemning it to the dustbin of modernity.

However, despite the fact that Confederate railroad policy was cut short by northern victory and proved incapable of propping up the southern war effort, it does not necessarily mean that Confederate railroad policy was devoid of modern attributes. The relationship between the Confederate government and railroad companies exhibited unmistakable characteristics of expedient corporatism. Political scientist Howard J. Wiarda summed up Confederate railroad policy in his description of corporatist systems. In an explanation of corporatist relationships Wiarda points out, "the state tries to structure . . . [and] control . . . to better integrate and organize state policy . . . [as] the corporate groups try to maintain some level of autonomy from the state and bargain [to] promote the best interests of their members." The power to formulate railroad policy, not immediately assumed by the government, was eagerly taken up by the railroad companies. This represents an example of a corporatist relationship. Railroads were a vital portion of the Confederate system, and the debate over what entity should control railroad policy symbolizes a key corporatist characteristic. As Wiarda notes, it is "this tension and struggle, [that] lies at the heart of the theory of corporatism."[95]

CONCLUSION

Myriad policies and institutions influenced the southern wartime experience, evident in the three pillars of the Confederate system that touched important aspects of southern life: conscription, the domestic passport system, and railroad policy. Each policy was created in an ad hoc atmosphere, and only in the later years of the war from 1863 to 1865 did these policies become operational on a standardized basis. Each new addition to the Confederate bureaucracy was an expedient response to wartime necessities. Unintentionally, Confederate leaders crafted a system that displayed many qualities of a modern corporatist state.

Conscription was a key element in the Confederate system, and without it the nation could not have survived until 1865. Conscription also established a modern-style mobilization of society and fundamentally altered the relationship between the national government and the southern people. However, to interpret conscription as merely a top-down despotic measure is an oversimplification. The southern draft was indeed an authoritarian measure marked with class conflict and inequity, but the basic notion that this was a "rich man's war and a poor man's fight" does not adequately describe the fundamental nature of the Confederate draft system. Conscription never could have been implemented without the assistance of the southern states, contrary to the hyperbole of historians who focus on states' rights. The national government simply did not possess enough coercive power to force southerners to fight. Local and state governments provided most of conscription's enforcement mechanisms, and the national government relied on local communities to comply. On its face Confederate conscription was a modern authoritarian policy, but it never achieved the full bureaucratic power and reach of twentieth-century examples. Yet conscription was arguably the most important element in the Confederate system because it allowed for unprecedented government intrusion into the lives of southerners.

The domestic passport system evolved in response to concerns about internal security. Passports initially were required to discover disloyalty near the front lines, but this policy morphed into a comprehensive bureaucracy that collected personal data and assessed loyalty throughout the Confederacy. Some southerners were outraged that the government used armed guards to regulate the travel of southern citizens, but most simply endured the challenge of obtaining passports and the humiliation of checkpoints. The domestic passport system is an excellent example of the gradual erosion of civil liberties under the Confederate system and similar to the step-by-step loss of civil liberties seen in other corporatist states.

Southern railroad policy is the strongest example that the Confederate system operated within a broad expedient corporatist scheme. From the outset Confederate leaders understood that the railroad network would be pivotal to victory, but they did not grasp the importance of immediate government control. The Confederate government refused to domineer the southern railroads, either through outright seizure or coercive threat. Instead, the lack of government policy created a power vacuum that was filled by the collective leadership of southern railroad managers in a corporatist manner. From 1861 through 1864 Confederate railroad policy was formulated by the several conventions of self-interested railroad managers. Due to a combination of ineffectual congressional oversight and the superiority of private sector knowledge of railroad system operations, the Confederate government failed to take control of the southern rail network until 1865.

The expanding conscription policy, the domestic passport system, and corporatist railroad policy all were important aspects of the Confederate system. As House Speaker Thomas Bocock mentioned in February 1862, the *submission to authority* was certainly required by the policies of conscription and the domestic passport system. Bocock could not have anticipated corporatist railroad policy in 1862 even though the foundation for it had been laid, but he did point out that the Confederate system was essentially *conservative* and part of a new *political philosophy.* The Confederate system represented the gradual development of an expedient corporatist state. Strong similarities exist between the modern precedents established by the Confederacy and later corporatist states.

---·❖·---

CONCLUSION

---·❖·---

Their ideas of political economy are enough to drive the venerable
A. [Adam] Smith out of his quiet resting place with a fresh
edition of the "Wealth of Nations" in his claw.
—Lord Lyons to Lord Russell, May 21, 1861

W hen making this statement to his superior, British ambassador to
the United States Lord Lyons was describing the Confederacy's
ill-considered policy of "King Cotton" diplomacy. However, Lyons's remark that the father of modern capitalism, Adam Smith, would be
upset by the Confederacy's distortion of long-standing economic principles, implied that Confederate political economy was not truly a capitalist
system. Lyons's critique of "King Cotton" diplomacy was understandable,
but his suggestion that the Confederacy was not a capitalist system was
inaccurate. Capitalism was the guiding philosophy of Confederate political
economy. It is debatable how much the existing system of slaveholding capitalism affected the war effort, but circumstances dictated that the wartime
version of Confederate capitalism be suited to national survival.[1] Confederate leaders were forced to adapt methods that anticipated future capitalist
development instead of mimicking established economic norms.

The Confederacy clearly fits the definition of a modern corporatist
economy. As noted by Nobel Laureate economist Edmund Phelps, "a modern economy . . . means not a present-day economy but rather an economy
with a considerable degree of dynamism—that is, the will and the capacity
to innovate." In the areas of political culture, industrial organization, and
railroad policy, the Confederacy attempted innovations that drastically departed from antebellum norms. Even though most of the technology was
borrowed, the Confederacy was very innovative; it had to be in order to

survive. Edmund Phelps also described the modernist style of Confederate innovation when he defined "the modern economy . . . [as] a vast *imaginarium*—a space for imagining new products and methods," and the Confederacy certainly exhibited numerous examples of how a modern economy's "innovation process draws on human resources not utilized by a premodern economy."[2] By almost any standard, the Confederacy was a distinctly modern economic experiment.

Admittedly, the expedient corporatism of the Confederacy differed in several important ways from full-fledged twentieth-century corporatist states. Highly developed corporatist systems typically imposed government control over a three-member alliance of the state, business, and labor. The Confederacy never reached this level of development. In addition, rebel leaders oversaw a race-based slave labor system instead of the trade union organizations in twentieth-century corporatist systems. For later corporatist governments, this government-controlled trio of institutions—state, business, and labor—was coordinated to achieve maximum output and benefits for all members.

Another partial difference between the Confederacy and twentieth-century corporatist examples is the motivation to create a system to counteract liberal modern economies of each era. Confederate leaders seceded and crafted an expedient corporatist system to move away from the North's liberal capitalist economy. In this respect Confederate leaders shared a deep revulsion to liberal capitalist economic systems with their twentieth-century counterparts, but the later group of corporatist leaders was also motivated by the rising tide of socialism after 1918. The threat of socialism spurred early twentieth-century conservative governments to pursue a corporatist alternative in order to preserve their traditional economic structures. To be sure, these corporatist leaders firmly believed that liberal capitalism was wasteful and prone to serious economic disruption, but it was the fear of socialism that represented an existential threat and sparked corporatist development.

Another obvious difference between the expedient corporatism of the Confederacy and twentieth-century corporatist states is time. The aspiring Confederacy stumbled onto aspects of corporatism but had little experience with the problems of modern political and economic policies. The embattled Confederate nation did not survive long enough to fully implement its corporatist policies. By the 1920s corporatist leaders could look back on decades of competing modern economies and create organized systems to achieve national goals. The only realistic goal of the Confederacy was to survive.

Did the Confederacy possess enough corporatist qualities to be categorized as a corporatist state? The Confederacy does not strictly fit all the criteria of twentieth-century corporatism. However, there is a great deal of evidence that shows Confederate leaders were unintentionally going down a path of corporatist development.

Confederate political culture provided the essential foundation for corporatist evolution. The Confederate Constitution corrected long-standing antebellum disputes and overtly protected slavery, but it also created an excessively powerful executive branch. This modification proved useful in conducting the war effort but also fostered an authoritarian political culture that diminished the power of the legislative branch and denied the enabling of a countervailing judicial branch. The Confederate Constitution was the wellspring of the expedient corporatist state, and far more modern than just the U.S. Constitution with protections for slavery. In certain instances, such as the failure to establish a Supreme Court, the executive and legislative branches simply ignored the Confederate Constitution when it did not suit their purposes. Contrary to the analysis of many historians, the most important aspect of the Confederate Constitution was not state sovereignty, but the immensely increased power of the executive branch. This concentration of executive power helped expand the Confederate bureaucracy and also facilitated the development of government-business arrangements. However, the authoritarian political culture does not necessarily mean that the Confederacy was undemocratic. The Confederacy was operationally a democracy, constructed by a large citizenry willing to endure an authoritarian government in pursuit of independence.[3]

The closest comparison in American political history to Confederate antiparty sentiment was the era of single-party rule under the Jeffersonian Republicans, the so-called "Era of Good Feelings" from 1815 to 1824.[4] Although there were political factions centered around either the approval or disapproval of Jefferson Davis's policies, there were not full-fledged national political parties in the Confederacy. Antiparty sentiment allowed executive dominance, created a legislative political culture more responsive to bureaucratic needs than to the needs of the people, and also allowed specific industrial sectors to effectively craft government policy.

The Confederacy was forced to experiment with an industrial policy that resulted in a curious mixture of both private firms and state-owned industries. Vital private companies like the Tredegar Iron Works and the Shelby Iron Company were subsidized by guaranteed government contracts and enjoyed a relatively competition-free business environment during the war. Government officials demanded priority production, but company managers effectively leveraged their importance to the war effort into a leading role in policy formulation. The relationship between essential private industries and the Confederate government was symbiotic; neither party could survive without the other. The Confederacy also used government-owned industrial facilities to fill production gaps in gunpowder and armaments. Whether it was constructing a factory from scratch like the Augusta Powder Works, or expanding production at a small facility, the Confederacy proved willing to use government ownership to meet wartime demand. Some historians argue that nationalization of these industries is an example of state socialism, but this unprecedented step in southern industrial policy more clearly represents the expedient nature of Confederate corporatism. In the determined effort to fill army ranks, Confederate leaders instituted conscription and began a relentless government intervention into civilian life. Another intrusion was the domestic passport system that amassed enormous quantities of personal information to assess the loyalty of southern travelers. Confederate provost guards could arrest any suspicious citizen at numerous checkpoints in cities and train stations across the South. Railroad transportation was vital for Confederate success, but government officials did not have sufficient know-how to manage the network, so they left primary control over the rail system in the hands of private management. In 1861 railroad companies behaved patriotically, but for the next three years conventions of railroad managers set Confederate policy and guaranteed their own economic security. When the Confederate government finally took control of the railroad network in 1865, it was too late to rehabilitate the crumbling rail system and reverse the effects of corporatist policy. The individual aspects of the Confederate system combined to extend the life of the Richmond government, but each element was a stopgap, an expedient means to achieve the immediate goal of survival.

CONFEDERATE MODERNIZATION REVISITED

Framing the American Civil War in the wider context of global modernization is a difficult task. The historical study of modernism is apparently inexhaustible. The historiographical controversy over the causes of the Civil War have been particularly relevant to discussions of modernization.[5] In discussing the Civil War's causes, historians typically use sectional themes and the strife-ridden coexistence of southern slavery with northern free labor principles. Analytical arguments about modernist causation appear to have ended with a clear winner in 1865, the northern wage labor model, and an obvious loser, the southern slave system. For historians seeking to explain the Civil War's modernist causes, the war itself is typically the endgame. When focusing on the war, some historians highlight the similar modern "statist" qualities of the Union and Confederacy, but tend to conveniently deemphasize the major differences.

Some historians view the Civil War as the spark that ignited large-scale industrial and financial capitalism in the North and the genesis of a more industrial New South. Each method provides a valuable perspective, but each also depends upon a linear historical model that implies a sense of inevitability. The war years of 1861–1865 forced both sections to reaffirm, reinforce, and innovate their institutions into more modern forms. A standard definition of modernity provided by historian Dorothy Ross is "a stage of history characterized by national state formation, industrialization, and the rise of new ideas or reason."[6] This standard definition assists with further analysis of both wartime sections. Union armies were victorious and the North's version of modernity continued into the twentieth century, but this does not mean that the Confederacy did not briefly create its own modern system replete with slave labor, centralized government, and innovative industrial development.

Decisive victory in the Civil War affirmed the North's antebellum claims to a superior style of modernity. The Civil War turned out to be the North's self-fulfilling modernist prophecy. There is little doubt the Civil War helped define the United States's modern identity as it sought to gauge its role in global affairs, but what about the Confederacy? The war certainly forced Confederate leaders into adopting modern institutions and, whether they approved or not, southern planters were immediately required to accommodate this new variation of southern reality. The war forced southerners to determine their own unique modern identity.[7] It was northern modernity that endured, but Confederate modernity was also developing, although doomed to military defeat in 1865.

The Confederacy adopted a hallmark of modern corporatist states in times of crisis, the willingness to seriously curtail civil liberties. This scale of government intervention into daily life was unheard of in the Old Republic.[8] Conscription overtly eroded civil liberties with forced enrollment and less conspicuously by causing habeas corpus to be suspended. The creation of a domestic passport system to regulate civilian travel and assess loyalty was a clear indication that the national government ranked civil liberties as a low priority. The possibility of unwarranted arrest by government officials was a constant threat in the wartime South.

How did the Confederacy modernize relative to other societies undergoing transitions into the modern era? This question has been a source of fascination for numerous historians and it requires that the Confederacy be categorized in the *long durée* of economic history. Although he did not put great effort into explaining Confederate modernization itself, Barrington Moore's seminal work *Social Origins of Dictatorship and Democracy: Lord and Peasant in the Making of the Modern World* (1966) compared the American Civil War to other important revolutions. Moore described the Civil War as "the last capitalist revolution" and "the last revolutionary offensive on the part of . . . urban or capitalist democracy." Moore focused on the revolutionary nature of northern liberal capitalism, but by implication he also describes the counterrevolutionary nature of the Confederacy. This is important because, by default, Moore's categorization aligns the Confederacy with several reactionary governments that pursued modernization using conservative methods.[9]

Barrington Moore's most famous example of conservative modernization is Prussia, and he laid out a model that historians have since termed the "Prussian Road." Moore categorized three "routes to the modern world": bourgeois capitalist revolution, top-down reactionary political forms, and peasant-induced communism. Prussia serves as one of the best examples of the second method, a reactionary "revolution from above" or the "Prussian Road."[10] This form of modern development is defined by a landed aristocracy, in this case the Junkers, that dominate the government

and use that power to oversee industrial development while simultaneously maintaining an oppressive system of agricultural production. The basic similarities to political and economic developments in the antebellum
American South are obvious, but require deeper investigation.[11] Historians
point out a loose comparison between the Prussian Road and the historical
experience in the American South, but they do not explicitly correlate corporatist developments in Prussia and the Confederacy.

Historical approaches to modernity and the Civil War have tended to
highlight the North's antebellum modern economy as the ultimate winner
in the struggle between two very different societies. From this perspective, the antiquated southern slave labor system was snuffed out by Union
victory, and the virtues of northern modernity were thereby vindicated.
By contrast, the antebellum South exemplified a premodern society based
upon a more traditional culture and repressive labor system that, so the
argument goes, shunned modernist tendencies. However, in the attempt
to break away from the North's version of modernity, the Confederacy embarked upon a bold modernist experiment of its own, with slave labor, government centralization, and several characteristics that paralleled those of
twentieth-century corporatist states.

CORPORATIST COMPARATIVE

The Confederate example does not perfectly match all other corporatist
examples. Glaring differences exist between the well-organized corporatist regimes of the early twentieth century and the expedient corporatist
system created by the Confederacy. Charles S. Maier, preeminent historian
of Western European corporatism in the years after World War I, pointed
out some of the contrasts between the different eras of corporatist development. In the 1920s the corporatism of Italy, Germany, and France was
predicated on widespread fear of socialism among bourgeois business and
political leaders. In addition, the growing radicalization of labor unions was
undermined and controlled by inclusion in the corporatist system. Confederate corporatism, by contrast, was instigated by an elitist upper class, not
by a bourgeoisie, and while there was a threat from a laboring class in the
form of slave revolt, the Confederacy did not have to negotiate or appease
organized labor as twentieth-century governments did. Another key differ-

ence between the two eras is that more advanced corporatist states create business syndicates or cartels to minimize the potential conflicts between management and labor.[12] It is possible that the Confederacy might have developed into this more modern type of corporatist state, but the South never came close to this more interwoven relationship between the government, private sector, and labor organizations.

Despite the obvious differences, the Confederacy shared some key characteristics with twentieth-century corporatist states. In his study of the interwar corporatist systems of France, Germany, and Italy, Maier pointed out the "decay of parliamentary influence" and development of governments that "sought consensus less through the approval of a mass public than through continued bargaining among organized interests." Confederate railroad policy and the power of private munitions firms both fit the description of powerful economic blocs successfully dominating their relationship with the government. Maier also notes that twentieth-century corporatist states were sparked by the "wartime erosion of the distinction between private and public sectors," which can be seen in the Confederacy's state-owned munitions facilities being operated in conjunction with various private munitions firms. One of the hallmarks of a corporatist system, according to Maier, was that "the state claimed important new powers to control prices, the movement of labor, and the allocation of raw materials, [but] it turned over this new regulatory authority to delegates of business . . . not merely through informal consultation but also through official supervisory boards and committees."[13] This corporatist characteristic also could be used to describe the relationship between the Confederate government and vital industrial sectors like iron companies and railroads.

Another similarity between the Confederacy and other avowed corporatist governments is inflation. Historian Charles Maier argues that corporatist states use inflation "as a tempting if spurious way to purchase social peace," and that inherently the "corporatist bargaining system entailed creeping inflation."[14] According to this argument, a government finds it much easier to simply print money with which to pay businesses and laborers than to limit or deny resources. Of course, this method of appeasing the other two partners in a corporatist structure might eventually prove detrimental to the overall health of the economy.

Like some other corporatist states, the Confederacy not only experienced typical wartime inflation, but implemented fiscal policies of hyperinflation. In the Confederacy's case the basic flaw in monetary policy was too little direct taxation, inadequate revenue from government bonds, and overreliance on printed money. This type of intentional hyperinflation can also be seen in the twentieth-century corporatist example of Germany's Weimar Republic (1919–1933), which pursued a policy of hyperinflation in 1923. Hyperinflation tends to be caused by a combination of internal policies and external pressures. In the case of the Weimar Republic, it was a combination of the enormous post–World War I war reparations owed by Germany and French occupation of the industrial Ruhr Valley from January 1923 until August 1925 that sparked a general strike and exacerbated German inflationary policy. In 1924 German finances began to stabilize after a return to a gold-backed currency, thanks in part to the efforts of Hjalmar Schacht, but this period of hyperinflation had already caused irreparable damage to the Weimar Republic's credibility.[15] A portion of the Confederacy's inflation was certainly caused by scarcity of goods, but by 1864 the Confederate government, whether intentionally or not, experienced hyperinflation in the face of external pressure from invading Union armies. One could argue that in response to increasingly successful Union military campaigns, by 1864 the Confederacy resorted to a hyperinflationary fiscal policy, a strategy of other desperate corporatist governments.

CONFEDERATE POLITICAL ECONOMY AND AMERICA IN THE FIRST WORLD WAR

Fifty-two years after the surrender at Appomattox, the United States was on the verge of its first full-scale mobilization since the Civil War. World War I forced American leaders to marshal vast amounts of manpower and industrial resources and ship them across the Atlantic Ocean. The only American example that even remotely compared to this enormous wartime task was the Civil War. One might assume that President Woodrow Wilson's cabinet tried to replicate Union mobilization and industrial policy since the North won the Civil War, but the exact opposite was true. America's World War I leaders imitated the Confederate corporatist system because it more closely fit their modern vision of mobilization.

President Wilson gave his blessing to the development of a corporatist system. Wilson's southern roots and deep knowledge of the Civil War era were only coincidental. Like Jefferson Davis, Wilson was widely accused of despotism and of overseeing an increasingly centralized government. However, as pointed out by historian David M. Kennedy, American political economy in the First World War exhibited a classic corporatist relationship in which "both businessmen and government officials, including above all Woodrow Wilson, were ambiguous and hesitant about expanding state control over the economy," and as a result American leaders developed a system with "closer business-government integration." In fact, Wilson's cabinet leaders openly espoused the corporatist philosophy and put it into action. Powerful bureaucrats like the head of the War Industries Board (Bernard Baruch), secretary of war (Newton Baker), secretary of the treasury (William McAdoo), and head of the Food Administration (Herbert Hoover) were, according to Kennedy, "the leading apostles of that corporatist vision that conjured a bright future of increased efficiency and prosperity through business combination and government cooperation."[16] When one looks at the operational details of America's corporatist political economy in the First World War, it bears a striking resemblance to the Confederacy's expedient corporatist state.

Bernard Baruch, a native of Camden, South Carolina, was arguably the most important figure in President Wilson's corporatist system. As head of the War Industries Board, Baruch oversaw business-government relations for wartime production. With war looming in early 1917, Baruch sought to coordinate the efforts of industry and government under a unified wartime economy. He understood that the spirit of voluntarism required not only cooperation, but also the coordination of business and government interests. In January 1918 Baruch took control of the War Industries Board, and like his Confederate counterparts Josiah Gorgas and Colin J. McRae, albeit on a much larger scale, he directed an array of production facilities that mixed public and private interests. In a description of the War Industries Board, historian Robert Cuff also aptly summarized the philosophy of Confederate industrial policy: "In a situation tending by its very nature toward centralization and integration, the trends toward the growth of economic interest groups, giant corporations, corporate ideology, and intimate alliances between businessmen and the state all received widespread encouragement."[17] Bernard Baruch's management of the War Industries Board resembled Confederate industrial policy in several fundamental ways.

As America entered World War I in April 1917, President Woodrow Wilson and his cabinet drew important lessons from the Civil War conscription experiences of both the North and the South. One might think the northern model was emulated by the Wilson administration, but the Selective Service experience of World War I actually more closely resembled the Confederate draft system. As historian David Kennedy points out, the Wilson cabinet was composed of several bureaucrats who "were careful students of the American Civil War." They fully realized that "the Union army's experiment with the draft . . . had been a disaster, providing fewer than 6 percent of Union troops and provoking wide and deep resentment." Wilson's national draft coordinator, Provost Marshal General Enoch H. Crowder, described the Union's Civil War draft as an institution that "bared the teeth of the Federal Government."[18]

Much like Confederate conscription, the Selective Service Act of 1917 depended on the cooperation of local draft boards to enroll eligible men and to initially enforce the law's provisions. Secretary of War Newton Baker worried that there would be a widespread revolt against conscription if it appeared to be coercion by the federal government. Local draft boards were headed by prominent citizens from each community or region. Local leadership lessened the visible hard hand of compulsory government service and minimized the perception of coercion. In May and June 1917, just as in the heady days of April 1861, American men voluntarily enrolled for military service, almost ten million on June 5th alone![19] But unlike the Confederacy, the Wilson administration did not need repeated calls for troops. American mobilization in World War I can be considered excessive. Drafted troops barely served one full year in combat, and one wonders how sturdy the local conscription network would have been if the war had lasted into the 1920s. But unlike the unprepared Confederacy in which a centralized conscription system slowly evolved, from the outset the United States possessed a strong draft law with the possibility of national enforcement should local voluntarism falter.

America's political leaders realized that the railroad network was the backbone of the American economy and would be a pivotal part of mobilization and victory. Again President Wilson and his cabinet looked to the

Civil War for lessons on how to mesh the common goals of winning the war without drastically changing the fundamental operations of America's railroad system. Wilson could have mimicked Lincoln's policy, which threatened railroad companies with outright takeover if they did not fully comply with government demands, but instead he opted for a corporatist relationship that paralleled Confederate railroad policy. Confederate leaders had been woefully unqualified in both technical expertise and practical experience in coordinating a railroad network, but American leaders in 1917 had the benefit of decades of hindsight and access to knowledgeable bureaucrats to help them create a comprehensive railroad policy.

During the First World War, the railroad network played a crucial role in mobilizing the economic and human resources of American society. Wilson's cabinet faced logistical obstacles that Confederate leaders would have found insurmountable. The scale and rapidity of American mobilization for the First World War was staggering.[20] Railroad managers complained about numerous problems amidst the competing claims of customers and labor unions, but just as in the Confederacy the indispensable nature of the railroad system dominated policy formulation. In December 1917 President Wilson nominally put the American railroad network under government control with the creation of the Railroad Administration, headed by Treasury Secretary William Gibbs McAdoo. What looked like government control was actually a corporatist system in which policy was primarily directed by railroad companies.

The 1917 Railroad Administration operated much like the Confederacy's Railroad Bureau. The limited attempt by Confederate leaders to direct railroad policy was headed by bureaucrats like William Wadley and Frederick Sims, who were selected from the private sector because of their extensive industry knowledge. In a telling departure from the Confederate experience, President Wilson selected McAdoo to head the Railroad Administration. McAdoo had limited experience as a railroad man, but Wilson's selection showed that the government viewed railroads as one important sector of overall economic policy, not a separate interest.[21] Despite creation of the Railroad Administration, the government still did not completely control railroad policy.

Railroad company managers worried that wartime government direction might transition into postwar national ownership. Some Progressives had advocated nationalization of the railroad companies based on the argument that they operated like utilities, a necessary aspect of economic life. Progressives also argued that rail companies conducted business in an uncompetitive, near-monopolistic atmosphere. In 1918 railroad managers flexed their political muscles and used the Railroad Administration to protect their own interests in a truly corporatist fashion.

The notion of top-down government direction from McAdoo was immediately discarded. Historian David Kennedy uses a wonderful analogy to explain the relationship: Railroad managers "were prepared to accept McAdoo only as a steamship captain receives a harbor pilot—welcoming his temporary aid to navigate a difficult passage without relinquishing permanent command of the vessel." Akin to the numerous southern railroad conventions during the Civil War, an advisory board composed of railroad executives was created to instruct McAdoo on railroad policy. The Wilson administration promised that government oversight would end after the war, and the government guaranteed payment based on average profits from the three previous years. Instead of government control, the Wilson administration allowed railroad companies to set wartime policy in much the same way that Confederate railroad policy had been crafted by the conventions of railroad managers.[22]

Another example of the powerful railroad lobby during World War I can be witnessed in draft exemptions. Just like the Confederate experience of preferential draft exemptions for railroad employees, the railroad advisory board persuaded McAdoo to use his leverage with Secretary of War Newton Baker to exempt railroad workers from Selective Service.[23] In many respects, America's First World War railroad policy was very similar to the Confederacy's.

The Confederacy abruptly ended in 1865, but America's wartime experiment with corporatist political economy from 1917 to 1919 had far-reaching consequences. The bureaucratic experience and organizational skills of a new generation of American leaders meant that the United States was prepared to embark on a new era of modern government. The nation resorted to a corporatist system in the name of efficiency and improved economic results with a much greater degree of cooperation between government and the private sector. The implications for modern American society were obvious. According to historian David Kennedy, in the following decades after "the [First World] war can be dated the origins of the modern practice of massive informal collusion between government and organized private enterprise."[24] This practice of "informal collusion" was also evident in the Confederacy's expedient corporatist state.

The main difference between Confederate expedient corporatism and the Wilson administration's corporatist organization in the First World War is intent. Confederate leaders did not begin the war intending to create a corporatist system. American leaders in World War I, however, were more informed about their options for wartime political economy and voluntarily constructed a corporatist apparatus. It is a curious irony of American history that in its first major conflict since the Civil War, the United States opted to implement a corporatist system that had strong similarities to Confederate political economy.

THE CONFEDERACY'S CORPORATIST LEGACY

What are the implications of applying a corporatist model to American political economy? Corporatism is troubling for some historians and students of American history. Several political scientists point out the reason Americans are uncomfortable with corporatism. Corporatist theory counters the esteemed American belief in representative government, and it conjures images of undemocratic institutions that control the economy. Corporatism has earned a bad reputation due to twentieth-century corporatist regimes in Europe, which include examples like Italy and Germany in the 1920s, both of which eventually evolved into fascist states.[25] This study does not argue or imply that the Confederacy was a proto-fascist state or that, had southern independence been achieved, the Confederacy would have evolved into a fascist regime. The most extreme analysis that should be inferred from this study is that the Confederacy used authoritarian methods similar to later twentieth-century examples to mobilize southern society and prosecute the war.

Political scientists also detail the nature of twentieth-century corporatism, showing common characteristics between the Confederacy and other corporatist governments. Peter J. Williamson provides impressive corporatist analysis of various twentieth-century corporatist governments. The underlying theme is that they "all have been authoritarian in character."

In addition, Williamson notes "It is . . . possible to identify a number of common socio-economic and political aspects regarding the conditions in which corporatism was established," which include "a limited and insecure establishment of liberal democracy . . . a political system characterized by a dominant ruling elite," and an economy "with industry playing only a minority part in national output and with agriculture . . . being predominant." All of these preconditions existed in the American South at the outset of the Civil War and greatly influenced Confederate corporatist development.

The Confederate war effort also conforms to other elements of the standard corporatist definition. Williamson points out that "corporatism . . . appears to have been established in response to growing tensions amidst transition from a relatively backward agrarian economy to an essentially modern industrial capitalist one."[26] The war forced the agrarian South to rapidly industrialize, and Confederate corporatism evolved as a method of survival.

Historian Barrington Moore laid out a basic framework of conservative modernization practiced by some twentieth-century reactionary governments. Moore argues that several "conditions" are needed for a modern counterrevolution. "It takes very able leadership," Moore asserts, "to drag along the less perceptive reactionary elements, concentrated among, though not necessarily confined to, the upper classes." This description resembles the fevered process of secession across the southern states in 1861. A wide variety of southern citizens, even some previously level-headed Unionists, from all classes of southern society were eventually persuaded to support the fledgling Confederacy. The capability of Confederate political leaders during the war has rightly been questioned, but the amazing skill with which secession was achieved should not be underestimated. Moore describes the next step on the path of conservative modernization as the establishment of "a strong conservative government . . . [to] both encourage and control economic growth . . . [and] see to it that the lower classes who pay the costs of modernization do not make too much trouble."[27] Confederate leaders used a conservative yet also democratic political culture to establish bureaucracies that organized industrial production, while simultaneously limiting civil liberties. Like some twentieth-century examples, the Confederacy meets Barrington Moore's model of a reactionary government embarking upon conservative modernization.

In economic terms, Confederate political economy was a reaction against the modern liberal capitalist economy of the North. Nobel Laureate economist Edmund Phelps describes one of the primary reasons for secession in his description of corporatist motivation: "Conservative corporatists sought not just order but the *old* order . . . as they saw it, the modern culture with its yen for change was eroding the economic order in traditional communities, where members had a sense that they were working toward the shared goals of their traditional culture."[28]

The South's traditional economic system of slave-based agriculture continued alongside accelerated industrial expansion. The methods used to develop wartime industrial policy resembled those of other corporatist states. Necessity required quick creation of a munitions infrastructure, and the Confederate government used national ownership in specific sectors to guarantee production of war materiel. Through the Ordnance Department headed by Josiah Gorgas, the Confederate government embarked upon an expedient program of nationalized industrialization that was dictated more by circumstance than by adherence to any plan. An unprecedented government-business relationship developed between the Confederate government and vital economic sectors like munitions plants, iron foundries, and railroad companies. But important firms could rebuff the government's authoritarian threats and actually guide policy. The resulting relationships reflected the power of private interests over the public good. Confederate political economy departed from the liberal capitalist model of the northern states, but was no less modern in its operations.

In the ultimately failed process of nation-building, the Confederate government evolved into a far more centralized state that implemented authoritarian measures. In the Confederate system, policies like mass conscription and domestic passports diminished civil liberties. However, the Confederate experiment was not a conspiracy of oligarchs. It was instead a temporary solution made necessary for survival. Confederate nationalists were willing to risk the perils of centralization for the continued hope of independence. Some influential business leaders, however, hedged their bets and balked at unqualified support as the prospects for independence faded. Southern civilians and government officials were open to experimentation, both in terms of nationalized war industries and limited civil liberties, if the combination would achieve Confederate victory. Richmond used authoritarian policies to control the populace and nonessential industries, but allowed essential industries like munitions producers and railroad companies to largely define their own economic role. This combination of authoritarian government control over civilians and secondary economic sectors, while simultaneously allowing private dominance of indispensable economic sectors, is one of the hallmarks of a modern corporatist regime.

EXPEDIENT CORPORATISM AND CONFEDERATE NATIONALISM

The nature of the short-lived Confederate nation has been the focus of several eminent scholars of the Civil War era.[29] Lengthy scholarly debate also exists about the extent of Confederate nationalism. Recent scholarship that argues that Confederate citizens exhibited a strong sense of nationalism typically focuses on the staggering sacrifices endured during the war. Victory and the shared suffering of soldiers and families connected individual southerners into the larger purpose of Confederate independence.[30]

One of the enduring controversies of Civil War scholarship is why so many southerners, many of them nonslaveholders, supported the Confederacy. It is clear that many nonslaveholders supported secession and the war effort, but Confederate nationalism had realistic limits. Union battlefield victories finally proved to many from this group of otherwise patriotic Confederates that further military resistance was futile.[31] The foundation of many arguments that support a high degree of Confederate nationalism is the fact that a large percentage of eligible southern males performed military service, and they not only kept an opponent with superior human and material resources at bay for four years, but they came close to winning the war on the battlefield.

Slavery was inextricably tied to the Confederate national project. Paternalistic proslavery arguments of the antebellum decades were now tested under the strain of a society at war. Secession forced a renewed ideological defense of the peculiar institution and also caused southerners to reassess definitions of both slavery and liberty. As witnessed by the heated southern debate over arming slaves in exchange for emancipation in 1864–1865, the idea of a Confederate nation without slavery was, to some, simply unthinkable. Slavery was extinguished in conjunction with the Confederate national experiment, and one wonders if it would have been possible for the Confederacy to sustain nationhood without it.[32]

The debatable extent of Confederate nationalism is inextricably tied to the question of why the Confederacy collapsed. Extensive scholarship argues that Confederate nationalism was inherently weak from the outset and grew weaker despite the efforts of Confederate leaders. Internal dissent existed in several forms: avowed Unionists in geographical pockets across the South, four million African American slaves, and, as the war dragged on, lower-class white southerners who grew increasingly weary of the "rich man's war, but poor man's fight." According to this interpretation, these groups exerted sufficient internal pressure, in conjunction with Union armies, to destroy the Confederacy from within.[33]

What effect did the creation of an expedient corporatist state have on Confederate nationalism? Did the Confederacy's corporatist policies bolster the war effort or provide impetus to internal opponents of the government? The components of the Confederacy's expedient corporatist state must be examined individually to analyze their effect on nationalism. Confederate political culture, influenced by the Constitution's approval of powerful executive prerogatives, exhibited nonpartisan characteristics in which President Davis and the Congress jointly pursued policies that bolstered the war effort. Certainly some politicians disagreed with Davis's methods, but the executive and legislative branches basically agreed on major policy decisions that ensured national survival. One should not forget that the Confederacy was a democracy, and a majority of southern civilians elected these leaders to pursue the very policies that sometimes caused popular complaint. The average southern civilian likely did not know that the Supreme Court was never empowered or that Congress routinely met in secret sessions to conduct important business. Political culture, as part of the larger expedient corporatist state, benefited the Confederacy by allowing for rapid policy development and implementation, thus greatly supporting the war effort. Internal opponents of the Confederacy would have likely opposed the new government no matter what policies were carried out, so to argue that the fruits of Confederate political culture created irreparable domestic dissension is somewhat questionable.

Industrial policy symbolizes one of the most innovative aspects of the

Confederacy's expedient corporatist state. Essential private munitions companies like the Tredegar Iron Works and the Shelby Iron Company benefited from generous government subsidies and lucrative government contracts. These firms used their crucial importance to the war effort to help craft government industrial policy and also to pursue self-interested actions. One might argue that this tendency to put the concerns of the company ahead of those of the nation makes the corporatist industrial policy a detriment to Confederate nationalism, but this is not the case. Government officials were bound by circumstances to allow these companies to operate with impunity because the alternative meant diminished production.[34] The expedient nature of the Confederacy's corporatist industrial policy is perhaps best represented by the state-owned industries. Far from being a socialist experiment, these industries, like the Augusta Powder Factory and the Selma Foundry, filled vital gaps in munitions production. The mixture of private and nationalized industrial production showed the innovative nature of Confederate industrial policy and, by keeping armies supplied at the front, contributed to Confederate nationalism.

Implementation of wartime policies, or the Confederate system, included conscription, a domestic passport system, and a corporatist railroad policy. The argument that Confederate conscription was simply a top-down centralized policy underestimates the important roles played by local and state governments in the enrollment of eligible men for military service. The country could not have survived past 1862 without conscription, so this policy definitely aided Confederate nationalism. The domestic passport system evolved in relation to external military threats and, despite some criticism from frustrated southern civilians and politicians, set a modern example of government supervision of transportation. Overall, the growth of a domestic passport system was more of an asset than a liability to the Confederacy. The lack of extensive experience with railroads caused Confederate leaders to acquiesce in private sector dominance of wartime railroad policy. The result was an arrangement that exhibited unmistakable corporatist characteristics and arguably put company interests ahead of patriotism. One might argue that government control of the railroads would have better served the war effort and buttressed Confederate nationalism, but that would be speculation. The elements of the Confederate system—conscription, the domestic passport system, and railroad policy—were all unprecedented and highlight the adaptability of Confederate corporatist policy.

The war forced Confederate leaders to be innovative in terms of political culture, industrial policy, and their methods of mobilization and handling of the transportation network for the war effort. Confederate leaders unintentionally created an early example of a modern political economy that has thrived in other nations throughout the twentieth century and still exists today. The major difference between the Confederacy's version of corporatism and later examples was slavery, but the existence of the South's peculiar institution was not necessarily a hindrance to Confederate modernity.[35] Necessity and circumstance pushed Confederate leaders to develop an expedient corporatist state. This ad hoc policy formulation resulted in one of the great ironies of Civil War history. In an attempt to forestall the alleged threat of the North's modern economy rooted in liberal capitalism and hostile to slavery, the South seceded in hopes of protecting its more traditional economic system. Under wartime pressures the Confederacy began an evolutionary process of creating a modern corporatist government. The ultimate irony of Confederate political economy is obvious; in order to fight modernization the Confederacy was forced to modernize, and in the process created an expedient corporatist state perfectly compatible with slavery.

Notes

ABBREVIATIONS

The following abbreviations represent the respective repositories or works:

ADAH	Alabama Division of Archives and History
BL	Battles and Leaders of the Civil War
DUK	Perkins Library, Duke University
JCC	Journal of the Confederate Congress
NA	National Archives, Washington, D.C.
OR	Official Records of the War of the Rebellion
SCCRRMM	South Carolina Confederate Relic Room & Military Museum
SHC	Southern Historical Collection, Wilson Library, UNC Chapel Hill
SHSP	Southern Historical Society Papers
UASC	University of Alabama, Special Collections, W. S. Hoole Library

INTRODUCTION

1. For a more detailed discussion of nineteenth-century political economy, see Paul K. Conkin, *Prophets of Prosperity: America's First Political Economists* (Bloomington: Indiana University Press, 1980).

2. C. E. Black, *The Dynamics of Modernization: A Study in Comparative History* (New York: Harper & Row, 1966), 7.

3. For extensive discussion of modernization and the Civil War, see Eric Foner, "The Causes of the American Civil War: Recent Interpretations and New Directions," *Civil War History* (September 1974); Emory Thomas, *The Confederacy as a Revolutionary Experience* (Englewood Cliffs, NJ: Prentice-Hall, 1971); Raimondo Luraghi, *The Rise and Fall of the Plantation South* (New York: New Viewpoints, 1978); Richard Franklin Bensel, *Yankee Leviathan: The Origins of Central State Authority in America, 1859–1877* (New York: Cambridge University Press, 1990).

4. For further discussion of antebellum arguments for modernization in the South and Confederate views of modernism, see John Majewski, *Modernizing a Slave Economy: The Economic Vision of the Confederate Nation* (Chapel Hill: University of North Carolina Press, 2009).

5. See Chad Morgan, *Planter's Progress: Modernizing Confederate Georgia* (Gainesville: University Press of Florida, 2005), for analysis of Confederate "command economy."

6. Stephanie McCurry, *Confederate Reckoning: Power and Politics in the Civil War South* (Cambridge, MA: Harvard University Press, 2010), 96. McCurry argues that southern white women, especially soldiers' wives, carved out a powerful role in the development of Confederate policy through organization and protest. To be sure, women accessed previously closed avenues of political opinion and activity during the war, but to argue that they were a pillar of Confederate political economy overstates the case. Women did garner state attention through protest and state assistance, but they did so mainly in the context of loyalty. The women's food riots typically targeted private food retailers, not government installations, and thus their actions were an attempt to win government recognition and relief. The common sense policy of state succor for starving soldiers' wives should not be construed as an essential element of Confederate political economy, but only one of several necessities forced upon the government due to the exigencies of war.

7. E. P. Thompson, "Customs in Common: Studies in Traditional Popular Culture," in *The Essential E. P. Thompson*, ed. Dorothy Thompson (New York: Free Press, 2001), 318. Thompson defines moral economy as a "traditional view of social norms and obligations, of the proper economic functions of several parties within the community, which taken together, can be said to constitute the moral economy of the poor"; Josiah Gorgas, *The Civil War Diary of General Josiah Gorgas,* ed. Frank Vandiver (Tuscaloosa: University of Alabama Press, 1947), 28–29.

8. Mary Chesnut, *Mary Chesnut's Civil War*, ed. C. Vann Woodward (New Haven, CT: Yale University Press, 1981), 43–44; Edmund Ruffin, *The Diary of Edmund Ruffin, vol. I Toward Independence, October 1856–April 1861,* ed. William Kauffman Scarborough (Baton Rouge: Louisiana State University Press, 1972), 557.

9. See Winthrop D. Jordan, *Tumult and Silence at Second Creek: An Inquiry into a Civil War Slave Conspiracy* (Baton Rouge: Louisiana State University Press, 1993), 5.

10. James Henry Hammond to Thomas Clarkson, January 28, 1845, in *The Ideology of Slavery: Proslavery Thought in the Antebellum South, 1830–1860,* ed. Drew Gilpin Faust (Baton Rouge: Louisiana State University Press, 1981), 178.

11. See Philippe C. Schmitter and Gerhard Lehmbruch, *Trends Toward Corporatist Intermediation* (London: Sage, 1979), 13. Schmitter's definition is widely recognized as the most fundamental description of state corporatism and is usually the foundation for other explorations of the topic. According to Schmitter and Lehmbruch, "corporatism can be defined as a system of interest representation in which the constituent units are organized into a limited number of singular, compulsory, noncompetitive, hierarchically ordered and functionally differentiated categories, recognized or licensed (if not created) by the state and granted deliberate representational monopoly within their respective categories in

exchange for certain controls on their selection of leaders and articulation of demands and supports."

12. For more detail about the relationship between corporatism and capitalism, see Bob Jessop, "Corporatism and Syndicalism," in *A Companion to Contemporary Political Philosophy*, ed. Robert E. Goodin and Philip Pettit (Malden, MA: Blackwell, 1993), 404–406.

13. For further discussion of the integration of private and public sectors in corporatist states, see Howard Wiarda, *Corporatism and Comparative Politics: The Other Great "Ism"* (Armonk, NY: M. E. Sharpe, 1997), 8.

14. For more discussion of corporatism spurred by crisis, see Jessop, "Corporatism and Syndicalism," 405–406.

15. Charles S. Maier, *Recasting Bourgeois Europe: Stabilization in France, Germany, and Italy in the Decade after World War I* (Princeton, NJ: Princeton University Press, 1975). The bourgeois corporatist experiments in these countries evolved into two vastly different political systems by the 1930s. In Italy and Germany, right-wing fascist dictatorships emerged, and in France, the Popular Front, a series of short-lived leftist governments, held power.

16. Barrington Moore perhaps best summed up the secession movement in economic terms when he stated that "the ultimate causes of the war are to be found in the growth of different economic systems leading to different (but still capitalist) civilizations with incompatible stands on slavery." Barrington Moore Jr., *Social Origins of Dictatorship and Democracy: Lord and Peasant in the Making of the Modern World* (Boston: Beacon, 1966), 141.

17. For a detailed analysis of the Confederacy as a preemptive counterrevolution, see James McPherson, *Drawn with the Sword: Reflections on the American Civil War* (New York: Oxford University Press, 1996), 23. Most historians recognize that slaveholders operated with a capitalist mentality even if their methods of labor coercion symbolize elements of precapitalist production. Harry Watson sums up this dilemma of ideology and practice by declaring that "to insist on 'capitalism' and 'pre-capitalism' . . . would shackle historians to a rigid and useless teleology. . . . [perhaps] the best solution is simply to say that the market sector of the South's dual economy was a slave society that depended on the technology and institutions of the capitalist world, even as its dominant individuals sometimes feared and resisted the subversive power of those same institutions." Watson, "Slavery and Development in a Dual Economy: The South and the Market Revolution," in *The Market Revolution in America: Social, Political, and Religious Expressions, 1800–1880*, ed. Melvyn Stokes and Stephen Conway (Charlottesville: University Press of Virginia, 1996), 49. For other views on secession as a counterrevolution, see Manisha Sinha, *The Counter-Revolution of Slavery: Politics and Ideology in Antebellum South Carolina* (Chapel Hill: University of North Carolina Press, 2000).

18. George Edgar Turner, *Victory Rode the Rails: The Strategic Place of Railroads in the Civil War* (Indianapolis and New York: Bobbs-Merrill, 1953), 233; Robert C. Black III, *The Railroads of the Confederacy* (Chapel Hill: University of North Carolina Press, 1952), 63–64. For another critical interpretation of Confederate railroad policy, see John E. Clark Jr., *Railroads in the Civil War: The Impact of Management on Victory and Defeat* (Baton Rouge: Louisiana State University Press, 2001).

CHAPTER ONE

1. See Gabriel A. Almond and Sidney Verba, *The Civic Culture: Political Attitudes and Democracy in Five Nations* (Princeton, NJ: Princeton University Press, 1963).

2. George C. Rable, *The Confederate Republic: A Revolution Against Politics* (Chapel Hill: University of North Carolina Press, 1994). Rable's work greatly influenced this study, but one should also see the following to assess the various styles of investigation: Jean H. Baker, *Affairs of Party: The Political Culture of Northern Democrats in the Mid-Nineteenth Century* (Ithaca, NY: Cornell University Press, 1983); Glenn Altshuler and Stuart Blumin, *Rude Republic: Americans and Their Politics in the Nineteenth Century* (Princeton, NJ: Princeton University Press, 2000); Joel H. Silbey, *The American Political Nation, 1838–1893* (Palo Alto, CA: Stanford University Press, 1991); Mark E. Neely Jr., *The Boundaries of American Political Culture in the Civil War Era* (Chapel Hill: University of North Carolina Press, 2005).

3. This sectional divide over national resources is called the distributive model of politics, which can be defined as the ways in which regional interest groups utilize the democratic system to generate policies that benefit their respective sections. For a detailed description of distributive political systems, see Randall G. Holcombe, "The Distributive Model of Government: Evidence from the Confederate Constitution," *Southern Economic Journal* 58, no. 3 (January 1992). Also see Christopher Johnsen, Kenneth A. Shepsle, and Barry Weingast, "The Political Economy of Benefits and Costs: A Neoclassical Approach to Distributive Politics," *Journal of Political Economy* 89, no. 4 (August 1981). Economist Randall Holcombe has asserted that "the authors of the Confederate constitution . . . were concerned about the use of legislative powers to impose costs on the general public in order to provide benefits to narrow constituencies" in the northern states. Holcombe, "Distributive Model of Government," 768. Marshall DeRosa argues that "the primary concern of the Confederate framers was the centralization of political power at the national level to the detriment of the states; it was this centralization inherent in the political principles of the Federalists which they rejected." DeRosa, *The Confederate Constitution of 1861: An Inquiry into American Constitutionalism* (Columbia: University of Missouri Press, 1991), 5. The distributive model argument maintains that the principle of centralization was not the main point of contention for secessionists. Southern slaveholders were content so long as they either dominated or felt protected by a centralized national government.

4. Don E. Fehrenbacher, *Sectional Crisis and Southern Constitutionalism* (Baton Rouge: Louisiana State University Press, 1995), 141.

5. See William C. Davis, *A Government of Our Own: The Making of the Confederacy* (New York: Free Press, 1994); DeRosa, *Confederate Constitution of 1861*; Charles Robert Lee Jr., *The Confederate Constitutions* (Chapel Hill: University of North Carolina Press, 1963).

6. In the U.S. Constitution, the Ninth Amendment reads, "certain rights, shall not be construed to deny or disparage others retained by the people," and the Tenth Amendment states, "powers not delegated to the United States by the Constitution . . . are reserved to the States respectively, or to the people." Confederate framers included strict construction protections in Article VI, Section 5 and 6, and declared, "The enumeration, in the Consti-

tution, of certain rights, shall not be construed to deny or disparage others retained by the people of the several States," and "the powers not delegated to the Confederate States by the Constitution . . . are reserved to the States, respectively, or to the people thereof."

7. James Muscoe Matthews, *The Statutes at Large of the Provisional Government of the Confederate States of America* (Richmond, VA: R. M. Smith, 1864), 11.

8. For further investigation of the dominant theme of states' rights in the Confederate constitution, see DeRosa, *Confederate Constitution of 1861.* DeRosa states, "the South's answer to sectional diversity and conflict was recognizing and politically insisting upon states' rights. . . . In order for the national government to implement national policy, the consent of the states was essential" (34). Charles Robert Lee Jr. in *Confederate Constitutions* (1963) asserted, "the Confederate constitutions . . . represent the ultimate constitutional expression of the state rights philosophy and the state sovereignty concept in nineteenth century America" (150).

9. For a more detailed interpretation of slavery and the U.S. Constitution, see Don E. Fehrenbacher, *The Slaveholding Republic: An Account of the United States Government's Relations to Slavery* (New York: Oxford University Press, 2001), 15–47, 253–294. In addition, Don E. Fehrenbacher, *Sectional Crisis and Southern Constitutionalism* (Baton Rouge: Louisiana State University Press, 1995). The chapters titled "The South and the Federal Constitution" and "The Confederacy as a Constitutional System" (113–161) are of particular importance to this topic. For the most in-depth analysis of the Supreme Court's views on slavery in the old republic, see Don E. Fehrenbacher, *The Dred Scott Case: Its Significance in American Law and Politics* (New York: Oxford University Press, 1978).

10. For the backgrounds of Confederate constitutional delegates, see Charles Robert Lee Jr., *The Confederate Constitutions* (Chapel Hill: University of North Carolina Press, 1963). William C. Davis, preeminent historian of the Confederate constitutional convention, calculated that, of the original thirty-seven delegates gathered in Montgomery in early February, "eight were not slaveholders," so there is some discrepancy between Lee's census count and Davis's knowledge of the participants. See William C. Davis, *Look Away: A History of the Confederate States of America* (New York: Free Press, 2002), 57; Matthews, *Statutes at Large,* 20.

11. Davis, *A Government of Our Own,* 105.

12. Matthews, *Statutes at Large,* 15.

13. Ibid., 14.

14. Ibid., 27–28, 68–69, 127–135.

15. Ibid., 14.

16. "The Confederate plan," writes Sean Wilentz, "weakened the executive branch (by limiting the president to a single six-year term)" but strengthened other presidential powers. Wilentz, *The Rise of American Democracy: Jefferson to Lincoln* (New York: W. W. Norton 2005), 778. William C. Davis, scholarly authority on the Confederate constitutional convention, points out that delegates "wanted no imperial Presidency, and the one way to curb the possibility was to limit any man's tenure." Davis, *A Government of Our Own,* 227.

17. Matthews, *Statutes at Large,* 21.

18. Ibid., 14, 16.

19. Matthews, ibid., 15. See Richard D. Goff, *Confederate Supply* (Durham, NC: Duke University Press, 1969). Marshall DeRosa did not overlook this crucial aspect of the Confederate constitution and summed up the partial transfer of appropriations as "a significant shift in the balance of power from the legislative to the executive concerning the fiscal policy of the central government." DeRosa, *Confederate Constitution of 1861,* 85–86.

20. *The Southern Recorder,* Milledgeville, GA, April 2, 1861. Historians usually focus on Stephens's oft-quoted remarks on slavery as the "cornerstone" of the new republic but ignore the other comments.

21. Mark E. Neely Jr., *Lincoln and the Triumph of the Nation: Constitutional Conflict in the American Civil War* (Chapel Hill: University of North Carolina Press, 2011), 238.

22. *Charleston Mercury,* February 9, 1861; R. Barnwell Rhett, "The Confederate Government at Montgomery," in *Battles and Leaders of the Civil War,* ed. Clarence Buel and Robert Johnson for "The Century War Series," *Century Magazine,* The Century Co., NY (1884–1887), 1:99.

23. *Richmond Enquirer,* July 30, 1861.

24. *Charleston Mercury,* August 9, 1861.

25. JCC, vol. 1, 460, 22, 60–61; JCC, vol. 2, 25. On February 27, 1862, Assistant Doorkeeper James Wadsworth took the oath of secrecy in conjunction with being sworn in for his regular duties, not because of any suspicions about his conduct.

26. SHSP, vol. 44, 44. It should be noted that a well-read southerner with access to one or more newspapers could follow details of open session proceedings. Eventually the available open debates, those accessible to diligent southern readers during the war, were compiled in SHSP. Fortunately for historians, the *Journal of the Congress of the Confederate States of America* provides some coverage of secret session deliberations, but this information was not available to the average Confederate citizen.

27. *Charleston Mercury,* January 31, 1862; SHSP, vol. 44, 20, 44–45. Foote apparently forgot his ideological protests against secret sessions rather quickly and himself called for reclusion on March 29, 1862; this was not to be Foote's only example of hypocrisy during the war. SHSP, vol. 45, 35.

28. SHSP, vol. 44, 89–92. Rule XVII, clause 9 of the House rules indicates that the requirements for secret sessions are similar to those for the Confederate Congress. The primary difference between the U.S. and Confederate congresses was not the method but the frequency of closed door debate. Although secret sessions were more common in the Early Republic, the U.S. House of Representatives has only met secretly six times since 1825.

29. SHSP, vol. 45, 177–183; JCC, vol. 5, 301. See Congressman Franklin Sexton's comments about changing the rules, in Mary Estill and F. B. Sexton, "Diary of a Confederate Congressman, 1862–1863, I," *Southwestern Historical Quarterly* 38, no. 4 (April 1935): 276.

30. SHSP, vol. 45, 201–202.

31. Newspaper clipping with no date or title, James Thomas Leach Papers, SHC; JCC, vol. 7, 283, 17, 29, 70. It should be noted that Leach, true to form, voted "yes" on Foote's

2/3 resolution. However, the matter did not completely end after the May 17th vote. John B. Baldwin, who voted against Foote's plan, introduced a curious double-layered initiation of secrecy on May 23rd—which involved the original majority vote—to close the doors, after which "an additional question shall be put 'Shall this matter be considered in secret session?' [and] upon the vote two-thirds be found for a secret session it shall be held." JCC, vol. 7, 87. This strange and seemingly redundant motion was referred to the Rules Committee.

32. SHSP, vol. 44, 42, 51–52, vol. 45, 96.

33. SHSP, vol. 44, 74–78.

34. SHSP, vol. 44, 146, vol. 45, 116; Mary Estill and F. B. Sexton, "Diary of a Confederate Congressman, 1862–1863, II," *The Southwestern Historical Quarterly* 39, no. 1 (July 1935): 46, 62.

35. Douglas Ball, *Financial Failure and Confederate Defeat* (Urbana and Chicago: University of Illinois Press, 1991), 183–184.

36. Archibald Arrington to Kate Arrington, January 4, 1864; Archibald Arrington to Kate Arrington, January 22, 1864, Archibald Arrington Papers, SHC.

37. SHSP, vol. 50, 310–311.

38. JCC, vol. 6, 744–746, 845, 847, 866.

39. William Yancey to Clement Clay, April 26, 1863, Clement Claiborne Clay Papers, Perkins Library, DUK.

40. *Charleston Mercury,* June 13, 1862.

41. Neely Jr., *Lincoln and the Triumph of the Nation,* 268.

42. For a more complete discussion and analysis, see Fehrenbacher, *Dred Scott Case,* 43–45, 260.

43. Untitled speech, location unknown, February 1861, Archibald Arrington Papers, SHC.

44. Matthews, *Statutes at Large,* 19–20. Historians have come to several conclusions as to why Confederate constitutional delegates did not immediately create and empower a Supreme Court in the early months of the war. Charles Robert Lee Jr. points out that Christopher Memminger "introduced a motion to include in the Permanent Constitution . . . 'the appellate Jurisdiction of the Supreme Court shall not extend to any case which shall have been ajudged in any court of a State' [and concluded that] although this motion failed it indicated a strong state rights persuasion concerning the judiciary branch"; DeRosa, *Confederate Constitution of 1861,* 108. One can only wonder why this motion to protect the sovereignty of state courts failed if the reason to deny a Supreme Court derived from the ideology of states' rights. Marshall DeRosa asserts that "the Confederate Congress chose to functionally decentralize the judiciary," which "resulted in a democratization of judicial processes"; DeRosa, *Confederate Constitution of 1861,* 104. It was fear of centralized power, according to DeRosa, that prevented creation of a Confederate Supreme Court. Fear of centralization also appears in William C. Davis's explanation for the lack of a Supreme Court. When constitutional delegates discussed the issues of secession and nullification, Benjamin Hill "suggested that when any state challenged a law of the nation, its constitutionality

should be tried by the Supreme Court," at which point the opposition complained that "the last thing they wanted was a high court once again 'interpreting' a constitution . . . that was part of why they left the old compact"; Davis, *A Government of Our Own*, 250. It is fair to say that "fear of centralization" and "states' rights" were two sides of the same coin, and it is clear that delegates hesitated on Supreme Court creation due to apprehension about judicial review powers at the national level.

45. Matthews, *Statutes at Large*, 75, 78.

46. Ibid., 83–87.

47. Davis, *A Government of Our Own*, 260. Only a few of the delegates signed on March 16th, "two each from Alabama and Georgia . . . and one from Louisiana [and] those missing would be allowed to sign later"; Buck Yearns, *The Confederate Congress* (Athens: University of Georgia Press, 1960), 37.

48. JCC, vol. 2, 23; SHSP, vol. 44, 137–138; JCC, vol. 2, 94; SHSP, vol. 45, 115.

49. SHSP, vol. 46, 175–176; Ezra Warner and Buck Yearns, *Biographical Register of the Confederate Congress* (Baton Rouge: Louisiana State University Press, 1975), 118–119; JCC, vol. 2, 336–337; SHSP, vol. 47, 2. It is somewhat unclear which votes Hill lost in support of deliberation that eventually went over to the side for postponement. In the September 26th vote, the ten senators who voted to bring the issue forward were Hill, George Davis (NC), Landon Carter Haynes (TN), Gustavus Henry (TN), Augustus Maxwell (FL), James Orr (SC), James Phelan (MS), William B. Preston (VA), Thomas Semmes (LA), and Louis Wigfall (TX). Since there was no roll call for the September 27th vote, it is difficult to determine exactly which senators reversed their previous support for debating the issue and chose to delay. In the next session, Wigfall and Semmes both came out strongly against the court's appellate powers, so they were possibly two of the switched votes. Preston died in November 1862 and was replaced by Allen Caperton, who held a spot on the Judiciary Committee in the Third Session and supported Hill's efforts to organize the court.

50. *Report of the Attorney General* (Richmond, 1863), January 1, 1863, as quoted in J. G. de Roulhac Hamilton, "The State Courts and the Confederate Constitution," *Journal of Southern History* 4, no. 4 (November 1938), 427.

51. JCC, vol. 3, 20, 32; SHSP, vol. 47, 197–198.

52. SHSP, vol. 47, 197–201.

53. SHSP, vol. 47, 206–210.

54. SHSP, vol. 44, 120; vol. 47, 210–211.

55. The Clay amendment sought to repeal Sections 45 and 46 of the Judiciary Act (1861), which read: "Sec. 45. *Be it further enacted*, That a final judgment or decree in any suit, in the highest court of law or equity of a state in which a decision in the suit could be had, where is drawn in question the validity of a treaty or statute of, or an authority exercised under the Confederate States; or where is drawn in question the validity of a statute of, or an authority exercised under any state, on the ground of their being repugnant to the constitution, treaties or law of the Confederate States; or where is drawn in question the construction of any clause of the constitution, ... the decision may be re-examined,

and reversed or affirmed in the Supreme Court of the Confederate States . . . in the same manner . . . as if the judgment or decree complained of had been rendered or passed in a district court of the Confederate States. . . . Sec. 46. All judgments . . . by any state court since the date of secession . . . which before secession was within the jurisdiction of the courts of the United States, shall have the force and effect of judgments . . . of the courts herein established." Matthews, *Statutes at Large,* 84.

56. SHSP, vol. 48, 1–3, 25–27.

57. SHSP, vol. 48, 13–16, 318–319, 76.

58. Eric H. Walther, *William Lowndes Yancey and the Coming of the Civil War* (Chapel Hill: University of North Carolina Press, 2006), 359–360; SHSP, vol. 19, 374–376. The common narrative of the Hill-Yancey episode does not ask the quintessential school-yard question "who started the fight" and precise details are somewhat sketchy. Yancey later claimed innocence in instigating the assault, but his revisionism is dubious. It is probable that both men were equally to blame for the attack, although Hill should perhaps shoulder a bit more of the responsibility for having crossed the line of dignified response and resorted to physical measures. Despite being attacked by Hill, the wounded Yancey was faulted for the incident by a Senate committee, which censured him in a 9 to 8 vote. This decision showed that although many of Hill's colleagues disagreed with his methods, some basically approved of his motivation to silence the overbearing Yancey. The feud between Hill and Yancey did not resurface during the remainder of the session, and Yancey died of a kidney infection on July 27, 1863.

59. SHSP, vol. 48, 322–325.

60. Burgess Gaither to Zebulon Vance, April 24, 1863, in *Papers of Zebulon Vance: Vol. 2, 1863,* ed. Joe A. Mobley (Raleigh, NC: Division of Archives and History, 1995), 132.

61. SHSP, vol. 50, 68–69.

62. JCC, vol. 7, 26, 101, 281, 310, 758.

63. Hamilton, "The State Courts and the Confederate Constitution," 433. Hamilton asserted, "nobody paid a great deal of attention to the Confederate district courts which, by the failure to create a Supreme Court, were kept hanging in the air," but declared that by contrast, "the rulings of the state supreme courts were awaited anxiously." This somewhat overstates the case, but the point is taken that many citizens viewed the state supreme courts as the final arbiter in legal matters, not the Confederate district courts.

64. Vance to Seddon, May 22, 1863, Seddon to Vance, May 27, 1863, Vance to Seddon, June 8, 1863, in *Papers of Zebulon Vance: vol. 2,* 164, 175–176, 186–187. For a more complete description of the relationship, see Hamilton, "The State Courts and the Confederate Constitution."

65. William M. Robinson Jr., *Justice in Grey: A History of the Judicial System of the Confederate States of America* (Cambridge, MA: Harvard University Press, 1941), 529.

66. Rembert Patrick, ed., *The Opinions of the Confederate Attorneys General, 1861–1865* (Buffalo: Denis, 1950), 273–274.

67. Ibid., 376.

68. Ibid., 505.

69. For a more detailed discussion of state judicial supremacy, see DeRosa, *Confederate Constitution of 1861,* 108, 119.

70. R. Kent Newmyer, *John Marshall and the Heroic Age of the Supreme Court* (Baton Rouge: Louisiana State University Press, 2001), 339.

71. The standard states' rights interpretation for failure to empower the Supreme Court can be found in Yearns, *Confederate Congress;* Charles Robert Lee Jr., *The Confederate Constitutions;* and Marshall DeRosa, *Confederate Constitution of 1861.* Lee holds that "the tendency of the state Supreme Courts to sustain the acts of the Confederate government, and not to emphasize state rights, helps explain why the movement for a federal supreme court did not become stronger" (109–110). DeRosa states that creation of the national Supreme Court failed as a "result of the Congress intentionally deferring to the prevalent states' rights position" (108).

72. DeRosa, *Confederate Constitution of 1861,* 100.

73. Silbey, *Partisan Imperative,* 49. As political historian Joel Silbey pointed out, some leaders remained dedicated to "the traditional and usually unshakable adherence . . . to the party of their fathers, come what may," but by 1860, this was the exception. George Rable highlighted the ironic development that decades of political maneuvering dedicated "to build and maintain political parties within a slave-based political culture undermined faith in political organizations and nourished anti-party ideology." Rable, *Confederate Republic,* 10–11. According to Mark Neely Jr., secession debates were "apolitical and elevated above the corrupt ways of the old political parties." Neely Jr., *Lincoln and the Triumph of the Nation,* 249.

74. According to Kermit Hall and James Ely Jr., republicanism "deeply influenced Confederate framers" who wanted to "preserve [it] by mitigating the influence of party, checking partisan politics, placing tight restraints on self-serving politicians, and guaranteeing that those in government acted in the public interest." Hall and Ely, *An Uncertain Tradition: Constitutionalism and the History of the South* (Athens: University of Georgia Press, 1989), 202, 206.

75. For a more detailed analysis of the links between slavery and republicanism, see Harris, *Plain Folk and Gentry.*

76. SHSP, vol. 44, 91; SHSP, vol. 48, 15.

77. SHSP, vol. 1, 24; Herschel Johnson to Alexander Stephens, March 10, 1864, Herschel V. Johnson Papers, Perkins Library, DUK.

78. SHSP, vol. 48, 141–142.

79. According to Marc Kruman, the antiadministration or Conservative party was "more than a bastardization of the Whig party but less than a brand new political organization." Kruman, *Parties and Politics,* 240; see 255 for a more detailed breakdown of the 1863 election.

80. Thomas B. Alexander and Richard E. Beringer described antiparty sentiment and concluded that "the Confederate Congress . . . showed only a bare remnant of two-party behavior and not even a relic of two-party organization, . . . [and] no form of analysis . . . has exposed more than a hint of two-party performance." Alexander and Beringer, *Anatomy of*

the Confederate Congress, 331. George Rable points out, however, that these "unbending defenders of civil liberty made little effort to rally their forces, much less create an organized opposition . . . [thus] avoiding the evils of political parties." Rable, *Confederate Republic*, 210. Some historians see a modicum of party division in Confederate political culture. William C. Davis asserts, "informal parties did form, parties with no constructive platforms, no policies, no issues even, other than their support for or opposition to Davis." *A Government of Our Own*, 406–407.

81. *Richmond Enquirer*, May 31, 1861.

CHAPTER TWO

1. For a comprehensive explanation of the underdevelopment thesis, see Bateman and Weiss, *Deplorable Scarcity*.

2. For a brief discussion of the industrial sufficiency argument, see Wilson, *Confederate Industry*, vii–viii.

3. Textile factories count as an industrial base but are only indirect resources for thwarting Union forces, by the tenuous argument that Confederate soldiers might desert if poorly supplied with tents and clothing. As Glatthaar masterfully points out in *The Army of Northern Virginia*, Lee's army fought four years with its clothing in a state of perpetual tatters, but only in the last months of the war did desertion become a serious problem.

4. *Richmond Enquirer*, July 2, 1861.

5. Bateman and Weiss, *Deplorable Scarcity*, 10–13.

6. Bateman and Weiss, *Deplorable Scarcity*, 10–13.

7. "To proceed down the path of economic modernization," Chad Morgan argues, "the Confederate government resorted to forced industrialization" and in the process developed a system of "statism." Far from being simply the victory of an industrial over an agrarian society, the Civil War was, according to Morgan, "the triumph of one vision of modernity over another." Morgan, *Planters' Progress*, 63–69. Morgan focuses on the effect of Confederate policies in Georgia and refers to quartermaster impressments as "what amounted to a command economy." Morgan also describes the path of wartime industrialization as "an inverted Prussian road" and argues that "the Confederate government resorted to forced industrialization and compounded the evils of slavery with those of statism." This argument will be addressed further in the conclusion. Also see Bensel, *Yankee Leviathan*.

8. *Charleston Daily Courier*, March 13, 1861, March 23, 1861.

9. Ibid.

10. Matthews, *Statutes at Large*, 28–29.

11. Ibid., 28–29.

12. Ibid., 28–29.

13. Ibid., 33, 38.

14. Shelby Iron Company Papers, UASC. This contract will be discussed in much more detail in the later portion of this chapter.

15. SHSP, vol. 45, 47–50. In a friendly jab at his colleague, Senator Haynes "said the Senate had heard a good deal of Georgia iron" and "she is no doubt a good deal in the wind question," referring to Hills's blustering, "and if the question was one of wind, then I would yield to pre-eminence." Hill replied, "there is good deal of wind coursing about in Georgia [but] she has no East quarter—no East Tennessee," perhaps referring to the notorious amount of Unionism in this self-defined portion of the Volunteer State. Haynes fired back, "then . . . she has a cardinal point blown off, and I don't think for this reason, she ought to have a foundry."

16. Charles B. Dew, *Ironmaker to the Confederacy: Joseph R. Anderson and the Tredegar Iron Works* (New Haven: Yale University Press, 1966), 6–9, 13.

17. Ibid., 40.

18. Ibid., 44.

19. Ibid., 50–58.

20. Ibid., 63.

21. Ibid., 69–70.

22. Ibid., 81.

23. Ibid., 84; see Luraghi, *Rise and Fall* (New York: New Viewpoints, 1978); Luraghi's assertion of sale in anticipation of state socialism conveniently fits a predetermined thesis and, like other theories, is possible but speculative.

24. Dew, *Ironmaker to the Confederacy*, 150–151.

25. Ibid., 283.

26. Ibid., 127.

27. Ibid., 130; see table 6. Each ton is 2,240 lbs. of iron.

28. Ibid., 106.

29. For a more detailed list of the wide variety of artillery pieces manufactured for the Confederacy, see ibid., 324–325, 118.

30. Ibid., 111.

31. Ibid., 125.

32. Ibid., 133, 147.

33. Ibid., 149; see table 7 on 166 for disparity in private and public iron receipts.

34. Ibid., 176–177, 152.

35. Ibid., 147.

36. Ibid., 147–148,

37. Ibid., 212.

38. Ibid., 213–214.

39. Ibid., 216–217.

40. Ibid., 226.

41. As pointed out by Charles Dew, the Confederate government clearly "needed the Tredegar's production much more than the company needed the government's business." In fact the firm was so important to the war effort that "Confederate officials were willing to grant almost any legal demand the Tredegar management might make." Ibid., 143.

42. Joyce Jackson, *History of the Shelby Iron Company, 1862–1868* (Brasher Publications with the Historic Shelby Association, 1990), 2–3.

43. Thos. McConaghey to Horace Ware, July 21, 1860, Colin J. McRae Papers, ADAH; John Fraser to Horace Ware, June 7, 1860, McRae Papers, ADAH.

44. As described by Jonathan Wiener, "there were seven blast furnaces in the state . . . with a total maximum daily output of forty tons of iron [and] . . . the iron they produced was strictly for local consumption . . . kettles, ovens, stoves, saws, and skillets." Wiener, *Social Origins of the New South: Alabama, 1860–1885* (Baton Rouge: Louisiana State University Press, 1978), 139.

45. Jackson, "History of the Shelby Iron Company," 10; investor John Lapsley described his associates with pride as "Judge McClanahan (a very substantial and respected man) of Shelby County, . . . A. J. Jones (Hard ware merchant) James W. Lapsley . . . John R. Kenan . . . [and] H. Ware, the present owner of the property." John W. Lapsley to Colin McRae, February 8, 1862, McRae Papers, ADAH.

46. J. W. Lapsley to Colin McRae, February 6, 1862, Colin McRae Papers, ADAH.

47. H. H. Ware to J. W. Lapsley, March 24, 1862, Shelby Iron Company Papers, UASC.

48. List of expenditures in 1862, Shelby Iron Company Papers, UASC. It should be noted that the Shelby Iron Company papers are not completely organized. At points, specific files have been arranged by topic, but some documents are loose in files or boxes simply labeled by year. That being said, the staff at W. S. Hoole Special Collections did a fantastic job of helping me find the materials necessary for this section.

49. J. W. Lapsley to Ware and Jones, March 12, 1862, Shelby Iron Company Papers, UASC.

50. J. W. Lapsley to Ware and Jones, March 12, 1862, Shelby Iron Company Papers, UASC.

51. Initial contract offer by Shelby Company—1862, Shelby Iron Company Papers, UASC.

52. Shelby Iron Company Papers, UASC; Colin McRae to H. H. Ware, March 24, 1862, Shelby Iron Company Papers, UASC.

53. 1862 contract, Shelby Iron Company Papers, UASC.

54. 1862 contract, Shelby Iron Company Papers, UASC.

55. 1862 contract, Shelby Iron Company Papers, UASC.

56. Shelby Board of Directors Minutes, June 14, 1862; Colin McRae to H. H. Ware, April 27, 1862, Shelby Iron Company Papers, UASC.

57. Colin McRae to A. J. Jones, June 24, 1862, Shelby Iron Company Papers, UASC.

58. Shelby Directors to Colin McRae, July 3, 1862, Shelby Iron Company Papers, UASC.

59. Shelby Directors to Colin McRae, July 3, 1862, Shelby Iron Company Papers, UASC.

60. Colin McRae to A. J. Jones, August 5, 1862, Shelby Iron Company Papers, UASC.

61. A. J. Jones to Josiah Gorgas, September 29, 1862, Shelby Iron Company Papers, UASC. Charcoal blooms are the product of a relatively primitive form of iron smelting compared to modern blast furnaces. Charcoal blooms are used in production of wrought iron.

62. Josiah Gorgas to A. J. Jones, October 1, 1862, Shelby Iron Company Papers, UASC.

63. Colin McRae to A. J. Jones, November 4, 1862, A. J. Jones to McRae, November 5, 1862, McRae to A. J. Jones, November 5, 1862; Shelby Iron Company Papers, UASC.

64. Colin McRae to A. J. Jones, November 5, 1862; Shelby Iron Company Papers, UASC.

65. Colin McRae to A. J. Jones, November 14, 1862, Shelby Iron Company Papers, UASC.

66. Colin McRae to A. J. Jones, December 12, 1862; C. J. Hazard to Colin McRae, December 20, 1862, Shelby Iron Company Papers, UASC.

67. Jackson, *History of the Shelby Iron Company,* 34–35.

68. Ibid., 34–35.

69. Matthews, *Statutes at Large,* 27–28.

70. Joyce Jackson argues that "the signing of the new [1863] contract and a reorganization within the Ordnance Department marked the end of any independence the Shelby Iron Company had claimed and demanded. . . . The subjugation of the Shelby Iron Company to the complete domination by Hunt's office came gradually and though the company resisted policy dictation, circumstances made it necessary for the company to yield its position as an independent establishment." Jackson, *History of the Shelby Iron Company,* 35. Frank Vandiver asserted that Shelby management acquiesced to government demands because it realized "the Confederate government exerted vast control over all war manufactories in the South . . . [and] by use of these various controls, became practically a socialistic state." See "The Shelby Iron Company in the Civil War: A Study of Confederate Industry," *Alabama Review* 1 (1948): 117–118. Both interpretations are examples of the "command economy" argument, which declares that the relationship between the Confederate government and the Shelby Iron Company was founded upon government threats of takeover or resource denial that symbolized a top-down industrial policy conducted in a dictatorial style by the state. Both of these interpretations overstate the power of the War Department and underestimate the determination of Shelby management to subordinate the interests of the government to its own needs in the corporatist style.

71. As noted by Joyce Jackson, "the government withheld twenty per cent of the monthly payments . . . as reservation for the purpose of reimbursing the advances," but the government also held back another "ten per cent" each month to make sure that Shelby upheld its "fulfillment of the contract." Jackson, *History of the Shelby Iron Company,* 38.

72. Shelby Directors to Major William Richardson Hunt, September 3, 1863, Shelby Iron Company Papers, UASC.

73. Shelby Directors to Major William Richardson Hunt, September 3, 1863, Shelby Iron Company Papers, UASC.

74. Letter to Col. I. M. St. John, October 12, 1863, Shelby Iron Company Papers, UASC.

75. Letter to Col. I. M. St. John, October 12, 1863, Shelby Iron Company Papers, UASC.

76. Matthews, *Statutes at Large,* First Congress, Session 2, 77–79.

77. Vandiver, "The Shelby Iron Company in the Civil War," 122, 127; Shelby Board of

Directors Minutes, March 13, 1863, Shelby Iron Company Papers, UASC; Vandiver, "The Shelby Iron Company in the Civil War," 204–205.

78. As noted by Charles Dew, in 1847 Tredegar founder Joseph Reid Anderson "won a total victory in his battle with" skilled white "strikers" who were fired and "not rehired" in an innovative, if not ruthless, example of using slaves as strikebreakers. Anderson proved that skilled slave labor could be effectively and profitably utilized in iron manufacturing, and the "slaves soon took up important positions in the [iron] mills." Dew, *Ironmaker to the Confederacy,* 26.

79. Shelby Board of Directors Minutes, June 14, 1862, January 26, 1863, Shelby Iron Company Papers, UASC.

80. As Joyce Jackson points out, "puddlers and foundrymen were rented from Richmond, the Cumberland Works in Tennessee, Etowah, Georgia and establishments in Mississippi." Over the course of the war, Shelby management "employed an average of three hundred and fifty to four hundred slaves" and "approximately one-fifth of this number were engaged in skilled work." Jackson, *History of the Shelby Iron Company,* 21–22; Board of Directors Minutes, August 20, 1864, Shelby Iron Company Papers, UASC.

81. As noted by Frank Vandiver, "by October 1864, Shelby had hired 63 white women over 18 years of age and 31 boys and girls between 12 and 18 in an attempt to solve the labor problems." Vandiver, "The Shelby Iron Company in the Civil War," 212. Also see Edwin L. Combs III, "Field or Workshop: A Study of Southern Industrial Labor in the Civil War," PhD diss., University of Alabama, 2003.

82. Shelby Board of Directors Minutes, June 14, 1862; Shelby directors, undated, Shelby Iron Company Papers, found in "Correspondence, 1862–1864" file, UASC; based upon the subjects discussed, it was likely written in late 1862 or early 1863.

83. Letter from Shelby to William Richardson Hunt, September 3, 1863; Shelby Board of Directors Minutes, February 4, 1864, Shelby Iron Company Papers, UASC.

84. Shelby Directors to Hon. Charles B. Mitchell of the Confederate States Senate, April 26, 1864. Copy of letter provided by Professor T. Michael Parrish, Baylor University.

85. Shelby Board of Directors to Major William Richardson Hunt, July 25, 1864, Shelby Iron Company Papers, UASC.

86. Jackson, *History of the Shelby Iron Company,* 43–44.

87. Shelby Board of Directors to Major William Richardson Hunt, July 25, 1864, Shelby Iron Company Papers, UASC.

88. Shelby Board of Directors to Major William Richardson Hunt, July 25, 1864, Shelby Iron Company Papers, UASC.

89. William Richardson Hunt to I. M. St. John, July 15, 1864, Shelby Iron Company Papers, as quoted in Lester Cappon, "Government and Private Industry in the Southern Confederacy," in *Humanistic Studies in Honor of John Calvin Metcalf* (Charlottesville: University of Virginia Press, 1941), 182–183.

90. Shelby Directors, undated, "Correspondence, 1862–1864," Shelby Iron Company Papers, UASC.

91. See Mary DeCredico, *Patriotism for Profit* (Chapel Hill: University of North Carolina Press, 1990).

92. Political philosopher Bob Jessop defined corporatism as "an ongoing, integrated, system of representation, policy-formation and policy implementation, which is organized in terms of the function in the division of labour of those involved." Jessop, "Corporatism and Syndicalism," 404.

CHAPTER THREE

1. State-owned facilities were vital additions to Confederate military supply and were the industrial examples that have spurred arguments of "state socialism" from some historians. Several historians interpret the Confederacy as an example of nineteenth-century state socialism. Louise B. Hill initiated the state socialism interpretation by asserting that the Confederacy represented "the most successful demonstration of State Socialism to be found up to the time of modern civilization." Hill focused on Confederate foreign commerce and government intervention into blockade running and remarked that "the experiment of 1864–65, by which the Confederate government controlled all foreign commerce . . . was devised and successfully carried on by state rights Southerners" who shared "an unwavering devotion to the policy of laissez-faire" economic development. Hill admits that state socialism "came slowly and with much travail" and that "rugged individualism disputed every step" but concludes that "had the experiment been undertaken at an earlier period of the war" there would have been a greater chance for "attaining and making permanent the larger objectives of secession." Louise B. Hill, "State Socialism in the Confederate States of America," in *Southern Sketches* (Charlottesville, VA: Historical Publishing, 1936), 3–4, 31.

The state socialism school was further advanced by Raimondo Luraghi and developed into a more comprehensive interpretive model of Confederate political economy. Luraghi argued that "the slaveholding class contrived with remarkable success not to lose control over the industrializing process," and that "no capitalistic class was allowed to rise." According to Luraghi, state socialism dominated wartime industrial policy because "the Confederate government relied mainly on manufactures directly owned." As for the limited privately owned industrial sector, he asserted that Richmond bureaucrats dominated the "existing private manufactures by means of contracts which amounted to quasi-nationalisation." Luraghi put this into historical perspective and claimed, "possibly never before had America seen so ruthless a violation of the sacred rights of private property" and that "no country, from the Inca Empire to Soviet Russia has ever possessed a similar government-owned (or controlled) kind of economy." Luraghi, "The Civil War and Modernization of American Society: Social Structure and Industrial Revolution in the Old South Before and During the Civil War," *Civil War History* 18, no. 3 (September 1972): 245–246.

In *The Rise and Fall of the Plantation South* (1978) Luraghi expanded the state socialism argument. In a chapter titled "Forced Industrialization Through State Socialism," Luraghi argued that "the Confederate government acted immediately to nationalize the whole productive power of existing manufactures as far as war production was concerned." Yet arguably the most important extant industrial plant, the Tredegar Iron Works in Richmond, was never nationalized during the war. Nationalization of other war-related industries, however, did occur. Luraghi contends that "never before in history had anything like this been seen . . . a backward agricultural country . . . had created a gigantic industry, investing millions of dollars, arming and supplying one of the largest armies in the world—and all this as national property or under national control, in a kind of quasi-socialist management." Key industries vital to the Confederate war effort were indeed nationalized due to expediency, but not as a result of a "quasi-socialist" outlook among rebel leaders.

Luraghi also argues that the private sector declined and as a consequence, "private firms were bought out by the Confederacy in what amounted to a true process of nationalization." National ownership only occurred among economic sectors in which there was little or no previous industrial capacity, like gunpowder manufacturing, armories, and the manufacture of other military accoutrements meant to support the war effort. These industries were required for immediate Confederate survival, and therefore might be considered examples of expedient nationalization. Luraghi concluded "that Confederate rulers did not want a private capitalist industry; they did not want to see a powerful industrial bourgeoisie rising in the Confederacy," and as a result, they "chose the way of 'state socialism,' a solution that is as far from capitalism as the earth is from the moon." As we have seen, Luraghi's interpretation underestimates the economic leverage of privately owned firms like the Tredegar Iron Works and the Shelby Iron Company. The historical examples in which Luraghi and Hill see plans of state socialism were only examples of industrial expediency within an otherwise corporatist-style system. Luraghi, *The Rise and Fall of the Plantation South,* 126–128, 132, 150.

2. Historian of the Confederate supply system Richard Goff pointed out, "only the Richmond arsenal was immediately equipped to manufacture small arms [and] the other establishments . . . at Nashville, Baton Rouge, Montgomery, Mount Vernon, Charleston, Augusta, and Savannah, were in a position to make only accoutrements, plus cartridges." Goff, *Confederate Supply* (Durham, NC: Duke University Press, 1969), 15.

3. For a more complete and detailed prewar biography of Josiah Gorgas, see Frank Vandiver, *Ploughshares into Swords: Josiah Gorgas and Confederate Ordnance* (Austin: University of Texas Press, 1952), 3–54.

4. Ibid., 75. In addition to these gunpowder sources, Confederate authorities sought expansion of the Sycamore powder mill in Nashville, and the state of North Carolina attempted to establish a powder operation in Raleigh. See John C. Barrett, *The Civil War in North Carolina* (Chapel Hill: University of North Carolina Press, 1963), 27.

5. The most complete study of George Washington Rains and the innovations implemented in the construction and management of the Augusta Powder Works is C. L. Bragg, Charles D. Ross, Gordon A. Blaker, Stephanie A. T. Jacobe, and Theodore P. Savas, *Never for Want of Powder: The Confederate Powder Works in Augusta, Georgia* (Columbia: University of South Carolina Press, 2007). This book contains detailed sketches of the powder works

along with excellent biographical data about Rains and his importance to the Confederate war effort.

6. George Washington Rains, "History of the Confederate Powder Works," *The New-burgh Daily News Print,* Newburgh, NY, 1882, 27, 3–4.

7. Gorgas to G. W. Rains, September 30, 1861, George Washington Rains Papers, SHC.

8. George Washington Rains, "Col. Rains Appeal for the Powder Works Obelisk," George Washington Rains Papers, SHC.

9. "Col. Rains Appeal."

10. Augusta Powder Factory Records, September 1861, National Archives, Washington, D.C., Record Group #109, Entry #35, vol. 1.

11. Augusta Powder Factory Records, September 1861, National Archives, Washington, D.C., Record Group #109, Entry #35, vol. 1.

12. For details of Rains's various duties and responsibilities, see Theodore P. Savas, in Bragg et al., *Never for Want of Powder,* 21–23.

13. In June 1862 the mixing house consumed 482,349 pounds of ingredients: 72,526 pounds of charcoal, 48,333 pounds of sulfur, and 361,490 pounds of saltpeter. These ingredients were combined as required by Rains's gunpowder recipe, which established a standard for the number of pounds "of each ingredient used in a 70 lb. charge, Saltpeter 53.5 oz, Sulfur 7 lbs., and Charcoal 9 lbs. and 13 ozs." Receipts and Issues at Mixing House, June 1862, Augusta Powder Factory Records, NA, Washington, D.C., Record Group #109, Entry #35, vol. 1. The statistics for powder shipped can be found in Bragg et al., *Never for Want of Powder,* 112–113. Table 1 is a compilation of the detailed ledger in the National Archives. Figure 21 is a graph that displays the amount of powder shipped.

14. As listed in Bragg et al., *Never for Want of Powder,* 112.

15. Ibid., 112.

16. "Daily Report of William Pendleton, Superintendent of the Powder Works, December [November] 1, 1862–Nov 28, 1863," NA, Record Group 109, Entry #32, vol. 4A.

17. Daily Report of William Pendleton, Superintendent of the Powder Works, December 7, 1863–April 25, 1865, NA, Record Group 109, Entry # 32, vol. 4B.

18. Bragg et al., *Never for Want of Powder,* 102; Daily Report of William Pendleton, Superintendent of the Powder Works, December 7, 1863–April 25, 1865, NA, Record Group 109, Entry # 32, vol. 4B.

19. Daily Report of William Pendleton, Superintendent of the Powder Works, December 7, 1863–April 25, 1865, NA, Record Group 109, Entry #32, vol. 4B. The labor data are incomplete for January 1864 (only six days recorded), February 1864 (only eight days recorded), and August 1864 (only five days recorded). There are no available data for the months of March, May, June, and July 1864. The numbers significantly drop the last week of December 1864, presumably because of the traditional holiday week for slave laborers between Christmas and New Year's, which would have caused a drastic decrease in the labor force.

20. Josiah Gorgas, January 21, 1864, *The Journals of Josiah Gorgas, 1857–1878,* ed. Sarah Woolfolk Wiggins (Tuscaloosa: University of Alabama Press, 1995), 92.

21. Josiah Gorgas to G. W. Rains, October 30, 1864, George Washington Rains Papers, SHC.

22. Josiah Gorgas to G. W. Rains, October 30, 1864, George Washington Rains Papers, SHC.

23. Daily Report of William Pendleton, Superintendent of the Powder Works, December 7, 1863–April 25, 1865, NA, Record Group 109, Entry # 32, vol. 4B.

24. Josiah Gorgas, November 21, 1864, *Civil War Diary of General Josiah Gorgas*, 151. For the possible transfer of the powder mill to Columbia, South Carolina, see Theodore Savas, in Bragg et al., *Never for Want of Powder*, 26–27.

25. Josiah Gorgas to G. W. Rains, February 23, 1865, March 4, 1865, March 14, 1865, George Washington Rains Papers, SHC.

26. Josiah Gorgas to G. W. Rains, February 27, 1862, George Washington Rains Papers, SHC.

27. James H. Hammond to G. W. Rains, May 21, 1862. Hammond offered to meet with Rains and give his military advice again on July 14th. It is unclear if Rains ever met with the controversial antebellum fire-eater. For a detailed description of the makeup of officers in the First Regiment Local Troops, Georgia Infantry, see C. L. Bragg in Bragg et al., *Never for Want of Powder*, 223–234.

28. Benjamin Huger to G. W. Rains, January 6, 1864, George Washington Rains Papers, SHC; Major McIntosh to G. W. Rains, September 23, 1864, George Washington Rains Papers, SHC.

29. Vandiver, *Ploughshares into Swords*, 231–232.

30. Warner and Yearns, *Biographical Register of the Confederate Congress* (Baton Rouge: Louisiana State University Press, 1975), 163–164.

31. *OR*, series IV, vol. 1, 107–108.

32. Colin McRae to Jefferson Davis, February 4, 1862, McRae Papers, SCCRRMM.

33. Colin McRae to Jefferson Davis, February 4, 1862, McRae Papers, SCCRRMM. Parentheses around the words—Ware Mines—were not added by the author but in the original letter, and presumably refer to Horace Ware.

34. Colin McRae to Jefferson Davis, February 4, 1862, McRae Papers, SCCRRMM.

35. Letter from McRae to J. P. Benjamin and S. R. Mallory, February 19, 1862, McRae Papers, SCCRRMM. In this letter McRae originally wrote, "I propose to do so provided I can have such patronage from the government" but crossed out "from the government"; Colin McRae to Jefferson Davis, February 24, 1862, McRae Papers, ADAH. The word *immediately* was underlined in the original letter.

36. Colin McRae to Josiah Gorgas, March 10, 1862; J. W. Lapsley to Colin McRae, March 22, 1862, Colin J. McRae Letters, SCCRRMM; George Minor to Colin McRae, March 25, 1862, Colin J. McRae Letters, ADAH.

37. Contract with CSA Government, Colin J. McRae Papers, SCCRRMM.

38. Wiener, *Social Origins of the New South*, 137.

39. Josiah Gorgas to Colin McRae, May 14, 1862. This information is contained in two separate letters on the same day.

40. John Gill Shorter to Colin McRae, November 13, 1862; Incorporation of Selma Iron Foundry Company, December 5, 1862, SCCRRMM; SHSP, vol. 12, 83; Contract of Sale, February 12, 1863, Colin J. McRae Papers, SCCRRMM.

41. William Still, "Selma and the Confederate States Navy," *Alabama Review* 15, no. 1 (January 1962): 22–24, 29, 37.

42. Vandiver, *Ploughshares into Swords,* 240–241.

43. J. Donald McKee and Mark Cooper Pope III, *Mark Anthony Cooper: The Iron Man of Georgia, A Biography* (Atlanta: Graphic Publishing, 2000), 159, 172, 178, 180, 185. The owners after Cooper were William T. Quimby and William A. Robinson. They still held some ownership interest in the facility, but the Confederate government held the mortgage and title to the Etowah Iron Works. This arrangement apparently was amenable to both parties, since the partners received $1,250,000 in Confederate funds for operation and the Ordnance Department increased its armament supply. The Etowah Iron Works was destroyed by Union forces in May 1864, so government production only lasted about twenty-one months. See McKee and Pope, *Mark Anthony Cooper,* 186–187.

44. The state socialism model contains two main flaws that should not be ignored in an overall assessment. First, the state socialism argument overlooks the capitalists, both the agricultural capitalist slaveholders and the growing class of industrial capitalists, who facilitated the dramatically increased production of war materiel. The state socialism argument depends entirely upon the phenomenon of nationalized industries to prove its existence and neglects one of the main points of any self-proclaimed socialist society: equality. Socialist societies may not be completely egalitarian in practice, but each one must at least make a pretense or rhetorical attempt of pursuing equality for all citizens. Southerners, however, were devoted to American-style capitalism. The Confederacy never espoused full equality, except perhaps political equality for white male property holders, and in fact a foundational core of inequality was its cornerstone. The state socialism model compels historians to contemplate the nature of industrial growth and come to terms with partial nationalization of war industries, but as a useful synthesis the state socialism argument is deficient.

45. Charles Beard and Mary Beard, *The Rise of American Civilization* (New York: MacMillan, 1927), vol. 2, 53–54; Louis Hacker, *The Triumph of American Capitalism: The Development of Forces in American History to the End of the Nineteenth Century* (New York: Columbia University Press, 1940); Roger Ransom, "Fact and Counterfact: The 'Second American Revolution' Revisited," *Civil War History* 45, no. 1 (March 1999); Roger Ransom, "War and Cliometrics: Adventures in Economic History," *Journal of Economic History* 66, no. 2 (June 2006): 272–274.

46. For a more detailed interpretive debate about the Hacker-Beard thesis, see Robert Gallman, "Commodity Output, 1839–1899," in *Output, Employment, and Productivity in the Nineteenth Century,* National Bureau of Economic Research (Princeton: Princeton University Press, 1960), and Robert Gallman, "Gross National Product in the United States after 1800," National Bureau of Economic Research (Princeton: Princeton University Press, 1966). Also see Thomas Cochran, "Did the Civil War Retard Industrialization?," *Mississippi*

Valley Historical Review 48 (September 1961); Stanley Engerman, "The Economic Impact of the Civil War," *Explorations in Entrepreneurial History,* series 2, vol. 3 (Spring 1966); and James McPherson, *Battle Cry of Freedom: America in the Civil War Era* (New York: Ballantine, 1988), 453.

47. For a more detailed discussion of this standard interpretation of the Union during the Civil War, see McPherson, *Battle Cry of Freedom,* 442–453.

48. Mark R. Wilson, *The Business of Civil War: Military Mobilization and the State, 1861–1865* (Baltimore: Johns Hopkins University Press, 2006), 105–106, 191–192.

49. McPherson, *Battle Cry of Freedom,* 442; Thomas, *Confederacy as a Revolutionary Experience,* 82.

50. For a detailed argument about the importance of Lee's Army of Northern Virginia to Confederate nationalism, see Gary Gallagher, *The Confederate* War (Cambridge: Harvard University Press, 1997), 63–111.

CHAPTER FOUR

1. SHSP, vol. 44, 10–14.

2. Albert Burton Moore, *Conscription and Conflict in the Confederacy* (New York: MacMillan, 1924), 6–8. It is quite remarkable that Moore's book is still the authoritative study on Confederate conscription policy.

3. Charles Edward Cauthen, *South Carolina Goes to War, 1860–1865* (Chapel Hill: University of North Carolina Press, 1950), 142–143. According to John Edmunds Jr., South Carolina's Executive Council "became more dictatorial than the governor and possessed almost unlimited powers . . . [that] encompassed both executive and legislative prerogatives." Edmunds, "South Carolina," in *Confederate Governors,* ed. Buck Yearns (Athens: University of Georgia Press, 1985), 171.

4. O.R., series 4, vol. I, no. 127, 973–977.

5. Matthews, *Statutes at Large,* 29–32. The Confederate Congress passed two strong symbols of the expedient corporatist state in consecutive days. The first conscription law passed on April 16th and the sweeping subsidies for munitions industries passed on April 17, 1862.

6. Ibid., 29–32.

7. Ibid., 51–52.

8. D. W. Hill to Thomas David Smith McDowell, August 25, 1862, Thomas David Smith McDowell Papers, SHC; E. Phillips to Archibald Arrington, January 20, 1864, Archibald Arrington Papers, SHC.

9. John Sacher points out, however, that principals were not necessarily derided as wealthy snobs who merely wanted to shirk their duty to the Confederate war effort; instead they were men who "followed the law and often provided services to the community and the Confederacy." According to Sacher, "principals would not be judged by their wealth and the fact that they had hired substitutes, but by what they supplied the community." Sacher

argues that southerners who hired substitutes were not "evaders and cowards who should be considered alongside deserters and Unionists"; in many communities they "could be patriotic Confederates." Sacher, "The Loyal Draft Dodger: A Reexamination of Confederate Substitution," *Civil War History* 57, no. 2 (June 2011): 154, 159, 178.

10. Josiah Gorgas, August 14th, 1862, *The Civil War Diary of General Josiah Gorgas,* ed. Frank Vandiver, 13.

11. Matthews, *Statutes at Large,* 61–62.

12. Ibid., 77–79.

13. Peter H. Wood, *Black Majority: Negroes in Colonial South Carolina from 1670 through the Stono Rebellion* (New York: Norton, 1974), 325; O.R., series 4, vol. IV, no. 127, 1106.

14. Matthews, *Statutes at Large,* 158–159.

15. Ibid., 213–214.

16. As James McPherson points out, "although only four or five thousand planters or overseers obtained exemptions under the law—representing about 15 percent of the eligible plantations and 3 percent of the men exempted for all causes—the symbolism of the law was powerful." McPherson, *Battle Cry of Freedom,* 612.

17. John Beauchamp Jones, *A Rebel War Clerk's Diary, vol. 1,* ed. Howard Swiggett (New York: Old Hickory Bookshop, 1935), 233–234. For more information about the innovative but controversial career of Gabriel J. Rains, see Michael Brem Bonner, "Gabriel J. Rains and the Ethical Controversy Over Confederate Land Mine Use," MA thesis, East Carolina University, 1998; Robert Garlick Hill Kean, *Inside the Confederate Government: The Diary of Robert Garlick Hill Kean,* ed. Edward Younger (New York: Oxford University Press, 1957), 84–85.

18. O.R., series IV, vol. 1, no. 127, 1104, 1107–1108, 1140–1141, 1144, 1153–1154; O.R., series IV, vol. 2, no. 128, 155–156. Ezra Warner attributed Preston's bureaucratic success to the fact that he "was an orator of great force, and perhaps for this reason, his management of the unpopular conscript bureau was extremely able." Warner, *Generals in Gray: Lives of the Confederate Commanders* (Baton Rouge: Louisiana State University Press, 1959), 246.

19. Josiah Gorgas, April 12th, 1863, *The Civil War Diary of General Josiah Gorgas,* ed. Frank Vandiver, 32.

20. Matthews, *Statutes at Large,* 211–215; Josiah Gorgas, January 31, 1864, *The Civil War Diary of General Josiah Gorgas,* 77.

21. Matthews, *Statutes at Large,* 211–215.

22. Ibid., 211–215.

23. Southern newspapers held a variety of opinions about conscription, but according to Albert Moore, "as a rule the leading newspapers supported the conscription act." Moore, *Conscription and Conflict in the Confederacy,* 21. For a sampling of newspaper opinions about conscription, see Moore, *Conscription and Conflict in the Confederacy,* 21–23.

24. Kenneth W. Noe provides a much-needed look into the motivations of rebel soldiers who enlisted after one full year of war. According to Noe, conscripts and late enlistees were not necessarily the shirkers and cowards of historical legend. Noe points out that this group of reluctant rebel soldiers may not have been inspired by the call of southern rights in 1861, but after they joined the army there was a "slow, final adjustment to the reality of

service." The evidence of what motivated late enlistees is by no means comprehensive; according to Noe's extensive sample, many of the volunteers were motivated by an "ideology and hatred of the enemy," but behind it all was the threat of conscription. There is little doubt that conscripts and mildly coerced volunteers were "less ideological than 1861 enlistees and less imbued with camaraderie and especially unit pride," but they did fight, and according to Noe, there is "no evidence" that they skedaddled like cowards during combat or deserted at higher rates than regular troops. Noe, *Reluctant Rebels: The Confederates Who Joined the Army after 1861* (Chapel Hill: University of North Carolina Press, 2010), 109, 120–121, 195, 207.

25. For a detailed analysis of the class conflict and internal collapse interpretation, see Paul D. Escott, *After Secession: Jefferson Davis and the Failure of Confederate Nationalism* (Baton Rouge: Louisiana State University Press, 1978) and more recently David Williams, *Bitterly Divided: The South's Inner Civil War* (New York: New Press, 2008). Other notable works that focus on internal division in the Confederacy as a major cause of defeat are David J. Eicher, *Dixie Betrayed: How the South Really Lost the Civil War* (New York: Little, Brown, 2006); McCurry, *Confederate Reckoning: Power and Politics in the Civil War South* (Cambridge: Harvard University Press, 2010); and Bruce Levine, *The Fall of the House of Dixie: The Civil War and the Social Revolution that Transformed the South* (New York: Random House, 2013).

26. McPherson, *Battle Cry of Freedom,* 605; James W. Geary, "Civil War Conscription in the North: A Historiographical Review," *Civil War History* 32, no. 3 (September 1986): 224–226. For a more detailed discussion of Union conscription, see James W. Geary, *We Need Men: The Union Draft in the Civil War* (DeKalb: Northern Illinois University Press, 1991). Geary argues that "with the combination of recruiting, bounties, drafting, and all of the attendant difficulties that resulted in obtaining men for the Union army, the methods employed in the Civil War North were indeed curious" (172).

27. NA, Record Group 109, Boxes 1–7.

28. For a more detailed description and analysis of the Provost Department, see Kenneth Radley, *Rebel Watchdog: The Confederate States Army Provost Guard* (Baton Rouge: Louisiana State University Press, 1989).

29. Major Griswold to Brig. Gen. Winder, January 22, 1864, Communication of the Secretary of War, Confederate States of America, War Department, Richmond, Va., January 27, 1864, Gorgas Library, University of Alabama.

30. *O.R.,* series 2, vol. III, 735; *O.R.,* series 1, vol. LI, no. 2, 491.

31. *O.R.,* series 1, vol. VI, 857–858. The provost assigned to the 2nd District of Orleans parish was Pierre Soule, former Democratic senator and architect of the Ostend Manifesto (1854); *O.R.,* series 2, vol. III, 877.

32. Major Griswold to Brig. Gen. Winder, January 22, 1864, Communication of the Secretary of War, Confederate States of America, War Department, Richmond, Va., January 27, 1864, Gorgas Library, University of Alabama.

33. For a more detailed discussion of Winder's early career and decision to side with the Confederacy, see Arch Frederic Blakey, *General John H. Winder* (Gainesville: University

Press of Florida, 1990), 6–65, 88–118; also for a quick summary of Winder's background and career, see Warner, *Generals in Gray*, 340–341.

34. As Arch Blakey points out, although "Winder had broad powers under martial law . . . he was not a dictator . . . [and] the Richmond police still functioned." Blakey, *General John H. Winder*, 122.

35. Jones, *A Rebel War Clerk's Diary*, vol. I, 113–114; Elizabeth R. Varon, *Southern Lady, Yankee Spy: The True Story of Elizabeth Van Lew, A Union Agent in the Heart of the Confederacy* (New York: Oxford University Press, 2003), 78–79.

36. Lewis Chamberlayne to Major J. H. Carrington, undated, NA, Record Group 109, Records of the Confederate Passport Office, Entry 10, Box 1.

37. Dr. W. Waugh passport, December 13, 1864, NA, Records of the Confederate Passport Office, Record Group 109, Entry 10, Box 3; see Central Rail Road and Fredericksburg Rail Road passes, NA, Records of the Confederate Passport Office, Record Group 109, Entry 10, Box 3.

38. Tredegar Iron Works Passport Applications, August 31, 1864, NA, Records of the Confederate Passport Office, Record Group 109, Box 1.

39. Tolson Application, July 18, 1864, NA, Record Group 109, Records of the Confederate Passport Office, Entry 10, Box 3.

40. Major J. H. Carrington, January 12, 1865, NA, Record Group 109, Records of the Confederate Passport Office, Entry 10, Box 3.

41. Griswold to Pegram, February 14, 1864, NA, Record Group 109, Records of the Confederate Passport Office, Box 7. It is difficult to make out the name of the addressee in this letter, but it looks like Major General Pegram. The most likely recipient of Griswold's letter was the ill-fated Brigadier General John Pegram. Since Pegram was transferred from a western theater cavalry assignment to command an infantry brigade in Lee's 2nd Corps in early 1864, he would have likely been unfamiliar with the stringent passport rules around the capital. Also as a native of Petersburg, he likely chafed at being required to ask permission to travel in his home region. The other problem is that John Pegram was never officially promoted to major general and even at the time of his death at Hatcher's Run (February 6, 1865), approximately one year after this letter, Pegram still held the rank of brigadier general. I opted not to assume that John Pegram was the intended reader of Griswold's letter because some uncertainty existed about not only the name, but the rank listed on the heading.

42. NA, Records of the Confederate Passport Office, Record Group 109, Box 1. The dates were not randomly selected but were arrived at by a combination of available evidence in the 1862 records and a comparable month two years later, when most of the same travel routes and options were still available to Richmond travelers. Examples of the number of passes issued on other days of the week in March 1862 are: Friday, March 21st—1,350, and Saturday, March 22nd—950.

43. JCC, vol. 6, 615.

44. Communication of the Secretary of War, Confederate States of America, War Department, Richmond, Va., January 27, 1864, Gorgas Library, University of Alabama, 1–2.

45. Ibid., 3–4.

46. Ibid., 4–5.

47. Ibid., 5; "List of Officers and Employees in the Office of Provost Marshal, Richmond, April 5, 1864," Confederate States of America Collection, Louisiana State University Special Collections.

48. NA, Records of the Confederate Passport Office, Record Group 109, Box 7.

49. Ibid. The column heading "Rec'd" is short for "Received." The column for "Signatures" has been left blank so as not to clutter the chart with the perfunctory validation of passport office clerks.

50. Rev. E. Lewiston passport, NA, Records of the Confederate Passport Office, Record Group 109, Box 1.

51. Estill and Sexton, "Diary of a Confederate Congressman, 1862–1863, I"; SHSP, vol. 45, 226.

52. SHSP, vol. 45, 224; SHSP, vol. 47, 46–47.

53. Jones, *A Rebel War Clerk's Diary,* vol. II, 20.

54. SHSP, vol. 47, 72–73; *O.R.,* series 4, vol. II, 640; *O.R.,* series 1, vol. 42, part 3, 1149–1150.

55. *O.R.,* series 1, vol. 39, part 3, 848–849.

56. *O.R.,* series 1, vol. LI, no. 2, 815–816.

57. *O.R.,* series 4, vol. II, 405. Jones put quotation marks around the phrase "patriotic contributions," and one could speculate that these funds might have been offered by private citizens to help smooth their passport office experiences in the future.

58. Jones, *A Rebel War Clerk's Diary,* vol. II, 77; Alfred Hoyt Bill, *The Beleaguered City: Richmond, 1861–1865* (New York: Knopf, 1946), 205. Bill gives a negative impression of the "elegant young assistant provost marshals [who] sat with their polished boots on their desks" and asserts that the "Provost Guard was as outrageous as it was active."

59. Communication of the Secretary of War, Confederate States of America, War Department, Richmond, Va., January 27, 1864, Gorgas Library, University of Alabama, 8.

60. Mark E. Neely Jr., *Southern Rights: Political Prisoners and the Myth of Confederate Constitutionalism* (Charlottesville: University of Virginia Press, 1999), 2.

61. Craig Robertson, *The Passport in America: The History of a Document* (Oxford: Oxford University Press, 2010), 142; also see appendix, 254, 294n41. For a more detailed description of Seward's agents, see James G. Randall, *Constitutional Problems under Lincoln* (New York: Appleton, 1926), 149–150.

62. For a detailed scholarly look at the Lincoln administration's record on civil liberties, see Mark E. Neely Jr., *The Fate of Liberty: Abraham Lincoln and Civil Liberties* (New York: Oxford University Press, 1991), and William A. Blair, *With Malice Toward Some: Treason and Loyalty in the Civil War Era* (Chapel Hill: University of North Carolina Press, 2014).

63. John Moody, *The Railroad Builders* (New Haven, CT: Yale University Press, 1919). Economist Milton Friedman once remarked in a 1996 television interview with Jim Lehrer that "there are two superpowers in the world today in my opinion. There's the United States and there's Moody's Bond Rating Service. The United States can destroy you by

dropping bombs, and Moody's can destroy you by downgrading your bonds. And believe me, it's not clear sometimes who's more powerful."

64. As described by Robert C. Black III, "the relative increase in railroad mileage between 1850 and 1860 was somewhat greater in the South than in the North." Black, *Railroads of the Confederacy*, 2. According to preeminent Civil War railroad historian George Edgar Turner, Confederate railroad "policy is difficult either to recognize or define, for it was in no sense comprehensive and its inconsistencies frequently cast doubt on its actual existence." Turner, *Victory Rode the Rails*, 233. James W. Ely Jr. also argued that Confederate railroad policy was essentially nonexistent. Ely asserted that "despite pledges of cooperation by railroad companies and the Herculean efforts of a few government officials, the Confederacy never formulated a coherent policy towards its railroads." The reasons for this lack of uniform railroad policy, according to Ely, were "states' rights ideology, pervasive localism, and disinclination of the Confederate government to forcefully assert control over the railroads." Ely, *Railroads and American Law* (Lawrence: University Press of Kansas, 2001), 44.

65. According to Robert Black, the Confederacy "was never to exert an effective supervision over its railways" due to a policy structure "wherein private interests were to remain inviolate." Black, *Railroads of the Confederacy*, 63–64.

66. Turner, *Victory Rode the Rails*, 246.

67. JCC, vol. 1, 379; Draft of Railroad Bill, August 21, 1861, Accounts of the Confederate Government with Railroads, 1861–1865, NA, Record Group 109, Entry 54, Box #2.

68. Draft of Railroad Bill, August 21, 1861, Accounts of the Confederate Government with Railroads, 1861–1865, NA, Record Group 109, Entry 54, Box 2. The remarks to the Military Affairs Committee, chaired by South Carolina congressman William Porcher Miles, are on the outside of the document draft and it is impossible to make out the name of the person who commented on the bill. There is no record of a vote on the Railroad Bill in the *Journals of the Confederate Congress*.

69. *Journals of the Confederate Congress*, vol. I, 379. George Edgar Turner aptly summarized the problem faced by Confederate leaders and declared that "perhaps it would have been too much to expect of the lords of the cotton kingdom . . . [to] suddenly become masters of mechanized transportation." Turner, *Victory Rode the Rails*, 318.

70. Charles Ramsdell, "The Confederate Government and Railroads," *American Historical Review* 22 (1917): 795–796.

71. *Official Records of the War of the Rebellion*, series 4, vol. 1, 269, 538.

72. As noted by Charles Ramsdell, southern railroad companies "were enjoying a government patronage which greatly exceeded their former business." Ramsdell, "The Confederate Government and Railroads," 796.

73. Lt. Col. Larkin Smith, January 13, 1862, NA, Accounts of the Confederate Government with Railroads, 1861–1865, Record Group #109, Entry # 54, Box 2.

74. *O.R.* series 4, vol. 1, 1010–1011; Josiah Gorgas, July 27, 1862, *The Diary of General Josiah Gorgas*, ed. Frank Vandiver, 10.

75. JCC, vol. 5, 82; SHSP, vol. 44, 188; JCC, vol. 5, 251–254; Black, *Railroads of the Confederacy*, 98–99.

76. *O.R.* series 4, vol. 2, 108–109.

77. *O.R.* series 4, vol. 1, 1048; Black, *Railroads of the Confederacy*, 65–70, 110.

78. Black, *Railroads of the Confederacy*, 111–112.

79. *O.R.* series 4, vol. 2, 270–273. Richard Black asserted that Wadley's ineffectual supervision was caused by the fact that he maintained "the prejudices of a railroad man" and "if Congress would not give him an effective law . . . he preferred that the railroads should stay in the hands of railroad men." Black, *Railroads of the Confederacy*, 116.

80. Black, *Railroads of the Confederacy*, 119–120.

81. Ibid., 120–121.

82. Wadley's departure, as noted by Robert C. Black, could have been linked to his northern birth, a case of antebellum "business revenge," or his obvious tendency to side with railroad companies in negotiations. Black, *Railroads of the Confederacy*, 121–123.

83. *O.R.* series 4, vol. 2, 881–883.

84. NA, Accounts of the Confederate Government with Railroads, 1861–1865, Record Group 109, Entry 54, Box 2. The five-man committee consisted of George W. Adams, superintendent of the Georgia Central Railroad; H. T. Peake, superintendent of the South Carolina Railroad; H. S. Haines, superintendent of the Charleston & Savannah Railroad; William Johnston, president of both the Charlotte & South Carolina Railroad and Atlantic, Tennessee, & Ohio Railroad; and D. H. Cram, superintendent of the Montgomery & West Point Railroad.

85. NA, Accounts of the Confederate Government with Railroads, 1861–1865, Record Group 109, Entry 54, Box 2.

86. NA, Accounts of the Confederate Government with Railroads, 1861–1865, Record Group 109, Entry 54, Box 2.

87. Robert C. Black summed up the power of the railroad companies' corporatist bloc when he declared that "the Government stood helpless before [the] determined railroad interest; to protect itself it possessed nothing save the impressment statute and the railroad variant of May 1, 1863, neither of which it cared or dared to invoke." Black, *Railroads of the Confederacy*, 172.

88. Josiah Gorgas, April 11, 1864, *Diary of General Josiah Gorgas*, 92; Robert E. Lee to Secretary of War James Seddon, April 12, 1864, as quoted in Gary Gallagher, *Becoming Confederates: Paths to a New National Loyalty* (Athens: University of Georgia Press, 2013), 24.

89. Matthews, *Statutes at Large*, 214–215.

90. Memorial to the Honorable Senate and House of Representatives of the Confederate States of America, May 9, 1864, NA, Accounts of the Confederate Government with Railroads, 1861–1865, Record Group 109, Entry 54, Box 2, item 2.

91. Ramsdell, "The Confederate Government and Railroads," 808–809.

92. Turner, *Victory Rode the Rails*, 246; Ramsdell, "The Confederate Government and Railroads," 799; Graham K. Wilson, "Why Is There No Corporatism in the United States?" in *Patterns of Corporatist Policy Making*, ed. Gerhard Lehmbruch and Philippe C. Schmitter (London: Sage, 1982), 221.

93. Black, *Railroads of the Confederacy*, 294–295.

94. Robert G. Angevine, *The Railroad and the State: War, Politics, and Technology in Nineteenth Century America* (Stanford, CA: Stanford University Press, 2004), 130, 151, 164. For another interpretation of Union railroad policy and its ramifications for the South and the postwar years, see William G. Thomas, *The Iron Way: Railroads, the Civil War, and the Making of Modern America* (New Haven, CT: Yale University Press, 2011).

95. Wiarda, *Corporatism and Comparative Politics*, 24.

CONCLUSION

Epigraph: Lord Lyons to Lord Russell, May 21, 1861, British National Archives, London, PRO 30/22/35.

1. Laurence Shore argues that adherence to slaveholding capitalism increased class conflict and "demoralization" in the Confederacy. Shore alleges the selfish motives of slaveholders undermined Confederate nationalism and states that "masters would not be masters and capitalists not capitalists if they had to share their labor resources with the poor." Laurence Shore, *Southern Capitalists: The Ideological Leadership of an Elite, 1832–1885* (Chapel Hill: University of North Carolina Press, 1986), 87.

2. Edmund Phelps, *Mass Flourishing: How Grassroots Innovation Created Jobs, Challenge, and Change* (Princeton, NJ: Princeton University Press, 2013), 19, 27.

3. For an alternate definition of this type of system, see Moore, *Social Origins of Dictatorship and Democracy*, 437–438. Moore called this type of state an "authoritarian semiparliamentary government," and with its tendency towards antiparty sentiment and an overly powerful executive branch, the Confederacy is arguably a good fit with Moore's definition.

4. George Dangerfield eloquently described why the absence of bipartisan competition in the American political system is a rarity: "one-party government cannot continue long in a political democracy without resorting to dictatorship or dissolving into anarchy . . . it is not flexible, not responsive to the people; it tends to produce a crusty political elite; and it is easily ensnared by any special interest strongly enough organized to make its wishes felt." Dangerfield, *The Era of Good Feelings* (New York: Harcourt Brace, 1952; repr., Chicago: I. R. Dee, 1980), foreword, section III.

5. As Frank Towers points out, the modernization thesis "endured in large part because its central problem facilitated a productive debate over the meaning and pace of change and proved amenable to repeated innovations in method and sources." Towers, "Partisans, New History, and Modernization: The Historiography of the Civil War's Causes, 1861–2011," *Journal of the Civil War Era* 1, no. 2 (June 2011): 247.

6. Dorothy Ross, "American Modernities, Past and Present," *American Historical Review* 116, no. 3 (June 2011): 702–703.

7. As Dorothy Ross points out, in the final decades of the nineteenth century "the United States captured the ideal generic modernity: the country need only fulfill its own identity to achieve it." "American Modernities," 702–703.

8. Gary Gallagher asserts, "until deep into the twentieth century no administration in American history proved so intrusive into its citizens' lives as that in Richmond during the Civil War." Gallagher, *Becoming Confederates*, 13.

9. Moore, *Social Origins of Dictatorship and Democracy*, 111–112.

10. Ibid., 435–442, 413–414. Moore's categories describe each method and several examples. The first way "combined capitalism and parliamentary democracy after a series of revolutions: the Puritan Revolution, the French Revolution, and the American Civil War . . . the bourgeois revolution, a route that England, France, and the United States entered. . . . The second path was also a capitalist one, but, in the absence of a strong revolutionary surge, it passed through reactionary political forms to culminate in fascism . . . through a revolution from above . . . The third route is of course the communist one."

11. Several historians have commented on the similar characteristics of nineteenth-century southern political economy to the "Prussian Road." Shearer Davis Bowman provides the strongest comparison between southern slave-owning leaders and their Junker counterparts in Prussia. Bowman focuses most of his comparison on antebellum southern planters' notion of slave-based republicanism and opposition to northern-style liberalizing democratic government, the common link between southern "masters" and Prussian "lords." However, Bowman notes that the Junkers oversaw development of a full-fledged corporatist government in the 1870s, and as a result the landed aristocracy continued to dominate a modernizing German nation. Despite the official end of the plantation slave labor system in 1865, the planter class in the American South also continued to dominate southern agricultural production even if their corporatist experiment failed in the Civil War. Bowman, *Masters and Lords: Mid-Nineteenth Century U.S. Planters and Prussian Junkers* (New York: Oxford University Press, 1993). For a more detailed discussion of the Prussian Road and corporatism, see 104, 113–114. Bowman does not declare that the Confederacy was corporatist, but his study certainly puts these two examples, Prussia and the Confederacy, in the same categorical vicinity with regard to the cultural background necessary for corporatist political economy. Jonathan Wiener focused on the postbellum qualities of the American South in relation to the Prussian Road paradigm. Wiener summarized the continued power of the southern landed class in the decades after the war:

> The planter class, rooted as it was in the antebellum elite, chose . . . the Prussian Road. The Black Codes passed in 1865–1867 expressed that choice; temporarily abolished by the Radicals, many were resurrected by the planter regimes that regained power in the seventies. . . . [Historians have] treated southern economic and political development as separate questions. The South's characteristic poverty and political oppression arose out of the same social relations: the Prussian Road, with its dominant planter class and its labor-repressive system of agricultural production.

Jonathan Wiener, *Social Origins of the New South*, 72–73. Chad Morgan argues that modernization in wartime Georgia represented an "inverted Prussian Road." Morgan, *Planter's Progress*, 67–68.

12. Frank J. Byrne argues that there was a continuity of bourgeois culture in the American South that has been largely overlooked by other historians. See Byrne, *Becoming Bourgeois: Merchant Culture in the South, 1820–1865* (Lexington: University Press of Kentucky, 2006); Phelps, *Mass Flourishing*, 24, 142.

13. Maier, *Recasting Bourgeois Europe*, 9–13.

14. Ibid., 590.

15. As economic historian Niall Ferguson points out, "inflation is a monetary phenomenon . . . but hyperinflation is always and everywhere a *political* phenomenon, in the sense that it cannot occur without a fundamental malfunction of a country's political economy." Niall Ferguson, *The Ascent of Money: A Financial History of the World* (New York: Penguin, 2008), 104. Richard J. Evans detailed the drastic nature of Germany's hyperinflation in 1923, when the number of marks it took to purchase one dollar skyrocketed from 17,000 in January to 4,200,000,000,000 in December! Evans, *The Coming of the Third Reich* (New York: Penguin, 2003), 105. For a comprehensive discussion and analysis of hyperinflation in the Weimar Republic, see Gerald Feldman, *The Great Disorder: Politics, Economics, and Society in the German Inflation, 1914–1924* (New York: Oxford University Press, 1993), 513–835. Feldman's account delves into many aspects of German society, and he concludes that the era of hyperinflation caused the Weimar Republic to be a "mortgaged democracy."

16. David M. Kennedy, *Over Here: The First World War and American Society* (New York: Oxford University Press, 1980), 137, 329.

17. Robert Cuff argues that "Baruch realized before April [1917] that various committees of big businessmen could contribute something far more important to the war effort than information, and acquire far more than an advisory role." Cuff, *The War Industries Board: Business-Government Relations During World War I* (Baltimore: Johns Hopkins University Press, 1973), 69–70, 273.

18. Kennedy, *Over Here*, 151.

19. Ibid., 152–155.

20. David Kennedy describes the wartime burdens on the rail system: "The mobilization-induced economic surge in 1917 . . . badly taxed the capacity of the rail network. Insufficient rolling stock, undermaintained roadbeds, antiquated terminal facilities, and inadequate coordination among the several lines all threatened to strangle commerce and paralyze the war effort." Ibid., 252–253.

21. Ibid., 253.

22. Ibid., 253–254.

23. Ibid., 154.

24. David Kennedy argues that the arrangements crafted to mobilize the American wartime economy represented "a marked shift toward corporatism in the nation's business affairs." Ibid., 141.

25. Political scientist Howard Wiarda argues that this uneasiness about corporatism derives from "the individualistic and liberal pluralist ethos and ideology [that] are so strongly ingrained in the American political consciousness [and] Americans are reluctant to admit the power of certain groups in our society to control the economic and political system

... but powerful interest groups tied to a strong state are precisely what corporatism is all about." Wiarda, *Corporatism and Comparative Politics*, viii–ix. For the negative interpretation of corporatist states, see Wyn Grant, *The Political Economy of Corporatism* (London: Macmillan, 1985), 27, and Wilson, "Why Is There No Corporatism in the United States?," 219.

26. Peter J. Williamson, *Corporatism in Perspective: An Introductory Guide to Corporatist Theory* (London: Sage, 1989), 41, 41–42.

27. Moore, *Social Origins of Dictatorship and Democracy*, 441–442.

28. Phelps, *Mass Flourishing*, 138.

29. Emory M. Thomas focused on the radical changes wrought by the war in his seminal work *The Confederacy as a Revolutionary Experience* (1971). Thomas's call to "take a long second look at the Confederate experience—to view it for what it was" remains a valid goal for current historians. Thomas trailblazed the path for other interpretations of Confederate modernity and argued that "present Americans have much in common with the Confederate past." In his grand narrative *The Confederate Nation, 1861–1865* (New York: Harper & Row, 1979), Thomas expanded upon the attributes of Confederate nationalism and described its antebellum foundations, vital link to battlefield victories, and eventual destruction by Union armies. One of the most important scholarly comparatives of Confederate nationalism is *Yankee Leviathan*. Bensel analyzes the "statist" tendencies of the Union and the Confederate governments and concludes that "in many respects, the Confederate state possessed more modern characteristics than this northern regime." Two important scholarly works on the nature of Confederate nationalism were published in 1994, *A Government of Our Own*, by William C. Davis, and *Confederate Republic*, by George C. Rable. Davis focuses on the moment that Confederate nationalism transitioned from an idea to a reality in early 1861. Rable analyzes Confederate political culture and describes the "anti-party sentiment" that characterized national politics. Both works bolster the argument that the Confederate nation was a constitutional democracy that tried to protect the institution of slavery while at the same time coping with the modernity imposed by wartime necessity. One of the most comprehensive scholarly works on the Confederacy is William C. Davis's *Look Away: A History of the Confederate States of America* (2002). Davis covers numerous aspects of Confederate policies and shows how the nation interacted with civilians. Each of these works combines to form an excellent foundation for understanding the Confederate nation in a comparative modern context. Thomas, *The Confederacy as a Revolutionary Experience*, ix, 138; Thomas, *Confederate Nation, 1861–1865*; Bensel, *Yankee Leviathan*, 236; Davis, *A Government of Our Own*; Rable, *Confederate Republic*; Davis, *Look Away*.

30. Gary Gallagher's *The Confederate War: How Popular Will, Nationalism, and Military Strategy Could Not Stave Off Defeat* (Cambridge, MA: Harvard University Press, 1997) asserts that battlefield victories imbued Confederate soldiers with a strong sense of nationalism that "in turn nourished patriotism and resolve among civilians." Gallagher, *The Confederate War*, 110–111. In his detailed narrative of the Army of Northern Virginia, *General Lee's Army: From Victory to Collapse* (New York: Free Press, 2008), Joseph T. Glatthaar reemphasizes the importance of southern armies to Confederate nationalism. Glatthaar argues that "General Lee's army . . . became the embodiment of the Rebel cause . . . [and] Lee and the Army of

Northern Virginia were the greatest nationalizing institution in the Confederacy." Glatthaar, *General Lee's Army*, xv.

31. Mark V. Wetherington addresses this complicated issue in *Plain Folks Fight: The Civil War and Reconstruction in Piney Woods Georgia* (Chapel Hill: University of North Carolina Press, 2005). Among these predominantly poor white Georgians, the Civil War sparked "a measure of artificial unity that had at its core the defense of family, home, and property." Wetherington, *Plain Folks Fight*, 305. In *Why Confederates Fought: Family and Nation in Civil War Virginia* (Chapel Hill: University of North Carolina Press, 2007), Aaron Sheehan-Dean argues that Virginians viewed their families in the context of "a slave society and the two were inseparable." Dean masterfully sums up the persistence of Confederate nationalism in Virginia and states, "the harder the North fought, the more vigorously the Confederacy resisted." Sheehan-Dean, *Why Confederates Fought*, 194–195.

32. For an excellent discussion of slavery's role in Confederate nationalism, see Robert E. Bonner, *Mastering America: Southern Slaveholders and the Crisis of American Nationhood* (New York: Cambridge University Press, 2009). In particular, see chapter 7—"The Anatomy of Confederate Nationhood," Chapter 8—"Reckoning With Confederate Purpose," and Chapter 9—"Liberty, Slavery, and the Burdens of Confederate Nationhood," 217–322.

33. Recent scholarship that argues the internal collapse thesis includes *The South vs. the South: How Anti-Confederate Southerners Shaped the Course of the Civil War* (New York: Oxford University Press, 2001) by William W. Freehling; *Dixie Betrayed: How the South Really Lost the Civil War* (New York: Little, Brown, 2006) by David J. Eicher; *Bitterly Divided: The South's Inner Civil War* (New York: New Press, 2008) by David Williams; *Confederate Reckoning: Power and Politics in the Civil War South* (Cambridge, MA: Harvard University Press, 2010) by Stephanie McCurry; and *The Fall of the House of Dixie: The Civil War and the Social Revolution That Transformed the South* (New York: Random House, 2013) by Bruce Levine.

34. As pointed out by Paul Escott, "military necessity was at the bottom of most of the startling innovations that altered the South's economy and society." Escott, *Military Necessity: Civil-Military Relations in the Confederacy* (Westport, CT: Praeger Security International, 2006), 177.

35. As Nicholas and Peter Onuf point out, "the Confederacy had a government, control over a territory, and impressive military successes; it *was* a modern nation." Nicholas Onuf and Peter Onuf, *Nations, Markets, and War: Modern History and the American Civil War* (Charlottesville: University of Virginia Press, 2006), 346. Edward E. Baptist argues that slavery was a crucial aspect of American economic modernization; for an in-depth discussion, see *The Half Has Not Been Told: Slavery and the Making of American Capitalism* (New York: Basic Books, 2014).

Works Cited

UNPUBLISHED PRIMARY SOURCES

National Archives—Washington, D. C.
Papers of the Augusta Powder Works, Record Group 109, Entry 35
Papers of the Confederate Passport Office, Record Group 109, Entry 10, Boxes 1–7
Papers of William Pendleton, Daily Report of William Pendleton, Superintendent of the Powder Works, Record Group 109, Entry 32

British National Archives—London
Papers of Lord Lyons—PRO 30/22/35

Southern Historical Collection, Wilson Library—Chapel Hill, NC
Archibald Arrington Papers
Battle Family Papers
Clingman and Puryear Family Papers
James Thomas Leach Papers
Thomas David Smith McDowell Papers
Richmond Mumford Pearson Papers
George Washington Rains Papers

Perkins Library—Durham, NC
Clement Claiborne Clay Papers
Herschel Vespasian Johnson Papers
Thomas Jenkins Semmes Papers
William Ephraim Smith Papers
William Nathan Harrell Smith Papers

W. S. Hoole Special Collections Library—Tuscaloosa, AL
Shelby Iron Company Papers

Alabama Division of Archives and History:
Colin J. McRae Papers

Louisiana State University Special Collections—Baton Rouge, LA
Confederate States of America Collection

South Carolina Confederate Relic Room and Museum
Colin J. McRae Papers

NEWSPAPERS

Charleston Daily Courier
Charleston Mercury
The Richmond Enquirer
The Southern Recorder (Milledgeville, Georgia)

PUBLISHED PRIMARY SOURCES

Buel, Clarence, and Robert Johnson, eds. *Battles and Leaders of the Civil War.* New York: Century, 1884–1887.

Chesnut, Mary. *Mary Chesnut's Civil War,* edited by C. Vann Woodward. New Haven, CT: Yale University Press, 1981.

Communication of the Secretary of War, Confederate States of America, War Department, Richmond, Va., January 27, 1864, Gorgas Library, University of Alabama.

Davis, Jefferson. *The Messages and Papers of Jefferson Davis and the Confederacy, Including Diplomatic Correspondences, 1861–1865.* Vols. 1 & 2, edited by James D. Richardson. New York: Chelsea House-Robert Hector, 1966.

———. *The Papers of Jefferson Davis.* Vols. 1–13, edited by Haskell M. Monroe, James T. McIntosh, and Lynda Lasswell Crist. Baton Rouge: Louisiana State University Press, 1971–2012.

Gorgas, Josiah. *The Civil War Diary of General Josiah Gorgas,* edited by Frank Vandiver. Tuscaloosa: University of Alabama Press, 1947.

———. *The Journals of Josiah Gorgas, 1857–1878,* edited by Sarah Woolfolk Wiggins. Tuscaloosa: University of Alabama Press, 1995.

Jones, John Beauchamp. *A Rebel War Clerk's Diary,* edited by Howard Swiggett. New York: Old Hickory Bookshop, 1935.

Journal of the Congress of the Confederate States of America. 7 vols. Washington, D.C.: Government Printing Office, 1904.

Kean, Robert Garlick Hill. *Inside the Confederate Government: The Diary of Robert Garlick Hill Kean,* edited by Edward Younger. New York: Oxford University Press, 1957.

Matthews, James Muscoe. *The Statutes at Large of the Provisional Government of the Confederate States of America.* Richmond, VA: R. M. Smith, 1864.

Rains, George Washington. "History of the Confederate Powder Works." *Newburgh Daily News Print,* Newburgh, NY, 1882.

Rembert, Patrick, ed. *The Opinions of the Confederate Attorneys General, 1861–1865.* Buffalo: Denis, 1951.

Ruffin, Edmund. *The Diary of Edmund Ruffin,* edited by William Kauffman Scarborough. Vol. I, *Toward Independence: October 1856–April 1861.* Baton Rouge: Louisiana State University Press, 1972.

———. *The Diary of Edmund Ruffin,* edited by William Kauffman Scarborough. Vol. II, *The Years of Hope: April 1861–June 1863.* Baton Rouge: Louisiana State University Press, 1976.

Southern Historical Society Papers. Vols. 44–52. Richmond: Virginia Historical Society, June 1923–1959.

Vance, Zebulon. *Papers of Zebulon Vance.* Vol. 1, 1843–1862, edited by Frontis Johnston. Raleigh, NC: Department of Archives and History, 1963.

———. *Papers of Zebulon Vance.* Vol. 2, 1863, edited by Joe A. Mobley. Raleigh, NC: Division of Archives and History, 1995.

The War of the Rebellion: A Compilation of the Official Records of the Union and Confederate Armies. 128 vols. in four series. Washington, D.C.: Government Printing Office, 1880–1901.

Wiggins, Sarah Woolfolk, ed. *The Journals of Josiah Gorgas, 1857–1878.* Tuscaloosa: University of Alabama Press, 1995.

SECONDARY SOURCES

Alexander, Thomas, and Richard Beringer. *The Anatomy of the Confederate Congress.* Nashville, TN: Vanderbilt University Press, 1972.

Almond, Gabriel A., and Sidney Verba. *The Civic Culture: Political Attitudes and Democracy in Five Nations.* Princeton, NJ: Princeton University Press, 1963.

Altshuler, Glenn, and Stuart Blumin. *Rude Republic: Americans and Their Politics in the Nineteenth Century.* Princeton, NJ: Princeton University Press, 2000.

Angevine, Robert G. *The Railroad and the State: War, Politics, and Technology in Nineteenth Century America.* Stanford: Stanford University Press, 2004.

Baker, Jean H. *Affairs of Party: The Political Culture of Northern Democrats in the Mid-Nineteenth Century.* Ithaca, NY: Cornell University Press, 1983.

Ball, Douglas. *Financial Failure and Confederate Defeat.* Urbana: University of Illinois Press, 1991.

Baptist, Edward E. *The Half Has Not Been Told: Slavery and the Making of American Capitalism.* New York: Basic Books, 2014.

Barnes, L. Diane, Brian Schoen, and Frank Towers, eds. *The Old South's Modern Worlds: Slavery, Region, and Nation in the Age of Progress.* New York: Oxford University Press, 2011.

Barrett, John C. *The Civil War in North Carolina.* Chapel Hill: University of North Carolina Press, 1963.

Bateman, Fred, and Thomas Weiss. *A Deplorable Scarcity: The Failure of Industrialization in the Slave Economy.* Chapel Hill: University of North Carolina Press, 1981.

Beard, Charles, and Mary Beard. *The Rise of American Civilization.* 2 vols. New York: Macmillan, 1927.

Bensel, Richard Franklin. *The American Ballot Box in the Mid-Nineteenth Century.* New York: Cambridge University Press, 2004.

———. *Yankee Leviathan: The Origins of Central State Authority in America, 1859–1877.* New York: Cambridge University Press, 1990.

Bernath, Michael T. *Confederate Minds: The Struggle for Intellectual Independence in The Civil War South.* Chapel Hill: University of North Carolina Press, 2010.

Bill, Alfred Hoyt. *The Beleaguered City: Richmond, 1861–1865.* New York: Knopf, 1946.

Black, C. E. *The Dynamics of Modernization: A Study in Comparative History.* New York: Harper & Row, 1966.

Black, Robert C. III. *The Railroads of the Confederacy.* Chapel Hill: University of North Carolina Press, 1952.

Blair, William A. *Virginia's Private War: Feeding Body and Soul in the Confederacy, 1861–1865.* Oxford & New York: Oxford University Press, 1998.

———. *With Malice Toward Some: Treason and Loyalty in the Civil War Era.* Chapel Hill: University of North Carolina Press, 2014.

Blakey, Arch Frederic. *General John H. Winder.* Gainesville: University Press of Florida, 1990.

Bonner, Robert E. *Mastering America: Southern Slaveholders and the Crisis of American Nationhood.* Cambridge and New York: Cambridge University Press, 2009.

Bowman, Shearer Davis. *Masters and Lords: Mid-Nineteenth Century U.S. Planters and Prussian Junkers.* New York: Oxford University Press, 1993.

Bragg, C. L., Charles D. Ross, Gordon A. Blaker, Stephanie A. T. Jacobe, and Theodore P. Savas. *Never for Want of Powder: The Confederate Powder Works in Augusta, Georgia.* Columbia: University of South Carolina Press, 2007.

Burke, James C. *The Wilmington and Weldon Railroad Company in the Civil War.* Jefferson, NC, and London: MacFarland, 2013.

Byrne, Frank J. *Becoming Bourgeois: Merchant Culture in the South, 1820–1865.* Lexington: University Press of Kentucky, 2006.

Carter, Dan. *The Politics of Rage: George Wallace, the Origins of the New Conservatism, and the Transformation of American Politics.* New York: Simon & Schuster, 1995.

Cauthen, Charles Edward. *South Carolina Goes to War, 1860–1865.* Chapel Hill: University of North Carolina Press, 1950.

Clark, John E. Jr. *Railroads in the Civil War: The Impact of Management on Victory and Defeat.* Baton Rouge: Louisiana State University Press, 2001.

Conkin, Paul K. *Prophets of Prosperity: America's First Political Economists.* Bloomington: Indiana University Press, 1980.

Craven, Avery. *The Coming of the Civil War.* Chicago: University of Chicago Press, 1957.

Cuff, Robert D. *The War Industries Board: Business-Government Relations during World War I.* Baltimore and London: Johns Hopkins University Press, 1973.

Dangerfield, George. *The Era of Good Feelings.* Chicago: I. R. Dee, 1980. First published 1952 by Harcourt, Brace.

Dattel, Eugene R. *Cotton and Race in the Making of America: The Human Costs of Economic Power.* Chicago: Ivan R. Dee, 2009.

Davis, Charles S. *Colin J. McRae: Confederate Financial Agent, Blockade Running in The Trans-Mississippi South as Affected by the Confederate Government's Direct European Procurement of Goods.* College Station, TX: Institute of Nautical Archaeology, 2008. Reprint, College Station, TX: Institute of Nautical Archaeology, 1961.

Davis, John Martin Jr., and George B. Tremmel. *Parole, Pardon, Pass and Amnesty Documents of the Civil War.* London: MacFarland, 2014.

Davis, William C. *A Government of Our Own: The Making of the Confederacy.* New York: Free Press, 1994.

———. *Look Away: A History of the Confederate States of America.* New York: Free Press, 2002.

DeCredico, Mary A. *Patriotism for Profit: Georgia's Urban Entrepreneurs and the Confederate War Effort.* Chapel Hill: University of North Carolina Press, 1990.

DeRosa, Marshall L. *The Confederate Constitution of 1861: An Inquiry into American Constitutionalism.* Columbia: University of Missouri Press, 1991.

Dew, Charles B. *Bond of Iron: Master and Slave at Buffalo Forge.* New York: W. W. Norton, 1994.

———. *Ironmaker to the Confederacy: Joseph R. Anderson and Tredegar Iron Works.* New Haven, CT: Yale University Press, 1966.

Eicher, David J. *Dixie Betrayed: How the South Really Lost the Civil War.* New York: Little, Brown, 2006.

Ely, James W. *Railroads and American Law.* Lawrence: University Press of Kansas, 2001.

Ely, James W., and Kermit L. Hall. *An Uncertain Tradition: Constitutionalism and the History of the South.* Athens: University of Georgia Press, 1989.

Escott, Paul D. *After Secession: Jefferson Davis and the Failure of Confederate Nationalism.* Baton Rouge: Louisiana State University Press, 1978.

———. *Military Necessity: Civil-Military Relations in the Confederacy.* Westport, CT, and London: Praeger Security International, 2006.

Evans, Richard J. *The Coming of the Third Reich.* New York: Penguin, 2003.

Faust, Drew Gilpin, ed. *The Creation of Confederate Nationalism: Ideology and Identity in the Civil War South.* Baton Rouge: Louisiana State University Press, 1988.

———. *The Ideology of Slavery: Proslavery Thought in the Antebellum South, 1830–1860.* Baton Rouge: Louisiana State University Press, 1981.

———. *This Republic of Suffering: Death and the American Civil War.* New York: Knopf, 2008.

Fehrenbacher, Don E. *The Dred Scott Case: Its Significance in American Law and Politics.* Oxford and New York: Oxford University Press, 1978.

———. *Sectional Crisis and Southern Constitutionalism.* Baton Rouge: Louisiana State University Press, 1995.

———. *The Slaveholding Republic: An Account of the United States Government's Relations to Slavery.* Oxford and New York: Oxford University Press, 2001.

Feldman, Gerald. *The Great Disorder: Politics, Economics, and Society in the German Inflation, 1914–1924.* Oxford and New York: Oxford University Press, 1993.

Ferguson, Niall. *The Ascent of Money: A Financial History of the World*. New York: Penguin, 2008.

Ford, Lacy K. *Deliver Us from Evil: The Slavery Question in the Old South*. New York: Oxford University Press, 2009.

——. *Origins of Southern Radicalism: The South Carolina Upcountry, 1800–1860*. Oxford and New York: Oxford University Press, 1988.

Fox-Genovese, Elizabeth, and Eugene Genovese. *The Mind of the Master Class: History and Faith in the Southern Slaveholders' Worldview*. New York: Cambridge University Press, 2005.

Freehling, William W. *The South vs. the South: How Anti-Confederate Southerners Shaped the Course of the Civil War*. Oxford and New York: Oxford University Press, 2001.

Gabel, Christopher R. *Rails to Oblivion: The Battle of Confederate Railroads in the Civil War*. Fort Leavenworth, KS: U.S. Army Command and General Staff College Press, 2002.

Gallagher, Gary. *Becoming Confederates: Paths to a New National Loyalty*. Athens: University of Georgia Press, 2013.

——. *The Confederate War: How Popular Will, Nationalism, and Military Strategy Could Not Stave Off Defeat*. Cambridge, MA, and London: Harvard University Press, 1997.

——. *The Union War*. Cambridge, MA, and London: Harvard University Press, 2011.

Geary, James W. *We Need Men: The Union Draft in the Civil War*. DeKalb: Northern Illinois University Press, 1991.

Glatthaar, Joseph T. *General Lee's Army: From Victory to Collapse*. New York: Free Press, 2008.

Goff, Richard D. *Confederate Supply*. Durham, NC: Duke University Press, 1969.

Goodin, Robert E., and Philip Pettit, eds. *A Companion to Contemporary Political Philosophy*. Malden, MA: Blackwell, 1993.

Gordon, Leslie, and John Inscoe, eds. *Inside the Confederate Nation: Essays in Honor of Emory M. Thomas*. Baton Rouge: Louisiana State University Press, 2005.

Grant, Wyn. *The Political Economy of Corporatism*. London: Macmillan, 1985.

Hacker, Louis. *The Triumph of American Capitalism: The Development of Forces in American History to the End of the Nineteenth Century*. New York: Columbia University Press, 1940.

Hall, Kernit L., and James W. Ely, eds. *An Uncertain Tradition: Constitutionalism and the History of the South*. Athens: University of Georgia Press, 1989.

Harris, J. William. *Plain Folk and Gentry in a Slave Society: White Society and Black Slavery in Augusta's Hinterland.* Middletown, CT: Wesleyan University Press, 1985.

Heidler, David S., and Jeanne T. Heidler, eds. *Encyclopedia of the American Civil War.* Volumes 1–5. Oxford: ABC-CLIO Press, 2000.

Jackson, Joyce. *History of the Shelby Iron Company: 1862–1868.* Brasher Publications with the Historic Shelby Association, c. 1990.

Jordan, Winthrop D. *Tumult and Silence at Second Creek: An Inquiry into a Civil War Slave Conspiracy.* Baton Rouge: Louisiana State University Press, 1993.

Kennedy, David M. *Over Here: The First World War and American Society.* New York: Oxford University Press, 1980.

Knowles, Anne Kelly. *Mastering Iron: The Struggle to Modernize an American Industry, 1800–1868.* Chicago: University of Chicago Press, 2013.

Koistenen, Paul A. C. *Beating Ploughshares into Swords: The Political Economy of American Warfare, 1606–1865.* Lawrence: University Press of Kansas, 1996.

Kruman, Marc W. *Parties and Politics in North Carolina, 1836–1865.* Baton Rouge: Louisiana State University Press, 1983.

Lee, Charles Robert Jr. *The Confederate Constitutions.* Chapel Hill: University of North Carolina Press, 1963.

Lehmbruch, Gerhard, and Philippe C. Schmitter, eds. *Patterns of Corporatist Policy Making.* London: Sage, 1982.

———. *Trends Toward Corporatist Intermediation.* London: Sage, 1979.

Levine, Bruce. *The Fall of the House of Dixie: The Civil War and the Social Revolution That Transformed the South.* New York: Random House, 2013.

Luraghi, Raimondo. *The Rise and Fall of the Plantation South.* New York: New Viewpoints, 1978.

Maier, Charles S. *Recasting Bourgeois Europe: Stabilization in France, Germany, and Italy in the Decade after World War I.* Princeton, NJ: Princeton University Press, 1975.

Majewski, John. *Modernizing a Slave Economy: The Economic Vision of the Confederate Nation.* Chapel Hill: University of North Carolina Press, 2009.

Martinez, Jaime Amanda. *Confederate Slave Impressment in the Upper South.* Chapel Hill: University of North Carolina Press, 2014.

McCurry, Stephanie. *Confederate Reckoning: Power and Politics in the Civil War South.* Cambridge, MA: Harvard University Press, 2010.

McKee, J. Donald, and Mark Cooper Pope III. *Mark Anthony Cooper: The Iron Man of Georgia, A Biography.* Atlanta: Graphic Publishing, 2000.

McPherson, James. *Battle Cry of Freedom: The Civil War Era.* New York: Ballantine, 1988.

———. *Drawn with the Sword: Reflections* on *the American Civil War*. New York: Oxford University Press, 1996.

Moody, John. *The Railroad Builders*. New Haven, CT: Yale University Press, 1919.

Moore, Albert Burton. *Conscription and Conflict in the Confederacy*. New York: MacMillan, 1924.

Moore, Barrington Jr. *Social Origins of Dictatorship and Democracy: Lord and Peasant in The Making of the Modern World*. Boston: Beacon, 1966.

Morgan, Chad. *Planters' Progress: Modernizing Confederate Georgia*. Gainesville: University Press of Florida, 2005.

Neely, Mark E. Jr. *The Boundaries of American Political Culture in the Civil War Era*. Chapel Hill: University of North Carolina Press, 2005.

———. *The Fate of Liberty: Abraham Lincoln and Civil Liberties*. New York: Oxford University Press, 1991.

———. *Lincoln and the Triumph of the Nation: Constitutional Conflict in the American Civil War*. Chapel Hill: University of North Carolina Press, 2011.

———. *Southern Rights: Political Prisoners and the Myth of Confederate Constitutionalism*. Charlottesville: University of Virginia Press, 1999.

Newmyer, R. Kent. *John Marshall and the Heroic Age of the Supreme Court*. Baton Rouge: Louisiana State University Press, 2001.

Noe, Kenneth W. *Reluctant Rebels: The Confederates Who Joined the Army after 1861*. Chapel Hill: University of North Carolina Press, 2010.

Onuf, Nicholas, and Peter Onuf. *Nations, Markets, and War: Modern History and the American Civil War*. Charlottesville: University of Virginia Press, 2006.

Patrick, Rembert. *Jefferson Davis and His Cabinet*. Baton Rouge: Louisiana State University Press, 1944.

———, ed. *The Opinions of the Confederate Attorneys General, 1861–1865*. Buffalo: Denis, 1950.

Phelps, Edmund. *Mass Flourishing: How Grassroots Innovation Created Jobs, Challenge, and Change*. Princeton, NJ: Princeton University Press, 2013.

Pope, Mark Cooper III, with J. Donald McKee. *Mark Anthony Cooper: The Iron Man of Georgia, A Biography*. Atlanta: Graphic Publishing, 2000.

Rable, George C. *The Confederate Republic: A Revolution Against Politics*. Chapel Hill: University of North Carolina Press, 1994.

———. *God's Almost Chosen People: A Religious History of the American Civil War*. Chapel Hill: University of North Carolina Press, 2010.

Radley, Kenneth. *Rebel Watchdog: The Confederate States Army Provost Guard*. Baton Rouge: Louisiana State University Press, 1989.

Randall, James G. *Constitutional Problems under Lincoln*. New York: Appleton, 1926.

Robertson, Craig. *The Passport in America: The History of a Document.* Oxford: Oxford University Press, 2010.

Robinson, William M. *Justice in Grey: A History of the Judicial System of the Confederate States of America.* Cambridge, MA: Harvard University Press, 1941.

Rogers, George C. Jr., and James C. Taylor. *A South Carolina Chronology: 1497–1992.* Columbia: University of South Carolina Press, 1994.

Sheehan-Dean, Aaron. *Why Confederates Fought: Family and Nation in Civil War Virginia.* Chapel Hill: University of North Carolina Press, 2007.

Shore, Laurence. *Southern Capitalists: The Ideological Leadership of an Elite, 1832–1885.* Chapel Hill: University of North Carolina Press, 1986.

Silbey, Joel H. *The American Political Nation, 1838–1893.* Palo Alto, CA: Stanford University Press, 1991.

———. *The Partisan Imperative: The Dynamics of American Politics Before the Civil War.* New York: Oxford University Press, 1985.

Sinha, Manisha. *The Counter-Revolution of Slavery: Politics and Ideology in Antebellum South Carolina.* Chapel Hill: University of North Carolina Press, 2000.

Stokes, Melvyn, and Stephen Conway, eds. *The Market Revolution in America: Social, Political, and Religious Expressions, 1800–1880.* Charlottesville: University Press of Virginia, 1996.

Thomas, Emory M. *The Confederacy as a Revolutionary Experience.* Englewood Cliffs, NJ:, Prentice-Hall, 1971.

———. *The Confederate Nation, 1861–1865.* New York: Harper and Row, 1979.

Thomas, William G. *The Iron Way: Railroads, the Civil War, and the Making of Modern America.* New Haven, CT, and London: Yale University Press, 2011.

Thompson, E. P. *The Essential E. P. Thompson,* edited by Dorothy Thompson. New York: Free Press, 2001.

Turner, George Edgar. *Victory Rode the Rails: The Strategic Place of Railroads in the Civil War.* Indianapolis and New York: Bobbs-Merrill, 1953.

Vandiver, Frank. *Ploughshares into Swords: Josiah Gorgas and Confederate Ordnance.* Austin: University of Texas Press, 1952.

Varon, Elizabeth R. *Southern Lady, Yankee Spy: The True Story of Elizabeth Van Lew, A Union Agent in the Heart of the Confederacy.* New York: Oxford University Press, 2003.

Walther, Eric H. *William Lowndes Yancey and the Coming of the Civil War.* Chapel Hill: University of North Carolina Press, 2006.

Warner, Ezra J. *Generals in Gray: Lives of the Confederate Commanders.* Baton Rouge: Louisiana State University Press, 1959.

Warner, Ezra J., and Buck Yearns. *Biographical Register of the Confederate Congress.* Baton Rouge: Louisiana State University Press, 1975.

Weber, Thomas. *The Northern Railroads in the Civil War, 1861–1865.* Bloomington: Indiana University Press, 1952.

Wetherington, Mark V. *Plain Folks Fight: The Civil War and Reconstruction in Piney Woods Georgia.* Chapel Hill: University of North Carolina Press, 2005.

Wiarda, Howard J. *Corporatism and Comparative Politics: The Other Great "Ism."* Armonk, NY: M. E. Sharpe, 1997.

Wiener, Jonathan. *Social Origins of the New South: Alabama 1860–1885.* Baton Rouge: Louisiana State University Press, 1978.

Wilentz, Sean. *The Rise of American Democracy: Jefferson to Lincoln.* New York: W. W. Norton, 2005.

Williams, David. *Bitterly Divided: The South's Inner Civil War.* New York: New Press, 2008.

Williamson, Peter J. *Corporatism in Perspective: An Introductory Guide to Corporatist Theory.* London: Sage, 1989.

———. *Varieties of Corporatism: Theory and Practice.* London: Cambridge University Press, 1985.

Wilson, Harold S. *Confederate Industry: Manufacturers and Quartermasters in the Civil War.* Jackson: University Press of Mississippi, 2002.

Wilson, Mark R. *The Business of Civil War: Military Mobilization and the State, 1861–1865.* Baltimore: Johns Hopkins University Press, 2006.

Wood, Peter H. *Black Majority: Negroes in Colonial South Carolina from 1670 through the Stono Rebellion.* New York: Norton, 1974.

Yearns, Buck. *The Confederate Congress.* Athens: University of Georgia Press, 1960.

———, ed. *The Confederate Governors.* Athens: University of Georgia Press, 1985.

ARTICLES

Anderson, John Nathan. "Money or Nothing: Confederate Postal System Collapse during the Civil War." *American Journalism* 30, no. 1 (Winter 2013).

Bernath, Michael T. "The Confederacy as a Moment of Possibility." *Journal of Southern History* 89, no. 2 (May 2013).

Cappon, Lester J. "Government and Private Industry in the Southern Confederacy." In *Humanistic Studies in Honor of John Calvin Metcalf.* Richmond: University of Virginia Press, 1941, 150–189.

Cochran, Thomas. "Did the Civil War Retard Industrialization?" *Mississippi Valley Historical Review* 48 (September 1961).

Collins, Steven G. "System in the South: John W. Mallet, Josiah Gorgas, and Uniform Production at the Confederate Ordnance Department." *Technology and Culture* 40, no. 3 (July 1999).

———. "Yankee Ingenuity in the South: James Burton and Confederate Ordnance Production." *The International Journal of the Social History of Military Technology* 1, no. 1 (2013).

Engerman, Stanley. "The Economic Impact of the Civil War." *Explorations in Entrepreneurial History,* series 2, vol. 3 (Spring 1966).

Estill, Mary S., and F. B. Sexton. "Diary of a Confederate Congressman, 1862–1863, I." *The Southwestern Historical Quarterly* 38, no. 4 (April 1935).

———. "Diary of a Confederate Congressman, 1862–1863, II." *Southwestern Historical Quarterly* 39, no. 1 (July 1935).

Foner, Eric. "The Causes of the American Civil War: Recent Interpretations and New Directions." *Civil War History* (September 1974).

Gallagher, Gary W. "Disaffection, Persistence, and Nation: Some Directions in Recent Scholarship on the Confederacy." *Civil War History* 55, no. 3 (September 2009).

Gallman, Robert. "Commodity Output, 1839–1899." In *Output, Employment, and Productivity in the Nineteenth Century.* National Bureau of Economic Research. Princeton, NJ: Princeton University Press, 1960.

———. "Gross National Product in the United States after 1800." National Bureau of Economic Research. Princeton, NJ: Princeton University Press, 1966.

Gavin, Michael Thomas. "War Comes to Iron Country: Middle Tennessee's Defense Industry during the Civil War." *West Tennessee Historical Society Papers* 63 (2009).

Geary, James W. "Civil War Conscription in the North: A Historiographical Review." *Civil War History* 32, no. 3 (September 1986).

Hamilton, J. G. de Roulhac. "The State Courts and the Confederate Constitution." *Journal of Southern History* 4, no. 4 (November 1938).

Harvey, A. D. "Was the American Civil War the First Modern War?" *History* 97, no. 326 (April 2012).

Hill, Louise B. "State Socialism in the Confederate States of America." In *Southern Sketches.* Charlottesville, VA: Historical Publishing, 1936.

Holcombe, Randall G. "The Distributive Model of Government: Evidence from the Confederate Constitution." *Southern Economic Journal* 58, issue 3 (January 1992).

Johnsen, Christopher, Kenneth A. Shepsle, and Barry Weingast. "The Political Economy of Benefits and Costs: A Neoclassical Approach to Distributive Politics." *Journal of Political Economy* 89, no. 4 (August 1981).

Keating, Ann Durkin. "Public-Private Partnerships in Public Works: A Bibliographic Essay." In *Essays in Public Works History*. Washington, D.C.: Public Works Historical Society, 1976.

Knowles, Anne Kelly. "Labor, Race, and Technology in the Confederate Iron Industry." *Technology and Culture* 42, no. 1 (January 2001).

Lamb, Parker. "A Macro-scale Look at Railroad History." *Railroad History* no. 207 (Fall/Winter 2012).

Layton, Edwin. "Colin J. McRae and the Selma Arsenal." *Alabama Review* 19, no. 2 (April 1966).

Leslie, William R. "The Confederate Constitution." *Michigan Quarterly Review* (1963).

Luraghi, Raimondo. "The Civil War and Modernization of American Society: Social Structure and Industrial Revolution in the Old South before and during the Civil War." *Civil War History* 18, no. 3 (September 1972).

Morgan, Chad. "The Public Nature of Private Industry in Confederate Georgia." *Civil War History* 50, no. 1 (March 2004).

———. "The Slave Works: Industrial Slavery and the Confederate Central Laboratory in Macon, Georgia." *Atlanta History: A Journal of Georgia & the South* 48, no. 1 (January 2006).

Nelson, Scott. "The Confederacy Serves the Southern: The Construction of the Southern Railway Network, 1861–1865." *Civil War History* 41, no. 3 (September 1995).

Ramsdell, Charles. "The Confederate Government and Railroads." *American Historical Review* 22 (1917).

Ransom, Roger. "Fact and Counterfact: The 'Second American Revolution' Revisited." *Civil War History* 45, no. 1 (March 1999).

———. "War and Cliometrics: Adventures in Economic History." *Journal of Economic History* 66, no. 2 (June 2006).

Ross, Dorothy. "American Modernities, Past and Present." *American Historical Review* 116, no. 3 (June 2011).

Sacher, John. "The Loyal Draft Dodger: A Reexamination of Confederate Substitution." *Civil War History* 57, no. 2 (June 2011).

Savas, Theodore P. "The Life Blood of the Confederate War Machine: George Washington Rains and the Augusta Powder Works." *Journal of Confederate History* no. 5 (1990).

Schoonover, Thomas. "Manpower, North and South, in 1860." *Civil War History* 6, no. 2 (June 1960).

Shoaf, Dana. "Tredegar Iron Works of Richmond, Virginia." *American History* 40, no. 5 (December 2005).

Still, William. "Selma and the Confederate States Navy." *Alabama Review* 15, no. 1 (January 1962).

Thomson, Ross, "The Continuity of Innovation: The Civil War Experience." *Enterprise and Society* 11, no. 1 (March 2010).

Towers, Frank. "Partisans, New History, and Modernization: The Historiography of the Civil War's Causes, 1861–2011." *Journal of the Civil War Era* 1, no. 2 (June 2011).

Vandiver, Frank E. "The Shelby Iron Company in the Civil War: A Study of a Confederate Industry." *Alabama Review* 1 (1948).

THESES AND DISSERTATIONS

Bonner, Michael Brem. "Confederate Political Economy: The Creation of an Expedient Corporatist State." PhD diss., University of California, Riverside, 2006.

———. "Gabriel J. Rains and the Ethical Controversy Over Confederate Land Mine Use." MA thesis, East Carolina University, 1998.

Bryant, Gary E. "Working Women in the Confederate South: White Southern Women in the Paid Labor Force during the Civil War." PhD diss., University of Houston, 2008.

Carlson, Robert D. "Breach of Faith: Conscription in Confederate Georgia." PhD diss., Emory University, 2009.

Combs, Edwin L. III. "Field or Workshop: A Study of Southern Industrial Labor in the Civil War." PhD diss., University of Alabama, 2003.

Davis, Robert Scott Jr. "Cotton, Fire, and Dreams: The Robert Findlay Iron Works and Heavy Industry in Macon, Georgia, 1839–1912." PhD diss., University of Alabama at Birmingham, 1996.

DeRosa, Marshall. "An Analysis of the Confederate States of American Constitution in Contradistinction to the United States Constitution as Explicated by Publius." PhD diss., University of Houston, 1987.

Garrett, Lynnette A. "Confederate Nationalism in Georgia, Louisiana, and Virginia During the American Civil War, 1861–1865." PhD diss., American University, 2012.

Hilleary, Lisa. "Richmond Iron: Tredegar's Role in Southern Industry during the Civil War and Reconstruction." MA thesis, Old Dominion University, 2011.

Johnson, Larry E. "Breakdown from Within: Virginia Railroads during the Civil War Era." PhD diss., University of Louisville, 2004.

Melton, Maurice Kaye. "Major Military Industries of the Confederate Government." PhD diss., Emory University, 1978.

Powell, Michael Albert. "Confederate Federalism: A View from the Governors." PhD diss., University of Maryland, 2004.

Ryan, Thomas Michael. "The Hardships of a Confederate Industry: Catesby Jones and the Selma Naval Ordnance Works." MA thesis, University of South Alabama, 1998.

.

Index